AA
DISCOVERING BRITAIN'S
LOST RAILWAYS

North Eastern Railway.
From YORK
PENRITH

AA
Discovering Britain's
Lost Railways

Paul Atterbury

Published by AA Publishing, a trading name of Automobile Association Developments Limited, whose registered office is Norfolk House, Priestley Road, Basingstoke, Hampshire RG24 2NY. Registered Number 1878835.

Conceived and designed by Julian Holland Publishing Ltd

A catalogue record for this book is available from the British Library.

ISBN 0 7495 1045 5 (hardback)
ISBN 0 7495 2264 X (softback)
Colour origination by Fotographics Ltd
Printed and bound in Italy by G. Canale SpA

The contents of this book are believed correct at the time of printing. Nevertheless, the Publishers cannot accept responsibility for errors or omissions, or for changes in details given.

Pages 2/3: Viaduct over the River Prysor, east of Trawsfynydd, on the old Bala Junction to Blaenau Ffestiniog line
Pages 4/5: Hulme End station looking towards Waterhouses, on the Leek & Manifold Valley Light Railway just before closure in August 1933. The L&MVLR is now a cycleway
Pages 6/7: Leekbrook Junction, awaiting restoration by the Cheddleton Railway Centre

PUBLIC ACCESS TO DISUSED RAILWAYS

It is, of course, essential that those who wish to explore Britain's lost railways for themselves should make sure that they are on public rights of way, or at least have the permission of the landowner. It is also important to keep off all disused and potentially dangerous structures, such as bridges and viaducts, that are not on official paths.

KEY TO MAPS

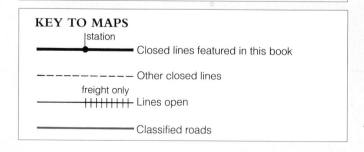

station
——●—— Closed lines featured in this book

– – – – – – – Other closed lines

freight only
++++++++++ Lines open

———————— Classified roads

CONTENTS

◆

INTRODUCTION

The earliest railways in Britain were built in the north of England, reflecting the industrial importance of this part of the country. There was no plan for a national network, and lines were built in isolation and usually for a particular flow of traffic, such as coal or other minerals. After the initial burst of building, which lasted through to the middle of the nineteenth century, the network remained relatively unchanged for 100 years until the 1960s, when wholesale cuts were made under the Beeching reorganisation.

You need to be into middle age, therefore, to remember the time when it was possible to reach every reasonably sized town by rail, and when most villages were but a short bus journey from a railway station. What this book helps to bring home is the sheer scale of the railway network that existed before Beeching. The surviving embankments, cuttings and bridges also underline the feats of engineering involved in building railways in the nineteenth century.

Line closures were not unknown in the days of the private companies, and this process continued after nationalisation in 1948. But the closure programme accelerated hugely under the Beeching reorganisation, when about one third of the network disappeared. It is beyond argument that the Beeching axe cut too deep. A survey of rural communities some twenty years after Beeching found there was still considerable anger in these communities over the loss of the rail link.

On the other hand, when visiting the site of some of the closed lines today it is easy to ask 'Why on earth did they build a line here?' Most were built to service a local industry, long since gone. But did the closure of the line lead to the death of the community or did the community disappear first, leaving the line without a reason for existence?

The importance of railways to rural communities lay not only in the contact they provided with the outside world, but also in the carriage of freight, including a range of farm produce. As a young railwayman, I recall one of the more pleasurable jobs on my line was to take fresh salmon, delivered by train, to the local hotel. A wee dram for your trouble at the end of the shift ensured that prompt delivery continued!

It is natural to look back on this period with more than a whiff of nostalgia. Yet in railway terms the pre-war times and the 1940s and 50s were a world apart from today.

As a young signalman in the early 1960s, I worked on the Ayr to Glasgow line and was made redundant four times when lines such as Dalry to Kilmarnock and Hurlford to Darvel were closed. The biggest change since Beeching has come in technological advance. At the time I worked the line there were more than thirty signal boxes between Ayr and Glasgow. Modern signalling means that these boxes have been replaced by just one.

Finding the site of an old railway station is usually straightforward for the experienced eye if the station building remains. Far more difficult is to pick out the site of old signal boxes. On the old-fashioned branch lines which even in pre-war days had only a limited service, signal boxes often had well-cultivated plots of land adjacent to them where the signalman, undervalued and underpaid even then, might spend an hour or two growing vegetables to help balance the household budget.

I have to confess that public fascination with railways never ceases to surprise me. Book follows book and video seems to follow video, each covering yet another aspect of railways. The truth, of course, as exemplified by this excellent book, is that the history of railways is far more than a chronology of lines opening and closing, or of advances – or failures – in engineering. Railways changed the world. As the Duke of Wellington reportedly said, expressing his disapproval: 'They encourage the lower classes to travel about.' The Iron Duke was certainly right about that!

The development of railways is an industrial, economic and social story of change and evolution, as we still see today. Perhaps I can illustrate this by mentioning that the rough draft of this introduction to a book on our forgotten railways was prepared on Eurostar, hurtling through the Channel Tunnel.

Puxton & Worle, Midsomer Norton, Evercreech and Wookey are names of stations, which, as the author eloquently states, are 'an anthem to the interwoven layers of England's cultural history'. Yesterday's railway perhaps, but, with the help of this book, not quite forgotten. The future will echo to a different song of praise, although the railway culture of Eurostar, Waterloo, Lille, Brussels and Paris still has its roots in our lost railways.

Jimmy Knapp
General Secretary
National Union of Rail, Maritime & Transport Workers
1995

ACROSS THE PENNINES TO THE LAKES

◆

Darlington to Penrith
Penrith to Cockermouth

At Stainmore Summit an old gangers' hut guards the line of the trackbed across the bleak landscape, with Lakeland hills in the distance

HISTORY

Few towns in Britain can compete with Darlington's claim to be the cradle of the railways. It was between here and Stockton that the world's first regular steam-hauled railway service was opened to the public in September 1825. Darlington's subsequent history as a railway town is well known, with the products of its railway works being exported all over the world. Inevitably, it also developed into a major junction, where lines converged from every point of the compass. Some of these lines were built by the Stockton & Darlington, part of a significant empire in the northeast of England that was the province of that company until its take-over, in 1863, by the much larger North Eastern Railway.

One of these lines was the Darlington & Barnard Castle Railway, authorised in July 1854 and completed exactly two years later. It ran from Hopetown, north of Darlington to Barnard Castle. Built by an independent company, it became a part of the Stockton & Darlington in 1858. At first, Barnard Castle was the end of the line, but this situation did not last long, for a much more important Stockton & Darlington scheme was its support for the ambitious South Durham & Lancashire Union Railway. This was a trans-Pennine line inspired by the need to forge a link between the coal and coke of the northeast and the haematite and ironworks of Cumbria. The route, from Spring Gardens Junction, near West Auckland, to Tebay, on the Lancaster & Carlisle Railway (now part of the West Coast main line), was completed in 1861. Heavily engineered, with many viaducts and a high Pennine summit at Stainmore, it passed through Barnard Castle and Kirkby Stephen on its way to Lancashire. As its promoters had intended, this

Above *By the end of 1966, Kirkby Stephen station was already a sad sight, with only a mineral line surviving. Today the scene is unrecognisable*

became a major trans-Pennine freight route, and remained so until its final closure in March 1965. The next link in the chain of railways between Darlington and Cockermouth was the Eden Valley Railway, another initially independent company that was to be absorbed ultimately by the Stockton & Darlington. Its route, along the valley of the River Eden from Kirkby Stephen to Clifton, south of Penrith, via Appleby, was completed in 1862. At Appleby there was a link with the Midland Railway's Settle & Carlisle route and at Clifton it joined the Lancaster & Carlisle for the last few miles into

Penrith. This was a lesser undertaking, and was single track for much of its route. It was also an early victim of the Beeching axe, closing just short of its centenary.

For many years the Lake District kept the railways at bay. A few branch lines had crept in, notably the Kendal & Windermere's route, opened from Oxenholme in 1847, and the short Coniston Railway completed twelve years later, but it was not until 1865 that passengers, and freight, were able to cross the Lakes by train. The Cockermouth, Keswick & Penrith Railway enjoyed a magnificent route, and it soon played its part in developing the Lake District's tourist potential. Initially single-tracked, it was doubled in 1900, by which time it was part of the London & North Western Railway. Despite its great appeal and obvious value, the line was ultimately sacrificed to the motor car, closing west of Keswick in 1966 and from Keswick to Penrith in 1972.

Although never planned as a through route, the series of railways that linked Darlington and Cockermouth offered a splendidly varied and frequently busy cross-country journey. In due time the line came to be a useful link between the LMS, on the west, and the LNER, on the east. In the days of British Railways, the traditional dominance of freight was gradually reduced, diminishing the line's importance as a through route. Passenger traffic was generally local, often handled, from the mid-1950s, by a new generation of diesel railcars. Despite the tourist potential of the Lakeland section, traffic was never enough to ensure the route's survival, and so from 1962 it closed progressively. The last part to remain open, the line runnin from Appleby to the military sidings near Warcop, was finally abandoned in the early 1990s.

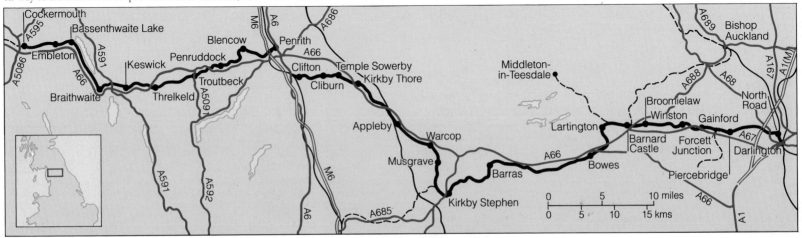

In 1955, when I was ten, my father took me to the north of England for the first time. He had clients to visit in Whitehaven and I must have been at a loose end during school holidays. We drove northwards in his black Citroen Light 15, hour after hour up the old A1 from London, until we reached Scotch Corner, where we spent the night. The next day we crossed the Pennines in bright sunshine to Penrith and then continued westwards through the Lakes to reach Whitehaven in time for tea. The rest of the visit is rather a blur but I do remember two things about Whitehaven. The first was the pleasure of watching old tank locomotives shunting up and down the quays, and the second was my astonishment at the extraordinary variety of things my father bought at an old junk shop, apparently well known to him from previous visits, and then crammed into the back of the car. Since then I have made that journey, and variations on it, many times. It was on one such trip, in 1968, that I saw for the last time a steam locomotive engaged in ordinary British Railway duties, dirty and unloved in the spring sunshine, pulling a line of wagons across a bridge over the road ahead of me. This apart, my railway experiences in the region were limited to a week's holiday in a camping coach at Seascale and a couple of visits to Darlington's North Road station, before and after its conversion to a museum.

DARLINGTON TO BARNARD CASTLE

It was, therefore, with a certain amount of trepidation that I set off in search some of the lost railways of northern England, well aware that this region was the lion's den of railway history. Darlington was, after all, the start of the whole thing. However, there was a satisfying sense of the cyclical nature of history as my friend (who had volunteered somewhat rashly to take on the duties of map reader and navigator) and I set off up the M1 from London, for my daughter, aged twelve rather than ten, had decided to come along too, it being school holidays and she being at a loose end. Four hours from London we were settled in our hotel near Darlington, after a journey now so simple that it made mockery of the epic I had experienced with my father.

As we set to work the next morning, the day was grey and unresolved, with a broken sky and sudden bursts of rain. Looking for lost railways is like any other kind of hunting, the first sight of the quarry being the essential spur to get the adrenalin flowing. In this case it was the stone abutments of a long-gone bridge over the A68 northwest of the town and the tantalising glimpse of an overgrown embankment that did the trick. From that point the day fell into place. Careful map reading, signposts and my memories of previous visits took us quickly to Darlington's North Road station. Set at the head of a curving drive, this symmetrical neo-classical building with its grand portico looks more like a minor country house than a railway station. Only the old wagons parked in the drive and the piles of railway paraphernalia that lay around it gave the game away. Built in 1842, to take the place of a less impressive warehouse structure that had served the needs of passengers since the line's opening in 1825, the station wears its mantle of history well. Retired now from conventional railway duties, although trains on British Rail's Bishop Auckland line still pass by, the station houses a museum devoted to the North Eastern Railway, the famous successor, from 1863, of the Stockton & Darlington, the world's first public railway to use steam locomotives. It is exciting to stand on the spot where it all began, visualising those scenes so familiar from old engravings and descriptions.

In those days trains went eastwards from Darlington to Stockton, whereas our interests lay to the west, in the line that crossed the country from Darlington to Cockermouth via Barnard Castle, Kirkby Stephen, Appleby, Penrith and Keswick. It was a complicated route, built in sections by a number of independent companies. The first of these was the Darlington & Barnard Castle Railway, incorporated in 1854 and completed two years later. Its independent life was short, for it became a part of the Stockton & Darlington in 1858. At Barnard Castle this met the grandly named South Durham & Lancashire Union

Below *Modern services to Bishop Auckland and Saltburn just about keep Darlington's North Road station alive. On a cold February morning in 1993, a class 153 diesel railcar emerges from the old train shed*

Railway, a trans-Pennine line from West Auckland to Tebay inspired by the need to bring together the coal and coke of Durham and the iron and haematite of Cumbria, and opened throughout in 1863. It also joined, briefly, the Stockton & Darlington empire, as did the next part of the route, the Eden Valley Railway, from Kirkby Stephen to a junction with the London & North Western main line at Clifton, south of Penrith, completed in 1862. The last part, the scenic 31-mile journey through the heart of the Lake District, was built by the Cockermouth, Keswick & Penrith Railway between 1861 and 1864. Never planned as a major trans-Pennine through route, it was always owned and operated by different companies. East of Penrith it became the property first of the North Eastern Railway and then, in 1923, it was absorbed into the LNER. West of Penrith it was taken over first by the London & North Western and then the LMS. Its survival, until the 1960s, was largely because of its importance for freight, its connections making it probably the most useful of the four trans-Pennine routes that used to exist in the north of England. Today, only one of these four, the line from Carlisle to Newcastle, survives and that faces a rather uncertain future. As a passenger route it was always leisurely, with only the Lakeland section having any real tourist appeal. This kept the Penrith to Keswick section open until 1972, the rest of the route having been closed progressively from 1962.

From North Road station the line shared the Bishop Auckland route for a short while to Hopetown Junction, where it branched away to the west. There is not much to be seen among the housing estates and industry of north Darlington and the best place to find the line is to the west of the former A68 crossing, where the trackbed becomes a footpath and cycleway. The starting point is fairly obscure, at the edge of a housing estate and unmarked by signposts or markers until you are virtually on it. It also has to be said that, as cycleways go, this one is not particularly gripping and so only real addicts need to seek it out. It continues westwards for a while, crossing a minor road and ending near the A1(M). Near by, a little to the west, is the site of Merrybent Junction, where a goods line ran southwards towards Barton, crossing the Tees at the point where the motorway now roars over it.

A bumpy and muddy bridleway turns south off the B6279 near Thornton Hall and comes, in due course, to the site of the railway. The trackbed, overgrown and scattered with builders' rubble and farm debris, curves across the fields in a slight cutting. Braving the puddles and the piles of soggy earth and cement, we got out of the car and explored, hoping to find something more tangible, some recognisable relic to justify the rich deposits of mud already covering our shoes and the car. It began to rain and we soon gave up, but not before my daughter

had begun to share the excitement of the chase. From that point on she proved herself a dedicated spotter of lost railways, quickly learning to pick out overgrown embankments and cuttings or the line of the trackbed across a field and, more importantly, to identify surviving structures and more specific remains. We drove on, pausing next at Carlbury where a much-extended house still contains, at its heart, the former crossing-keeper's cottage. A shout from behind drew my attention to an old cast-iron plaque, attached to a newish brick wall, bearing in relief below a large number the magic initials, S&DR. This was a major breakthrough, and the spotting of similar plaques throughout the day enabled positive identification of former Stockton & Darlington structures to be made.

At Piercebridge there was a station to seek out, and we did not have to look for long before finding the large timber-framed building enjoying a new life as a kennels and cattery, and conveniently called Station House. Decorative barge boarding and generous proportions set a standard followed by other surviving station houses and established a distinctive style for this part of the line. Across the road and occupying what had clearly once been railway sheds and the goods yard is a road freight depot. Lorries stood in serried ranks in the rain, as though underscoring their conquest of the transport system, but in one corner there was the battered body of an old wooden goods wagon, now used as a store but still keeping the railway flag flying.

Our next target was the site of the former junction with the branch that used to run southwards for a few miles to serve some quarries near Forcett. This branch was built in

Above With closure threatening, the line was attracting its share of specials. In October 1964 the preserved LNER K4 The Great Marquess, at the head of a typical special, is passed at Hopetown by the regular diesel Darlington to Barnard Castle service

N. E. R.

BARRAS.

the bridge there was a pile of ancient sleepers, neatly stacked thirty years ago by the demolition gangs and quietly returning to nature. We spent a long time enjoying it all.

The next stop was Gainford, which we approached as the sun broke through. First we followed a little lane to a bridge just to the east of the village. The bridge is still there, although it has been filled in, and on one side the track has disappeared completely. On the other side it survives, though completely overgrown. However, far more exciting was the discovery in an adjacent field of a group of old wagons, long abandoned after a period of post-railway duty as stabling. Some of them were metal, some wood, some had been burned, some taken over by bushes, and on one or two the old identification numbers were still readable. It was a picturesque scene of gentle decay.

In the village the station house was easily found, a handsome stone building in the characteristic style of the line, standing above a length of platform and surrounded by recent housing. It is now a private house, but a

Above *The site of the old junction with the Forcett line is a secret world of railway relics and memories*

Right *Old wagons quietly crumbling away in a field near Gainford maintain a link with railway days*

1866 as an independent line, the Forcett Railway, and it remained so, rather surprisingly, until the 1923 groupings. It then became part of the LNER and in due course part of British Railways, before finally closing in 1966. On the OS map a footpath off the A67, through East Greystone, appears to lead in half a mile or so directly to the junction. This, clearly marked from the road, started well but then went straight into a farmyard. We pressed on, negotiating various friendly but noisy dogs, a horse or two and finally a farmer on a tractor who pointed out the hedge we had to follow. A short distance on, we came to a fine stone bridge spanning a shallow cutting. In the field across the bridge a line of old brown stoneware sinks, mottled with moss and now in service as animal troughs, stretched away from the path, which turned left to follow the trackbed, finally dropping down to cross it right by the junction. It is a wonderful, secret spot, full of railway magic, all greens and greys under the lightening sky. The old main line, a low grass-covered embankment lined with bushes, goes straight on across the fields, while the branch swings away to the south, well defined but mysterious. Various grassy mounds, atmospheric, almost prehistoric, mark the sites of buildings and other now unfathomable railway structures. Every now and then some piece of old ironwork could be seen sticking out of the grass, a hint of something huge and deeply buried. Towards

plaque on the platform fence commemorates its previous life. Gainford is set in a bend of the Tees, looking out across the valley that by now was alive in the bright winter sunshine. To the west of the village the line makes two crossings of the meandering river. Both bridges were well-known features of the line and, remarkably, both are still there. The first, easily seen from a layby on the A67, is a fine stone structure of four graceful arches on rusticated pillars, in the sunshine soft gold against the shimmering blue of the fast-flowing river. There is

no way on to it, but it can be fully enjoyed from the fields near by. The road then climbs high above the river and from the woods at its crest there is an exciting view of the second bridge, a more conventional iron viaduct well placed on the curving river and framed by the surrounding trees.

The next station was at Winston, well to the north of its village, and once again its remains were easily identified, spread around the site of the former level crossing on the B6274. On one side an attractive single-storey stone building stands beside the grassy trackbed, while across the road there is another typical station house, this time shuttered, disused and half hidden by encroaching trees. There is also a magnificent stone goods shed and, overlooking the platform and now housing a coal merchant, a long low timber station complete with the old round station clock. From here a minor road follows the line westwards towards Little Newsham, to the site of a bridge long ago replaced by an embankment. On one side the trackbed stretches away into the distance, while on the other its route across a grassy field was made distinct by the sunlight throwing into shadow the soft but regular indentations left by the sleepers.

The line now makes its own way across the landscape for a few miles, inaccessible and private, while we followed the A688, a road that gave us a distant view of Raby Castle. According to my handy reprint of the 1947 Sectional Maps of British Railways (an essential tool for route and relic hunting), the next station was at Broomielaw, a place that on the modern Ordnance Survey map barely exists. A couple of buildings are shown at the end of a very minor white road, standing either side of the dotted line that indicates the 'dismtd rly'. We drove down the little road, barely more than a track, wondering if there really was a station here and, if so, who had ever used it. At the bottom of a wooded dip, below a gaunt stone house that might once have had railway connections, we stopped. At first there appeared to be nothing to see other than the trackbed, clearly visible on one side of the filled-in bridge. The view from the other side, partly hidden by trees, looked unpromising, but I persevered while the others stayed in the warmth of the car.

It was well worth it. Deep in the cutting beyond the bridge and surrounded by bushes and trees that would have hidden it from view in the summer was the station. The platform, liberally covered with grass and wild plants, curves away towards the distant fields and against the bank of the cutting are all the wooden station buildings. The canopy spreads its shelter over the platform and on the wooden walls are the panels that used to display the timetables and travel posters. All the name plates have gone and all the colour from the bleached and weatherbeaten wood, but what remains is romantic beyond belief, something straight out of *Sleeping Beauty*. I dragged my companions from the car and we all looked for a long time, enjoying the vision, before we left it to slumber in the soft sunlight.

Above *A fine stone bridge carried the railway across the Tees to the west of Gainford. Today it is one of the line's most impressive memorials*

Above *Cast-iron plaques like this one with the S&DR initials are still vital clues to former railway buildings. This plaque is all that remains at Barnard Castle*

BARNARD CASTLE TO KIRKBY STEPHEN

By comparison Barnard Castle was something of a disappointment. The town was as lovely as ever and miraculously unchanged by heritage mania. We explored a bit, had a satisfactory lunch in an old café, and then I showed my team the ruined castle, its broken golden walls rising high above the hump-backed bridge over the Tees. It was very stirring and, against the pattern of such things, better and grander than I remembered. However, when it came to the railway, there was nothing. We toured up and down the estates to the north of the town searching for the point where the Barnard Castle line joined the South Durham & Lancashire Union, but everything seemed to have vanished beneath a huge Glaxo factory. We were about to give up when my daughter spotted, on the side of an unremarkable cottage, one of the S&DR iron plaques. At least we knew where the railway had been, even if there was nothing much to see.

North of the town we found the line again, in the form of a viaduct that used to carry it over the Black Beck, but this is now private, part of a stables complex. We pressed on westwards along the B6277 and were rewarded by a distant view of the line high above the steep, wooded valley of the Tees. Originally it crossed on a big iron viaduct, one of the major engineering features for which the South Durham was justly famous, but this has long gone, leaving just the great stone abutments towering above the chasm. It must have been an exciting journey. From here the line goes in a great loop across the hills towards Lartington, passing the site of the junction with the branch that continued up along the Tees Valley to Middleton-in-Teesdale. Lartington station, surprisingly large and impressive and now a substantial private house, stands in a cutting just north of the road bridge in the centre of the village. A battered railway gate that used to lead down to the platform swung off its hinges and near by, hidden in the undergrowth, was a real treasure, a cast-iron North Eastern Railway boundary marker. After Lartington the line swings south again, climbing through cuttings and embankments away from the surrounding woodland and fields. From the bridge that carries the A67 there are good views of the grassy trackbed curving away against a backdrop of hills and moorland.

Below *At Barnard Castle on a summer's day in July 1957, the 11.02 local to Middleton-in-Teesdale waits in the bay platform, while Standard class 4 No. 76020 starts the long haul up to Stainmore at the head of a freight train. Not a trace of this scene remains today*

We could not find much at Bowes, the station and the line having vanished beneath a new road complex where the A67 met the A66, and we drove on out across the empty vastness of Bowes Moor and Stainmore Forest, the colours all around beautiful in the low afternoon sun. From the A66, high above the Greta, the trackbed is almost always in view, though tantalisingly unapproachable, as it climbs up the river valley towards its 1,370ft summit. This was a hard line, much used by heavy freight trains, with the locomotives having to fight against the wind and the weather. In winter, snow regularly closed it for days on end, despite the efforts of the ploughs and the clearance gangs, and it was unremitting in its bleakness. As we crossed the Pennine Way, deceptively alluring in the sunshine, the wind was like a knife.

The A66 sweeps on, following the route established by its Roman precursor, with the trackbed always in view below and then, at the moor's western edge, the two come together briefly before the road swings away to the north. We followed a minor road alongside the track to a stone overbridge, with spectacular views westwards towards the distant hills. In this empty fastness a farm gate gives access to the trackbed, taken over as so often for farm use, and on the gate a big sign says 'Beware of the Bull'. In a landscape devoted entirely to sheep, this can only be aimed at marauding urban railway enthusiasts, or walkers tempted by the level trackbed cutting across the hills. Visible from the road, the track curves round to Barras where another station lay waiting for us. High on a hillside, and serving a community of a handful of isolated farms and cottages, Barras station must always have been a bleak and windswept place. From the road above we had a wonderful view of the big station house, the tumbledown stone station on its platform and beyond it an infinite pattern of colourful fields and copses stretching towards a horizon of distant Lakeland hills.

Above *The station buildings at Barras survive today as a private house, with a spectacular view*

Below *Shortly before the line's closure, Standard class 4 No. 76048 hauls a Penrith to Darlington train out of Barras, with plenty of passengers soaking up the atmosphere*

After Barras the line follows a more secret route, cut into the steep hillside, carried by viaducts and embankments and through cuttings. A tunnel takes it under the rocky course of the River Belah. Footpaths cross by the tunnel mouths and farm tracks sometimes lead to the line, but broadly it is an inaccessible stretch, not to be taken lightly.

Returning to civilisation at Hartley, the line swings round east of Kirkby Stephen to drop down into the Eden Valley. The station, well to the south of the town centre, is in a yard taken over by industry, and little remained to attract our attention. Further to the south is another Kirkby Stephen station, still in use on the famous Settle to Carlisle line. We went westwards to a more evocative spot, on a minor road near Galebars, where the old South Durham line towards Tebay swung away to the right, to pass under the Settle & Carlisle at Smardale. Here was the junction with the Eden Valley Railway's line northwards to Appleby and Penrith. We looked at both lines from the tall bridges that crossed them, almost side by side, marvelling at the huge cuttings, and the endeavour it all represented, gone for ever beyond recall.

Left *One of the line's highlights was the American-style iron trestle viaduct at Belah. This view of it, taken shortly before closure, shows a class 2MT No. 46422 blasting across with a mixed freight, banked in the rear for the climb to Stainmore. Nothing remains of this remarkable structure*

Right *As the February light dwindles away in 1961, a diesel railcar on the Penrith to Darlington service drifts into Kirkby Stephen's distinctive train shed*

Lower Right *The train shed also features in this wood engraving of Kirkby Stephen and its staff, published in 1873 by the poet, John Close, in his* New Lakes Book

KIRKBY STEPHEN TO PENRITH

With the light beginning to go, we pushed on northwards across the softer landscape of the Eden Valley, catching occasional glimpses of the trackbed from a series of overbridges on minor roads. South of Great Musgrave an embankment takes it across the fields to the site of the bridge over the Eden. The embankment led us quickly to Musgrave station, now the outbuildings of a smart new house behind a smart new beech hedge. A neat plaque on a wall carries its name, Beech Ings, an unusually subtle variation on the familiar form.

At Warcop we had a surprise for, pulling in to what had been the station yard to the east of the village, we found the track still in place, a single line and some short sidings. Rusty and overgrown railway track always has a particular appeal, even when totally disused, as this clearly was, and we had a good time playing with the points levers, exploring the remains of the old signal box and standing on the platform waiting for a train that would never come. Demolition was under way, and some of the track had been lifted and left in heaps to await the scrapmen, but there was plenty there to allow the imagination to run riot. Until its recent, final closure this part of the line, from Flitholme east of Warcop and up to Appleby, had been kept open for military use, and so trains were by no means the distant memory

Poet Close's 4th Lake and Christmas Book.

RAILWAY OFFICIALS AT KIRKBY-STEPHEN STATION.

No. 1, Cameron ; 2, Murray ; 3, Herd ; 4, Moorhouse ; 5, Taylor ; 6, Dobson ; 7, Braithwaite, Booking-Clerk ; 8, Mr. Hogg, Station Master ; 9, Askew, Booking-Clerk, (now Station Master at Appleby): 10, Slee, (dead) ; 11, Davison ; 12, Hughes ; 13, Dixon ; 14, Staff-Porter Brunskill ; 15, Poet Close.
(Some of the above are gone.)

that they were everywhere else on the route.

A mile or so further on we left the car to walk the track for a while and came presently to a place where a footpath crossed over. Big notices told us to 'Stop Look and Listen'. We did so, but no trains came.

The A66 took us into Appleby alongside the railway and we carried on until we could see the spur that linked it to the Settle & Carlisle line. We called it a day then and found somewhere to spend the night, before visiting a friend whose house had a wonderful view of the raised embankment that carries the Settle

& Carlisle. He told us that they were now so used to seeing steam trains that they often did not bother to look up as they passed. He also told us that he had once seen, on a remote road that followed our route, an old signal box standing on its own in a field. He could not remember where, and so this became the challenge for the next day.

Leaving Appleby the next morning, we had some difficulty in finding our line as it had disappeared beneath the A66 north of the town. We finally tracked it down in farm use near Crackenthorpe and from here its route beside the A66 is easily followed, along the flat farmland of the Eden Valley and framed by distant snow-capped hills. We could not find much at Kirkby Thore, but at Temple Sowerby the station is readily identifiable, a white-painted house seen across the fields at the end of a tree-covered embankment, and a long way from its village. Who can ever have used these country stations, miles from anywhere?

Our navigator now took us on a slightly roundabout route in order to cross the Eden, and we followed remote and empty lanes for a while. At Cliburn we turned north again and climbed a hill out of the village. As we reached its summit, the road ahead dropped down into a little valley before climbing

again into Whinfell Forest. There, sitting in the valley, was the signal box, by the site of the level crossing it used to guard. It is not quite as remote as my friend had described it, nor as derelict, for it was clearly cared for, and not far away was Cliburn station, a pretty red stone building proudly dated 1866, now a private house, and the only one on the whole route to boast its own signal box.

From here the trackbed continues to the south of the forest, to cross under a minor road just by the Wetheriggs Pottery, and then a tree-covered embankment carries it across the fields towards Clifton, where it joins the main line for the run into Penrith. There is one more road bridge, completely filled in to the parapets so that a flock of Jacob sheep was standing on what would have been the roof of the train, and another, extremely decrepit, bridge that marks the route of a long abandoned link line to the south, and then the overgrown trackbed running past what used to be Clifton Moor station towards the overhead power lines of what is now the West Coast main line to Scotland.

PENRITH TO COCKERMOUTH

The sight and the noise of the modern trains on this line provided an almost aggressive sense of railway reality for a while as we hunted for the first traces of the old Cockermouth, Keswick & Penrith. Penrith station, of course, survives, but there is little of much relevance to be seen there and so we concentrated the search to the south, where the old line branched away westwards towards the Lakes. As so often, new roads and roundabouts have successfully buried the railway, but we eventually tracked it down in a field by the A66. From here its route, largely agricultural now, is easily followed as it loops up past Newbiggin and towards Great Blencow. An old signpost still indicated Blencow Stn 1½, but when we got there we were too late by twenty years or so and lorries stood about where the station had been. West of Penruddock the line was tenanted by sheep, but in the village it is a different story. The station is still to be seen, in an advanced state of decay, but much more striking is the big stone viaduct still striding above the cottages and farms. All that was missing were the trains.

Troutbeck station is also there, now a private house, on the A5091 just south of the junction with the A66, and the trackbed is well defined as it continues westwards into an increasingly dramatic landscape dominated by Souther Fell to the north and Great Mell to the south. The route is along a river

Left *Now a garden shed with a difference, Cliburn's former signal box marks the route of the track round Whinfell Forest*

Right *A Penrith-bound Ivatt class 2 runs east of Keswick in 1965, on what is now part of the Threlkeld to Keswick walkway*

Cockermouth, Keswick and Penrith Railway.

Date 27 - 5 -- 191 5

From THRELKELD

To

Via

Consignee,

Owner and No. of Waggon,

Owner and No. of Sheets and Under Sheets,

Above *A wagon consignment ticket, issued in August 1915, lives on long after the railway whose name it carries*

Right *Near Brundholme, half-way between Keswick and Threlkeld, an old girder bridge keeps railway memories alive for walkers enjoying the trackbed trail*

Far Right *Surrounded by overnight snow in April 1966, the 7.18am Penrith to Workington diesel railcar pauses at Cockermouth. No trace of this station remains today*

valley with fields to the north and a broad expanse of rising moorland to the south, framed by spectacular peaks. The fresh dusting of snow glittered in the sunshine. From a minor road there is a wonderful view of the trackbed crossing the moorland on a low embankment, with bridges intact and even a linesman's hut outlined against the white horizon of the Matterdale peaks. Increasingly remote and inaccessible, the line continues onwards to Threlkeld.

Threlkeld station, recognisable and complete with parts of platforms, is used by the County Council, but the station yard is now a car park for those wanting to join the official walkway along the track into Keswick. It is a wonderful walk, alongside and frequently crossing on old girder bridges the River Greta, in a narrow twisting valley framed by woodland and precipitous rock walls. For those not wanting to make the four-mile walk, there is an exciting drive on minor roads along the north side of the valley via Wescoe, Brundholme and Briery, high above the trackbed and with fine views down on to it. When the railway was built, there was plenty of well-orchestrated opposition, and for many its route straight through the Lakes was seen as

desecration. In the context of the desecration wrought on the Lakes on an annual basis by cars and coaches today, the railway was very small beer indeed. Had it survived, it could have played a major role in keeping the motorised hordes at bay. It was probably a dawning realisation of this that kept it open, at least from Penrith to Keswick, long after the rest of the route had gone, but it all came too late, and it was swept away in 1972. There must now be a very strong case for putting this railway back, as part of the battle to keep road traffic under control.

The walk continues right to the platform in Keswick's station, itself a remarkable and unexpected survivor. The building is intact, but rather disgracefully unused. Standing on the platform under the glazed canopy, we looked out over the paths and flower beds that had been carefully laid over the trackbed. There is no way through the boarded-up doors and windows, and the only way to see the station façade is to take a rather circuitous tour round the backyards of the Keswick Hotel. It is, however, essential to make the effort, for the station is a fine building, a symmetrical structure in rough stone looking rather like an old manor or a grand farm, and with its

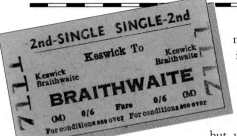

name in decorative wrought iron. Adjacent is the imposing bulk of the hotel, a flamboyant pile of architectural styles dating from 1869, whose sheer scale and bravura shows just how important the railway was in the development of Lakeland tourism.

The railway's route through the town is hard to track, but we found it again to the north, as an embankment running parallel to the new A66 ring road. This section is also a footpath, but not a very exciting one, enjoyed mainly by local dog-walkers. It is then traceable, but not approachable in any practical way, as it crosses the floodplain of the Derwent and curves round towards Braithwaite. Hurtling and impatient lorries on the A66 make looking for the possible site of Braithwaite station a hazardous activity, but we survived, just,

and found it up a little lane enjoying a new life as a private house. The platform, now well concealed as a fine terrace, looks out over a decorative garden.

From this point the railway completely vanishes, its destruction so complete that it is hard to believe it ever went any further. The secret, we soon discovered, is the A66, which has been built over the trackbed from here almost all the way to Cockermouth. Bassenthwaite Lake station seems to have disappeared and all we could find at Embleton was the crossing-keeper's cottage, much altered but still recognisable. Just east of Cockermouth, where the A66 swings away to the south, the railway reappears as an overgrown cutting and a low, tree-lined embankment seen across the fields. It follows the little valley of the Tom Rudd Beck straight into the town and so, not

Below *Two diesel railcars, one bound for Penrith and the other for Workington, meet at Bassenthwaite Lake station in 1963*

Right *Double-headed by two Ivatt class 2 locomotives, one of the many specials that were run over the line towards the end of its life comes into Cockermouth on a bright spring day in 1966*

Below Right *A page from the 1922 Bradshaw shows the timetable for the Penrith, Cockermouth and Whitehaven services with connection to and from London Euston*

surprisingly, its last mile or so has become a well-established, if not official, footpath. I walked along this for a while and was pleased to find tangible railway relics still surviving – the usual range of concrete fence and gate posts, some fine old iron gates and the lichen-decorated remains of a gradient post. We drove into Cockermouth and it did not take long to find Station Road, close by the old cattle market. Outside a junk shop just by the market entrance, was an old porter's trolley, in fading British Railways maroon. Inside the shop were old lamps and railway signs, but none had come from Cockermouth's station, flattened by bulldozers years ago. However, there were plenty of other things which my daughter wanted to cram into the car. Old habits die hard, even if on this occasion they skipped a generation.

This was the rather disappointing end of our journey but it was not, of course, the end of the line. In 1845 the building of a railway was authorised from Workington to Cockermouth and two years later its eight-mile route along the Derwent Valley was finally completed. It was this line that initially roused the ire of the Lakeland poets, a notable objector being Wordsworth's son John, the rector of Brigham. It appears he had some cause for complaint, for the projected route of the line went virtually through his garden and the Cockermouth & Workington Railway was obliged in the end to build a new rectory for him. For nearly twenty years Cockermouth was the end of the line, an isolated but rapidly expanding outpost of the extensive railway network that flourished along the Cumbrian coast. The arrival of the Cockermouth, Keswick & Penrith, which met it head-on in the town's station, ended that and opened a new route to the east, a line built, ironically in the light of later developments, more for freight than for passengers.

TARKA COUNTRY

♦

Halwill Junction to Barnstaple
Barnstaple to Ilfracombe
Lynton to Barnstaple (the Lynton & Barnstaple Railway)

A perfect setting for a country railway scene: class 2 tank locomotive No. 41238 hauls a mixed train over the Torridge near Torrington on a glorious late summer day in 1962

HISTORY

One of North Devon's earliest railways was the horse-drawn link, opened in 1848, between the town of Barnstaple and the quay at Fremington, a few miles west. When the main line from Exeter via Crediton joined this line at Barnstaple in 1854, the station became Barnstaple Junction. Pressure from the citizens of Bideford encouraged the extension of the Fremington line westwards and this was completed in 1855.

Many schemes were then drawn up for an extension south from Bideford towards Okehampton, but little happened until 1872 when the railway finally reached Torrington. The next stage took the form of a 3ft narrow gauge industrial line from Torrington southwards to Marland, built by the North Devon Clay Company in 1880 to provide an outlet for its products. Later, this was relaid as a standard gauge line and after much prevarication the final link between Marland, the end of the clay line, and Halwill, on the main Okehampton to Bude railway, was completed in 1925. Never a busy route, and one whose tourist potential remained unrealised, the line survived largely on its freight activities. In 1965 passenger services were withdrawn between Torrington and Halwill Junction and when the track was removed from Meeth southwards this section of the line, after a short life of only forty years, disappeared altogether. Passenger services from Torrington to Bideford and Barnstaple lingered on, but were soon withdrawn and by the early 1970s it was only the clay trains that kept the line alive. In 1982 these were also withdrawn and the line closed for good.

In a region dominated by the London & South Western Railway's networks, North Devon and the Atlantic coast were always a strong lure for the Great Western Railway. One of the many schemes that were considered was for a line from Bristol to Ilfracombe via Taunton, Dulverton and Barnstaple. In 1864 work began on a modified version of this, to a terminus in the centre of Barnstaple. Construction proved slow and expensive, and it was not until 1873 that the first train from Bristol was able to reach Barnstaple's new Victoria Road station, along what was in effect a 43-mile branch line from Taunton. In 1881 the Great Western once again set its sights on Ilfracombe; in 1885 a direct link was opened between the Taunton line and Barnstaple Junction, via a new bridge over the Taw, and by the early years of this century Great Western trains were able to run direct to Ilfracombe. This shared arrangement continued until 1960, when the Victoria Road station

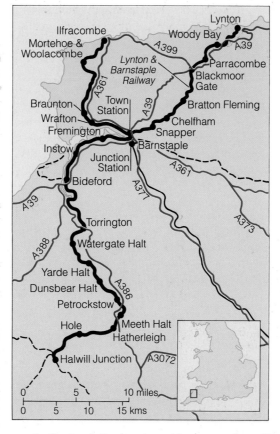

was finally closed. By then the writing was on the wall for the whole route, and the line from Taunton to Barnstaple was closed in 1966.

The Great Western's enthusiasm for Ilfracombe was shared by the London & South Western, but local opposition hindered plans for the building of its route until the early 1870s and the line was not completed until 1874. Major features in its construction were the

new bridge over the Taw that provided the link to Barnstaple Junction, and the rebuilding of the quays in Barnstaple that enabled to company to open a new station right by the river. Originally known as the Quay station, this was much extended and rebuilt in the late 1890s and renamed Barnstaple Town; it was also shared by the newly built Lynton & Barnstaple Railway. Rapidly successful, the Ilfracombe branch played an important part in the town's development as a major resort, but its busiest period was between the two World Wars, when Ilfracombe became part of the Southern Railway's Atlantic Coast Express network, as well as the terminus for other expresses from Waterloo, Paddington, Bristol and the Midlands. Some of these continued to run until the 1960s, but by then the resort's appeal had been eclipsed by cheap Continental package tours and in 1970 the line was closed. Track remained in place until 1975 while various attempts were made to acquire the line for preservation, but it was then removed, and in 1978 there followed the demolition of the bridge across the Taw.

For the citizens of Barnstaple, the only railway they really considered their own was the narrow gauge Lynton & Barnstaple. Sponsored by the publisher Sir Georges Newnes and opened in 1898, this little railway, with its 1ft 11½in gauge and its smart locomotives and carriages, always aroused strong local support even if it never made much money. Despite its slow and meandering route, it did much to develop the tourist potential of Lynton and Lynmouth, and it carried a respectable amount of freight. Subject from the 1920s to increasing competition from road traffic, especially motor coaches, it finally gave up the struggle and closed in 1935 despite considerable investment by the Southern Railway, who had taken control of it in 1923.

Left Exe, No. E760, one of the distinctive Lynton & Barnstaple locomotives, busies itself with shunting duties at Woody Bay station in April 1934. The station buildings survive, complete with grassy platforms, and now face a new future as the museum and headquarters for the Lynton & Barnstaple Railway Society

IN THE SPRING of 1973 I spent some time in North Devon on the trail of two subjects of particular interest to me, namely Victorian potteries and the author, Henry Williamson – topics wildly disparate in nature and linked only by geography. Helped by libraries, museums, Ordnance Survey maps and some entertaining exploration, the potteries, or at least their limited remains, proved quite easy to track down. Henry Williamson seemed likely to be more of a problem. A good knowledge of his novels and his landscape writing was all very well, but on its own could hardly be expected to conjure out of the air a man of considerable privacy. I did not even know his address. With no real thoughts as to how to proceed, I had virtually given up any idea of achieving something that seemed unreasonable, if not impossible. Then, incredibly enough, having stopped my car one day at the side of a road in Barnstaple to look at the map, I happened to glance in the mirror and recognised the man himself walking down the pavement towards me. Overcoming my natural instinct to let him walk by unmolested, I seized this extraordinary chance and leapt out of the car. The brief conversation that followed was insubstantial to say the least, but it enabled me to cross one long-held ambition off the list.

A certain amount of time was also happily wasted on that trip in the pursuit of canals. Highlights included the relics of the Bude Canal's eccentric engineering, notably the inclined planes that enabled the small wheeled barges to overcome the undulations of the landscape. Equally exciting was the Beam aqueduct which carried the Rolle Canal over the Torridge, a fine stone structure whose magnificence is quite disproportionate to the insignificant waterway it was laboriously built to serve.

Back on the Victorian potteries trail, I also began to look at railways, for curiosity had taken me to the clay pits of North Devon, the source of the raw material that was vital to the industry not only locally, but in much of North Staffordshire as well. Clay was even shipped to North America, a surprising but lucrative and long-lasting trade. At that time, the clay was still transported by train, rather than in the thundering English China Clay trucks that now block the lanes and threaten the villages of this area, and I well remember my first sight of lines of old wooden-sided wagons filling the sidings that served the pits at Meeth and Peters Marland. I decided there and then that the Victorian potters had had enough of my time and I switched my attention to the railways.

Starting from those sidings, deep in the moorland south of Torrington, I followed the railway line northwards to Barnstaple via Bideford. The rusty tracks, carrying only the irregular clay trains, wound their way through woodland and then along the valley of the Torridge towards its estuary. It was a line of great appeal and diversity, particularly in its semi-derelict state, making its way across a continually changing landscape by cuttings, embankments and bridges, with some surprisingly steep gradients and sharp curves. Passenger services had ceased several years before, after the closure of the southern link to Okehampton and Exeter via Halwill Junction, but plenty remained to be discovered and brought back to life with a bit of imagination. Some of the larger stations were intact, notably Torrington and Bideford, and even some of the smaller halts were still there. Buried in woods beside a tumbling stream was a small single platform, marked by typical Southern Railway concrete name boards. In 1973, at the height of President Nixon's débâcle, it was curious to be standing at a remote and long-forgotten station called Watergate.

Bideford's station, set high above the Torridge's western shore and flanked by old warehouses and hotels, offered a marvellous view across the river to the town, spread along the ancient quays. It must have been a beautiful place to wait for a train, watching the tide racing through the narrow arches of the stone

Below *A single platform among the trees is all that remains of Watergate, once a typical North Devon halt*

bridge. From here the line curved along beside the ever-widening estuary, that great expanse of tidal water formed by the confluence of the Torridge and the Taw, past Instow and Fremington, with mudflats and water birds, marshy creeks and rotting hulks, and the old army sidings for company, before swinging eastwards towards Barnstaple. Once the meeting point for five lines, Barnstaple in the early 1970s was well on the way to becoming a town of railway ghosts. Three lines still came together at Barnstaple Junction, the station well to the south of the town, the most important of which was the former main route south to Exeter via Crediton, now little more than a long branch. The others were the clay line to Torrington and beyond, with its occasional trains keeping the weeds and bushes at bay, and the once-busy branch northwards to Ilfracombe, by then closed but with its tracks still in place. Already gone was the former Great Western line to Taunton, another long branch born out of Victorian competition, whose trains ran originally to Barnstaple's third station, Victoria Road, and then later crossed the Taw on an iron viaduct that took them into the Junction station. This meandering last link in the Great Western's long haul to the Atlantic coast from Paddington closed in 1963 and had already disappeared into history. Even more of a fading memory was the narrow gauge Lynton & Barnstaple Railway, whose leisurely route to the north Devon coast from Barnstaple Town station, across the Taw, had been driven to oblivion in the mid-1930s by cars and motor buses.

The Town station, well placed near the centre of Barnstaple and greatly expanded since the opening of the Ilfracombe branch, was all still there in 1973, ranged along the Taw's north bank immediately after the curved iron bridge that carried the line over the river. After over two years of disuse, the bridge, the station and the line as a whole were showing clear signs of decay, and had that particular and rather romantic quality that is part of the appeal of the abandoned railway. I decided to follow its route, at first westwards along the estuary, passing the airfield at Chivenor, then swinging north towards Braunton. From here it ran along a little wooded valley beside a stream, at first between bungalows and suburban gardens that were already planning their take-overs of the track, and then into the hills. I remember the feeling of melancholy when I stopped at level crossings or bridges to examine the line in the soft evening light. Everything was still in place, waiting silently for the pounding, rattling roar of a passing express hauled by its chunky, green West Country class steam locomotive, a part of daily life gone for ever. A few years earlier, this line had been part of the complex network of the Atlantic Coast Express, one of the Southern's proudest trains. Now there was just the sound of the birds, the gentle wind and the ghosts of all that once had been.

Leaving the hills and swinging west, the line ran through the

surprisingly large station called Mortehoe and Woolacombe which was built to serve those resorts a few miles away on the coast. A big hotel stood by the station, a stranded whale abandoned by all those passengers who must once have booked in to avoid missing the early train. The railway then began its long descent down to Ilfracombe, and I followed this final stretch on foot. It was a fine walk, along the already weed-strewn single track, first through a cutting and then through the woods that flanked the Slade reservoirs, their waters filled with the golden green light of the spring evening. I marched through the short tunnel, imagining the heavy holiday trains, double-headed with a banking engine, blasting their way up the hill out of Ilfracombe, and then I followed the line down through woods to its terminus high above the town and the distant spread of the sea. Ilfracombe station at that time had a *Marie Celeste* quality, everything in place but suddenly deserted. The concrete 1930s name boards stood guard over the empty platforms while the paint on the awnings slowly faded and the sea air turned the tracks a soft orange brown.

Above *After the line's closure, Ilfracombe station lingered on for a while, a ghostly reminder of the great days of the 1930s. Since 1973, when this photograph was taken, the site has been completely flattened and redeveloped*

London and South Western Ry. 787
—
FROM WATERLOO TO
FREMINGTON

Above *Today Halwill Junction is just a name on a map, the station having vanished beneath a housing estate. Its former life is shown in this 1962 view, with the arrival of the 9.56am Okehampton to Padstow train under the control of class N No. 31843*

Below *A section from British Railways' 1963 summer timetable*

heart of rural Devon, some 500 feet above sea level, was busy with West Country expresses, local stopping trains and all kinds of goods traffic, with services to Plymouth, Exeter and London, Bude and Padstow, Bideford and Barnstaple stopping at its platforms. Here the great Atlantic Coast Express would pause while the coaches for Bude were detached from the train that went on to Wadebridge and Padstow. From the mid-1960s Halwill Junction began to lose its trains and its tracks, and now there are no railways there at all.

Precious little remains today even to hint that trains ever came to central Devon. Halwill Junction station and all its buildings have disappeared completely beneath a new housing estate, appropriately called Stationfields and with a road named Beeching Close. Only the Junction Inn, with its locomotive sign and its collection of old photographs and relics inside, gives a clue to what used to be here. The raised mound that marks the track of the line from the south, now a footpath curving away past the village recreation ground, can be seen disappearing into the trees towards Okehampton, but there is nothing in the village itself. The first traces of the lines that used to run north and west from Halwill Junction can be found in an overgrown cutting just beyond the new estate, which opens out into a wide expanse of former sidings partly cleared for local walkers, courting couples and dog exercisers. Discernible first is the branch that swung westwards towards Padstow, disappearing into the bushes. The path, still well defined, crosses a more open landscape, with farmland views to the west, and then enters a thicket of bushes through a round hole that from a distance looks like a tiny tunnel. It soon peters out in dense woodland and even the most determined of explorers quickly finds the way barred by a wire fence and a red 'No Entry' sign. Just beyond here is the point where the route northwards to Barnstaple branched away, leaving the main line for the holiday traffic to Bude.

The first few miles northwards from Halwill Junction are secret, impenetrable and largely private, a hidden world whose dense coverage of brambles and trees makes it hard to believe that trains ever ran here, let alone as recently as thirty years ago. The only way to see the line is from the parapets of road bridges, or from the place where a road bridge used to be, where there are glimpses of the trackbed curving away into a tantalisingly inaccessible wooded wilderness. Buried in this is what used to be the first station, Hole. Miles from any village, it can never have seen much traffic. Yet, old photographs show the double track, two platforms, and a number of people getting on and off the trains. The railway trackbed is at the heart of a nature reserve, a new use into which many former railways seem naturally to slip. Near Highampton there were two level crossings, of which no trace remains today. Such crossings were

HALWILL JUNCTION TO BARNSTAPLE

Returning twenty years later, I found that first visit had become a distant dream, memories made uncertain by the discovery that everything has changed almost beyond recognition. Deciding to do more than merely retrace my steps along the clay line from Meeth, I went first to Halwill Junction, now just a small hinterland village hard even to find on the map, but formerly an important railway junction and the meeting point for four lines. Once upon a time this remote spot in the

HALWILL, HATHERLEIGH and TORRINGTON

Miles			Week Days only					Miles			Week Days only				
			am	am SX		am SO	pm SX	pm				am	am		pm SX	pm SO
				1038		1052	6 30				dep	6 25	8 52		4 40	
	Halwill	dep		1047			6 39			Torrington		6 32	8 59		4 47	
3	Hole			11 1	11 5		6 57		1½	Watergate Halt		6 46	9 13		4 20 5	
7½	Hatherleigh		7 55	1126	1119		7 8		4¼	Yarde Halt		6½52 9 18			4 25 5	
10	Meeth Halt		8 4	1136	1132	4 37	7 18		5½	Dunsbear Halt			9 28		4 34 5 16	
12½	Petrockstow		8 10	1141	1142	4 46	7 28		7½	Petrockstow			9 38		4 44 5 26	
14½	Dunsbear Halt		8 24	1155	1152	4 52	7 34		10½	Meeth Halt			9 48		4 54 5 36	
16	Yarde Halt				1157	5 6	7 48		12½	Hatherleigh			10 8		5 13 5 56	
18½	Watergate Halt				1211	5 14	7 56		17½	Hole			1018		5 23 6 6	
20½	Torrington	arr	8 32	12 2	1218				20½	Halwill	arr					

SX Mondays to Fridays **SO** Saturdays only **†** Arrival

(7/89) SOUTHERN RAILWAY.
— FROM WATERLOO TO (787)
HOLE

traffic has been destroying the little roads of Devon. Clay pits and quarries usually had their own internal railway systems and the North Devon ones were no different. What was different was the construction in 1880 by the North Devon Clay Company of its own 3ft gauge line from Marland north to Torrington, where it met the branch line that had opened eight years earlier. While clay was the major traffic, also important were the pale yellow Marland bricks, a great industry that gave distinctive colour to many North Devon towns and villages. In due course this clay line was relaid to standard gauge and finally, after much public pressure, was extended southwards to meet the Southern Railway's Atlantic Coast line at Halwill Junction. This final link

Above *Halwill Junction today is just a trackbed path through the woods*

Right *Hatherleigh station, seen here in September 1962, is now a private house*

a feature of the line and there were plenty of them, sometimes over farm tracks and minor roads where the lack of gates forced the trains to crawl along with whistles shrieking. Cutting through the hills and following a brook that leads to the Torridge, the track makes its secret way eastwards, running close to the A3072, past Hatherleigh, whose remote station is now a private house. This is a pretty area of wooded fields, winding rivers and small lakes given over to trout fishing, rural Devon at its best. The line of a hedge, a wooded embankment or a tree-filled cutting seen from a bridge are often the only clues to the railway's former existence.

The A386 crosses the trackbed near Hele Bridge and then runs parallel for a mile or so before a sharply curving cutting brought the line into next station, Meeth. Meeth never boasted more than a single platform and a little shed-like waiting room, and it is surprising to find the platform virtually intact, albeit hidden beneath a mass of rampant blackberries. What was the station yard is now the entrance to one of the great clay pits of this area. It was these that brought the railway into being and kept it alive for some years after all the passengers had gone, and it is an irony – and a reflection upon our sense of values – that since the short-sighted closure of the railway, the ideal carrier for this kind of mineral traffic, in the early 1980s the huge clay

Above *The 8.52am Torrington to Halwill Junction train at Dunsbear Halt in 1962. Now Dunsbear is just a grassy platform on the Tarka Trail*

Far Right *Class 2 No. 41310 takes on water at Torrington in September 1962, while milk tankers in the sidings reflect the station's major cargo*

was not completed until 1925 and its active passenger-carrying life of only forty years was one of the shortest in West Country history. Now, the clay pits of Meeth and Marland continue to thrive, but their railway is just a dotted line on a map, an overgrown track across the fields, largely invisible.

It all changes at the next station, Petrockstow, ¾ of a mile northeast from the village, on a minor road running up to the A386. Suddenly the bushes and trees have been swept away, and the track becomes a broad path through the landscape, initially grassy and then giving way to a firmer surface. Though its buildings have gone, Petrockstow still has its platforms, all tidy and trim, and adjacent in the former goods yard is a car park and picnic site. A map and information panel announce this as the official start of the 23-mile bridle- and cycleway that leads all the way to Barnstaple, itself part of the 180-mile long Tarka Trail long-distance footpath, an exploration of the moorland, coastline and remote countryside of the Taw and Torridge rivers that is the setting for Henry Williamson's book, *Tarka the Otter*. The track proper starts just the other side of the road, over what used to be a level crossing. When the clay line to Meeth was finally closed in 1982, the route was taken over by the local authority and turned into a splendid long-distance path. It was opened in two stages, Barnstaple to Bideford in 1987, and Bideford to Petrockstow two years later. If a railway has to close, this is the perfect use for the track, and this one has been notably successful. Even out of season it carries a

continuous traffic of cyclists, and along the route a number of cycle hire depots have been opened, catering for both casual users and dedicated enthusiasts.

Easily followed from here thanks to its firm surface, sometimes tarmac, sometimes gravel and sometimes grass, the track's route is a reminder of the steep gradients and sharp curves that made the line so challenging for engine drivers in the days of steam. Platforms and other traces remain of the next stations, Dunsbear (on a minor road east of Winswell) and Yarde (on a minor road that turns south off the A386 at Gribble Inn). At the latter another car park and picnic site is overlooked by a line of terraced houses redolent of Victorian industry and rather out of place in the Devon landscape. An attractive wooded stretch drops the track down to Watergate, on the B3227, and then it twists and turns its way alongside a little river and on to the viaduct that carries it to Torrington. The hilltop town of Torrington is away to the east, high above its riverside station, which is still remarkably intact. There is even a short stretch of track to provoke the illusion of railway reality, but the traffic now is all two-wheeled. Long gone are the days when tank wagons would carry two million gallons of Torrington milk to London each year.

From Torrington the track follows the Torridge closely, initially criss-crossing the winding river. It is always a strange feeling to walk or ride across a former railway bridge, with the enjoyment of the views curiously heightened by an irrational sense of trespassing on forbidden territory. From one bridge there is a magnificent view of the great stone arches of the former Beam aqueduct, which now carries nothing more than the drive to Beam House. Beyond here, past Weare Giffard, the track clings to the side of the river valley, following the line of the old Rolle Canal, a minor and short-lived waterway that featured the same wheeled tub boats as the Bude network, carrying the same agricultural cargoes. Next comes the short tunnel that takes the track under the A386. This road runs parallel to the railway, at a higher level. Little can be seen from it, it is very busy, and anyone paying more attention to old railways and canals than to modern coaches and lorries runs the risk of an untimely end. The track then drops down through Landcross and over the river on the big curving iron viaduct. The last mile into Bideford is beside the ever-widening river, through an open landscape. With its little signal box, two old maroon carriages parked at the platform and its restored station buildings, Bideford is a deliberate time-warp (one carriage serves in summer as an information centre and tea room, and the station buildings are now home to the Devon Countryside Service and Tarka Trail offices). There is double track and a set of points, a signal, a couple of milk churns, a porter's trolley. The sense of railway reality was underlined on my visit by a

Above *The delightful signal box at Instow, preserved complete with all its fittings and a short section of track, is smartened up for the 1995 season*

an artist was hard at work depicting the box and its seaside setting as it might have been in the days of steam, and without the procession of passing cyclists. The station itself has gone, replaced by the more down-to-earth needs of the local sailing club. After Instow the track runs through the bungalows and chalets that face out over the dunes and the great expanse of golden sands and then passes a power station as it curves round across a remote region of saltmarsh and mudflats, well away from the main road sprawl of Yelland and Fremington. A short cutting leads to Fremington Quay and another iron viaduct that takes the track over the inlet with its moored boats and elderly hulks quietly decaying into the mud. This was once army territory, with extensive sidings to serve the camps and the old stone quays, but little now remains except a water tower, so completely covered by ivy that it looks like a squared-up piece of topiary, and some old sheds that bear traces of recent travellers' tales and house parties. Another remote stretch completes the journey to Barnstaple Junction, now a sad station isolated from its town by a modern factory estate, very much the end of the line where previously there had been a thriving centre of railway activity.

couple of old ladies sitting on a seat, apparently waiting for a train, and a man busy earthing up and replanting the waiting room window boxes. The illusion was rather shattered by the track's abrupt ending just beyond the platform and by the continuous stream of bicycles passing along it, paying little attention to the signal that gave them a clear road. Almost adjacent to the station is the grandiose Royal Hotel, which still boasts its private access to the platform.

Bideford once had, of course, another railway, independent, unconnected to the main line, and remarkably short-lived. Promoted in the 1860s, but not built until 1901, it ran from Bideford Quay near the town centre to Westward Ho! Inspired by a holiday traffic that never really materialised, it was later extended to Appledore, with eleven stations on its seven-mile route, much of which was right beside the Atlantic. Never fulfilling even a fraction of its promoters' hopes, the line was closed and dismantled during World War I, but plenty of clues were left behind for the keen-eyed explorer.

Bleak and windswept in winter, the route of the main line from Bideford to Barnstaple follows the river and the A39 northwards, with the huge new road bridge spawned by the demands of holiday traffic looking like an out-of-scale monster. At Instow the trains used to run through the heart of the village and once again a platform with concrete name board, a signal, a length of track and a little signal box, now a listed building with all its machinery, creates a sense of suspended reality. When I arrived, the signal box was having its annual repaint, and near by

BARNSTAPLE TO ILFRACOMBE

Beyond the buffers that now mark the end of the modern railway journey from Exeter to Barnstaple are the remains of two lines, both making their way under the A39. The one on the left is the end of the cycle track from Petrockstowe, the former line south to Halwill Junction, while the one on the right used to curve sharply round to cross the Taw to Barnstaple Town station and the start of the line to Ilfracombe. In 1978 the curving iron bridge over the Taw was removed, and today it is quite hard even to see where it used to be. Any modern exploration of the Ilfracombe branch has, therefore, to start at the Town station which, with its preserved station buildings, canopy, platform and signal box, is as good a place as any. Where there used to be trains there are now old people's flats and a riverside walkway, but hanging over the platform are green enamel signs saying suitable things such as 'Way Out' and 'Ladies', and the signal box contains a museum of relics of the Lynton & Barnstaple Railway, whose little trains also used to set off from the Town station, dwarfed by the huge expresses from London, Bristol and even further afield.

The first six miles or so of the route to Ilfracombe, from Barnstaple to Braunton along the Taw Estuary, are also a cycleway and so the track is still in good shape, well surfaced, with trimmed hedgerows and fine views out across the tideway. The route starts on Barnstaple's old quays and crosses the mouth of the River Yeo where originally there was a swing bridge to allow boats in and

out of the river moorings. With railways once running along both sides of the Taw westwards from Barnstaple, there must have been plenty of opportunities for train-to-train views across the widening mudflats. Now both tracks are cycleways but the distance is too great for cyclists to wave at each other across the water. At Chivenor the track runs inland, turning northwards as it passes the runways and hangars of the RAF base, and then enters Braunton alongside a little river whose quays at Velator, just south of the town, were home to the town's famous fleet of ketches that sailed to the Bristol Channel ports, and far further afield. North of Braunton it is a very different story. When the rails were finally lifted in 1975, after all the attempts to preserve the line had collapsed, those householders whose predatory intentions I had noted two years earlier moved in for the kill and much of the trackbed was absorbed into gardens big and small. Detailed exploration is, therefore, impossible now, even though the main A361 runs right beside the line for much of the route. There are glimpses from bridges and at some former level crossings on minor roads the rails are still there, embedded in asphalt and framed by gateways that lead directly into private gardens. One boasts a signal and other railway relics now incorporated into a complex horticultural scheme. After a few miles the map shows the track swinging westwards, away from the A361 and the river valley, but thick woods and the folds of the landscape make it hard to see very much and from here the route is largely inaccessible across farmland.

The line next appears near Turnpike Cross, off the B3231, at what was once Mortehoe and Woolacombe station. No longer derelict, the station is born again as part of the Once Upon A

Above *In August 1964 a Great Western visitor, No. 6363, drops the Taunton to Ilfracombe train down the slope from Mortehoe, while* (**below**) *a former Southern Railway class N and a Great Western 4300 class haul the Taunton train in tandem up the steep incline from Ilfracombe*

Time theme park, where 'dreams come true'. Pigs are the theme of this particular fantasy park, to be seen in every shape and form all over the place. When I was there, long after closing time on an autumn evening, the place was overlaid by a strong smell of real pigs. Whether this was part of the porcine experience I shall never know. The former station buildings are all there, but taken over by play areas and restaurants. Sitting by the platform two real carriages now house fairy-tale favourites, trapped for ever in this piggy world. Elsewhere there is a piggy train and a fantasy train ride, but there is little to link the site with any reality to the great days of the Ilfracombe line. Even the view from the football field behind the park, with the station standing high against the horizon, is marked by a giant totem-like plastic pig.

Soon after the station the line completely disappears and only a grassy slope marks the site of the bridge that carried the road from Mortehoe and Woolacombe to Turnpike Cross. The track soon reappears, and from here there is a semi-official footpath to the next bridge, at Lee Cross. Here, beside the B3231 ⅓ mile north of the junction with the B3343, a car park and notice boards announce the start of the official walkway and cycleway all the way along the track to the Cairns nature reserve just outside Ilfracombe. This is the walk I did years before, and now, with its firm surface, it certainly makes for easier walking than the unnatural stride imposed by sleepers. It has, of course, ceased to be in any sense a railway, and that makes the walking more prosaic; it is now a country path with lovely views rather than a track bearing the tangible memory of thundering

Above *An embankment carried the line to Ilfracombe past the Slade reservoirs. Today the embankment, pierced now and then by accommodation tunnels, carries a footpath through the woods*

I had seen in 1973. I walked around the grassy wasteland behind the factory, trying to work out the location of sidings, goods sheds, turntable and all that other railway paraphernalia. All I found was a great mound of spoil, roughly levelled, but far higher than the tracks had been. Wandering across this, I suddenly noticed contained within it and on its surface all sorts of railway bits, sections of rail, rusty spikes, broken ceramic electrical sockets, old stoneware bottles, parts of a porcelain sink, lumps of shattered concrete that were part of the 1930s Southern Railway detailing I remembered, and even broken cups from a refreshment room. This mound was clearly Ilfracombe station, bulldozed regardless, smashed into little bits and just piled up out of the way. Perhaps in a thousand years archaeologists will put it all together again.

LYNTON TO BARNSTAPLE

In 1973 I ran out of time before I could complete my railway tour of North Devon and I failed to look at the Lynton & Barnstaple Railway. I knew about it as a phenomenon and a curiosity, and I suppose I left it alone on the basis that whatever was still there then, forty years after it had closed, was likely to remain there for some time to come. As it turned out, I was right to concentrate on lines that were at least in existence, even if not particularly active, and whose future seemed uncertain.

Looking for the Lynton & Barnstaple is real railway hunting, with much more to it than simply following the dotted line on the Ordnance Survey map. There are no footpaths or cycleways to make it easy and some sections have completely disappeared back into the landscape. Others have become country lanes or sunk beneath reservoirs. It was a small-scale railway built with simple engineering, and so its track is often little more than a narrow path or a line of broken walling across a field. Sometimes it is just the lie of a hedge that is the give-away. In its own way it was a stylish railway, with good standards and a distinctive look, and this helps the identification of those structures that still stand. Its rather Swiss-style stations, for example, look just like houses by some minor Arts and Crafts architect, but are easy to spot once you know what to look for.

For no particular reason I started at the Lynton end, and did not take long to find the terminus station, high above the town's precipitous streets, and now just one more house in a row of prosperous villas and cottages. The style was unmistakable, but any lingering doubts were removed by the platform in the back garden, the railway signs and the unusual presence in the garden of a retired diesel narrow gauge locomotive, bright red and proudly bearing the name *Brunel*. There is also a plaque on the front of the house explaining its significance. Not much else remains, and on leaving the station the track goes straight into

locomotives. However, it is still a wonderful walk, with the colours reflected in the Slade reservoirs better than ever, and one bore of the Slade tunnel still part of the route. The winding walk down to Ilfracombe, with the distant views of the sea, and the town's suburban streets hidden by trees, is a delight. The cycleway stops rather suddenly, in the middle of nowhere, and there is then just a footpath across an area of grassy wasteland. Cyclists are supposed to wheel their machines across this and then down a gloomy little path that runs beside the huge warehouse and factory complex standing exactly where the station used to be. With its barbed wire perimeter fence and its security gates, it is a sad comment on our modern age, and a very poor replacement for the romantic and forlorn station that

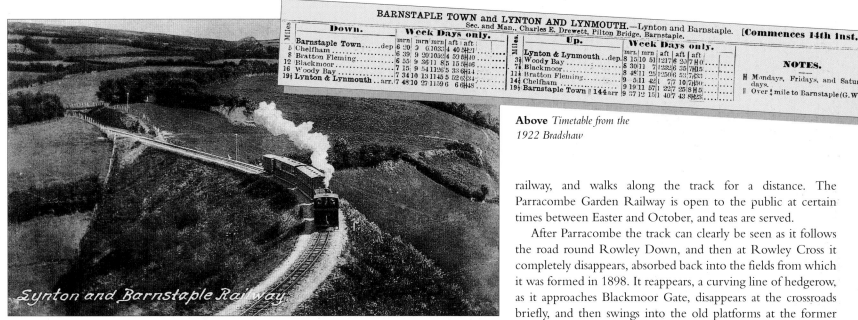

Lynton and Barnstaple Railway

BARNSTAPLE TOWN and LYNTON AND LYNMOUTH.—Lynton and Barnstaple.									[Commences 14th inst.

Sec. and Man., Charles E. Drewett, Pilton Bridge, Barnstaple.

Down.

Miles		Week Days only.					
		mrn	mrn	mrn	aft	aft	aft
	Barnstaple Town......dep	6 20	9 0	10 33	4 40	5 21	......
5	Chelfham	6 39	9 20	10 52	4 59	5 40	......
8	Bratton Fleming	6 55	9 36	11 8	5 15	5 46	......
12	Blackmoor	7 15	9 54	11 26	5 33	6 4	......
16	Woody Bay	7 34	10 13	11 45	5 52	6 34	......
19¼	Lynton & Lynmouth ...arr	7 48	10 27	11 59	6 6	6 48	......

Up.

Miles		Week Days only.				
		mrn	mrn	aft	aft	aft
	Lynton & Lynmouth ..dep	8 15	10 51	12 17	6 20	7 0
3¼	Woody Bay	8 30	11 7	12 32	6 35	7 15
7¼	Blackmoor	8 48	11 25	12 50	6 53	7 33
11¼	Bratton Fleming	9 5	11 42	1 7	7 10	7 50
14¼	Chelfham	9 19	11 57	1 22	7 25	8 5
19¼	Barnstaple Town ‖ 144 arr	9 37	12 15	1 40	7 43	8 23

NOTES.

H Mondays, Fridays, and Saturdays.

‖ Over ¼ mile to Barnstaple (G.W.)

Above *Timetable from the 1922 Bradshaw*

Above *A 1920s postcard view of Parracombe Bank*

Below *The former trackbed near Bratton Fleming in 1994*

railway, and walks along the track for a distance. The Parracombe Garden Railway is open to the public at certain times between Easter and October, and teas are served.

After Parracombe the track can clearly be seen as it follows the road round Rowley Down, and then at Rowley Cross it completely disappears, absorbed back into the fields from which it was formed in 1898. It reappears, a curving line of hedgerow, as it approaches Blackmoor Gate, disappears at the crossroads briefly, and then swings into the old platforms at the former station, now the Station Inn, a sort of roadhouse and restaurant that has made the most of the railway relics and associations of the site. Leaving the station, the track curves away along the side of the hill, to disappear again into the woods and beneath the waters of Wistlandpound Reservoir.

the garden next door and disappears. The route is then out of sight and out of mind in thick woods, high above but parallel to the A39 as it starts the descent towards Barnstaple. After a while a grassy mound can be discerned beside the road, as can the place where there used to be a level crossing, and then its route through the fields can be picked out among the sheep, to the south of Caffyns Down. Nothing remains of the halt built at Caffyns for the golf links, but isolated by a farm to the south of the road is an overbridge, now crossing nothing and with the road it used to carry long gone. It looks, as result, like some medieval relic, far older than its hundred years. There is not much to be seen where the line went over the road at Martinhoe Cross, but just to the west is the former Woody Bay station. From the road the station building looks like just another turn-of-the-century house, but in the garden are the original platforms and even the upright posts from the concrete name plates installed by the Southern Railway after its 1923 take-over of the line. This station was built to serve the planned development of Woody Bay, a few miles north, as a coastal resort, but the scheme never really got off the ground.

From the end of Woody Bay station's garden the just discernible track wanders off across the fields and cannot be easily defined again until Parracombe, where the large embankment was one of the line's major engineering features. The village of Parracombe is spread over the steep hillside, and the line wanders round the back of it. Up near Churchtown, a detached part of the village just west of the A39, is an old bridge. On one side a new bungalow straddles the track, but on the other is the start of a cleared section, with a length of garden

The route south from the reservoir is clearer, with country lanes now taking the railway's route past Hunnacott, Sprecott and Narracott. This lane ends at a road junction, with the track going straight on through a very picturesque and ivy-covered old bridge and along a farm path across a field. Now, following the folds of the hills, the trackbed twists and turns, in and out of overgrown cuttings, and only to be glimpsed from the overbridges on the little roads north of Bratton Fleming. Looking over the parapet of one such bridge and expecting the usual tangle of brambles and bushes, I was surprised to see instead a completely cleared trackbed, and laid along it a small narrow gauge railway. Further exploration via an adjacent footpath revealed a line extending over several hundred yards, complete with stations and passing loops, most of which was in the cuttings that characterised this section. It was a wonderful secret world, with the well-laid rails bright against the carpet of autumn leaves. At the end of the cutting it stopped, and a gate stood across the track, marked with a notice that said simply 'The End'. Beyond the gate was a thicket of bushes covering the curving track, and beyond that a field where cows wandered across the track and into the muddy swamp beneath a derelict overbridge. In the other direction the railway made its private way towards Bratton Fleming station, now a house, whose gardens have taken over the former sidings.

From here the track wanders across fields, with overbridges on minor roads southwest of Bratton Fleming being the only accessible clues to its existence, and then it enters the steep and twisting valley of the River Yeo. Woods lead to the grand Chelfham viaduct, whose curving arches stand as a lasting memorial to the Lynton & Barnstaple. Elegantly built in the local pale-coloured brick, it was the line's major structure, and the only one of this scale on any narrow gauge line in Britain. Seventy feet high, it towers over the narrow river valley. Near by is Chelfham station, now a private house. From here the river, the old railway line and a minor road run side by side, following the valley's twists and turns to Snapper, with the track sometimes discernible and sometimes not. As woods give way to a more open landscape, the track straightens up and heads for Barnstaple. At Pilton the company had its workshops and carriage sheds, the base for the five locomotives, seventeen coaches and twenty-nine wagons that operated the railway, and some of the buildings can still be identified. From here the railway used to swing round to the west of the town, crossing the Braunton road and leaving the Yeo for the Taw, before coming to the end of its line in Barnstaple's Town station. Today, there is virtually nothing to be seen of this final section and long memories and old photographs are all that can bring back the narrow gauge railway's route to the terminus in the heart of its town.

PRACTICAL INFORMATION

OS Landrangers
180, 190, 191

Information points
Barnstaple Tourist Information Centre: North Devon Library, Tuly Street, Barnstaple, Devon EX31 1EL. Tel 01271 388583/4, fax 01271 388599. Ilfracombe Tourist Information Centre: The Promenade, Ilfracombe, Devon EX34 9BX. Tel 01271 863001, fax 01271 862586.
Lynton Tourist Information Centre: Town Hall, Lee Road, Lynton, Devon EX35 6BT. Tel 01598 752225.
Tarka Trail: Devon Countryside Service, Bideford Station, Railway Terrace, East-the-Water, Bideford EX39 4BB. Tel 01237 471870.

Official cycle/walkways
Petrockstow to Barnstaple Junction (23 miles).
Bideford to Barnstaple (9 miles).
Barnstaple Town Station to Braunton (5¾ miles).
Lee Cross (Lee Bridge car park, grid reference SS 492 446) to Cairns Nature Reserve, Ilfracombe (2½ miles).

Cycle hire
During the summer months it is always advisable to arrive by 10am or to book bicycles in advance.
Barnstaple: Tarka Trail Cycle Hire, Railway Station. Tel 01271 24202. End Mar–end Oct daily, 9.15–5.
Bideford: Bideford Cycle Hire, Torrington Street, East-the-Water. Tel 01237 424123. All year, daily 9–5.

Braunton: Otter Cycle Hire, Station Road. Tel 01271 813339. All year, daily 9–5.
Torrington: Torrington Cycle Hire, Unit 1, Station Yard. Tel 01805 622633. Daily 9.15–5.
Yelland: Yelland Cycle Hire, West Yelland. Tel 01271 861424. Easter–Oct, daily 9–5; Nov–Easter, weekends only or by arrangement.

Nearby attractions
Exmoor Steam Railway: Cape of Good Hope Farm, near Bratton Fleming (on A399 1 mile east of Bratton Fleming. Tel 01598 710711. 12¼in gauge railway (approximately 1 mile). Open Mar, Sun 9–1; Easter holidays, daily 9–1; May–end Sep, Sun–Fri 9–1; Oct, Tue–Wed, Sun 9–1; Christmas specials.
Parracombe Churchtown Garden Railway: Fair View, Churchtown, Parracombe. Tel 01598 763478. 0 gauge working model of the Lynton & Barnstaple, model village. Open Easter–end Sep, Sat–Sun 11–6.
Lynton & Lynmouth Cliff Railway: Lynton's Esplanade to main street. Tel 01598 752318. 1:1¾ gradient, panoramic views of coast. Open Mar–Nov, Mon–Sat 8–7; Easter and May–Sep, also Sun, 10–7.
Great Torrington Railway: On B3220, next to Rosemoor RHS Garden. Tel 01805 623328. Miniature steam train rides. Open Easter holidays and end May–mid Sep, daily 10–5, end Apr–end May and late Sep, Sat–Sun 10–5 (weather permitting).

Left *Still impressive today, Chelfham viaduct is a remarkable structure to find on an essentially local narrow gauge line*

Inset Left *Looking smart in its new Southern Railway livery, E188 Lew poses outside the Pilton shed with its crew, ready for work in the summer of 1926*

THE SLOW AND DIRTY

The Somerset & Dorset Joint Railway main line from
Bath Green Park to Templecombe via Evercreech Junction

The Somerset & Dorset's greatest memorial is the massive Charlton viaduct in Shepton Mallet, seen in Gaymer's garden setting

HISTORY

Apart from pioneering lines such as the Bristol & Exeter, railways came quite late to Somerset and Dorset. From the 1850s, however, there were a number of schemes for the building of lines that would link the main towns in the rural heart of these counties. Inspiration came from two main sources, the Somerset coal field, and the belief in the traffic potential of a line from the Bristol Channel to the south coast. First off the mark was the Wiltshire, Somerset & Weymouth Railway, a protégé of the Great Western, incorporated in 1845 but not completed until 1857. Three years earlier, the Somerset Central Railway had opened its line from Glastonbury to Highbridge. The Great Western was also involved in this and so, like the Wiltshire, Somerset & Weymouth, it was built originally as a broad gauge line. A few years later, branches were built to Burnham-on-Sea, where the company established a steamer quay, and Wells. In due course the main line was also extended southwards beyond Glastonbury. Further south, the similarly named Dorset Central Railway was completing its line from Wimborne to Blandford,. Opened in 1860, this gradually extended itself northwards, reaching Templecombe and Cole by 1862, where it met the Somerset Central, now converted to standard gauge. The same year the two companies merged to form the Somerset & Dorset Railway and, thanks to an arrangement with the London & South Western which gave access via their rails to the south coast, trains were then able to run between the Bristol Channel and the English Channel.

The Somerset & Dorset's great hopes of profitable through traffic proved to be over-optimistic and the company was often in financial difficulties. It was in receivership in 1866 but recovered, and in 1870 decided to rescue its fortunes by building a 26-mile branch from Evercreech to Bath, with links to Bristol and thus to the Midlands and the North. Completed in 1874, this new line with its dramatic crossing of the Mendips via tunnels, embankments and heavy gradients proved to

be very expensive and traffic receipts were not enough to save the company from bankruptcy. It was then taken over by the Midland Railway and the London & South Western Railway in partnership, who leased the line and in 1876 created a new company, the Somerset & Dorset Joint Railway. With new investment this proved to be a success, and rapidly expanding traffic on the new Bath route turned it into the main line. There was regular heavy use by both passenger and freight trains and, thanks to a policy of doubling some of the sections that had been built as single track, and the opening in 1885 of a new direct line from Corfe Mullen to Broadstone that bypassed Wimborne, the Somerset & Dorset was soon seeing the first of the through holiday expresses between the Midlands and the North and the south coast resorts. In due course these trains were to became the most famous feature of the line, in particular the Pines Express.

In 1923 the London & South Western and the Midland were grouped into the Southern and the LMS respectively, but the Somerset & Dorset, while operated now by the Southern and the LMS, managed to remain largely independent, in spirit if not in fact. It retained its own livery for a while and its own locomotives and, even after nationalisation, it continued to be known as the Somerset & Dorset.

This individuality was one reason for the line's lasting popularity with railway enthusiasts, but also important was the nature of the trains that used the route. Frequent traffic and the steep gradients, with long stretches of 1 in 50 where the railway climbed over the Mendips, made double-heading and banking engines essential, and there was therefore always plenty to watch. Heavy use of the line continued through the 1950s and into the early 1960s, but by 1962 much of the through freight traffic was being routed elsewhere. Most of the through passenger traffic ceased in 1964 and, with only the little-used local services to keep it going, the Somerset & Dorset was soon in decline. Once railway services in western England had been decimated in the Beeching years, the S&D could not hope to survive and in March 1966 the line was finally closed. Much of the route was rapidly demolished and the structures sold off. While the coal mines were still in use, a section at Radstock survived as a freight line, but this was finally adandoned in the early 1970s along with the last of the pits that had inspired the building of the line in the first place.

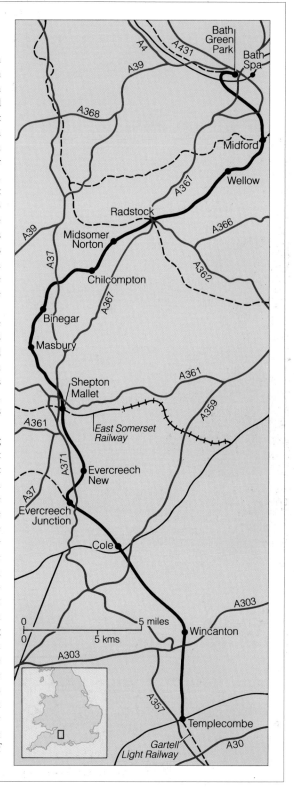

SOUTHERN RAILWAY.
(7/27)
FROM WATERLOO TO
CHILCOMPTON
(787)
(Via TEMPLECOMBE.)

For a county apparently so rural, Somerset once had a surprising number of railways. Maps of the pre-Beeching era show a rich patterning of lines winding along the river valleys, climbing over the Mendips and the Polden Hills and reaching into every corner. Particularly dense was the triangle formed by Taunton in the west, Bristol in the north and Yeovil in the south, a network whose labyrinthine complexity was often the result of stiff competition between the Great Western Railway and its rivals. South of Yeovil there was very little, with the London & South Western's route westwards from Salisbury towards Exeter and beyond forming a kind of railway frontier. Dorset never had the same appeal to the railway builders and few of those lines that were constructed are still there today.

In Somerset, however, it seemed they could never build enough, despite the expensive and demanding challenge posed by the county's hilly landscape. The costs were high but so were the rewards, thanks largely to the presence of the Somersetshire coal field which spread southwards from Bristol in a broad band. In the eighteenth and early nineteenth centuries, coal and canals had brought prosperity to the region, a sure foundation for the enormous growth that took place during the railway age. Coal, with the help of stone, fuller's earth and other products torn from the ground, kept the railways busy over many decades as generations of tough locomotives ground their way up the steep gradients and pounded through the tunnels and over the great viaducts demanded by the landscape.

The needs of passengers were rather a secondary consideration but there were, inevitably, numerous stations. Their names are an anthem to the interwoven layers of England's linguistic and cultural history: Bleadon & Uphill, Puxton & Worle, Pylle, Charlton Mackrell, Athelney, Binegar, Midsomer Norton, Congresbury, Yatton, Hallatrow, Vobster, Keinton Mandeville, Evercreech, Shoscombe & Single Hill, Bason Bridge, Flax Bourton and Wookey. None of these exists today; nor do any of the lines on which they stood. As coal had brought the railways to life, so the decline and closure of the coal field killed them. By the time Dr Beeching got to work in Somerset, there was precious little worth keeping and the whole network that lay between the Bath to Bristol, Bristol to Taunton and Taunton to Westbury main lines was swept away. Few places on the English railway map experienced such wholesale devastation.

Many of the lines that disappeared were part of the Great Western network, but there was one that was particularly unusual, even eccentric − a railway whose determined and long-lasting individuality had given it more than a local significance. It all started in the early 1850s with a number of schemes for railways in Somerset and Dorset, most of which made little progress. One which did succeed was the Somerset Central Railway, whose line from Highbridge to Glastonbury opened in 1854 and was then extended to Burnham-on-Sea, Wells and southwards to Cole. A few years later another company, the Dorset Central Railway, completed its line from Wimborne, where there were connections with routes to Bournemouth and the coast, to Blandford. This in turn was extended northwards to Templecombe and then onwards to Cole, where it met the Somerset Central. This meeting brought the two companies into a close association, formalised at the end of 1862 as the Somerset & Dorset Railway. From its early days this railway, whose main line from Highbridge to Wimborne was finally completed in 1863, showed a marked spirit of independence. Its operations were based more on hope than commercial realism and, when the expected cross-country traffic from the Bristol Channel to the south coast failed to materialise, it staggered from one financial crisis to another. The development of a steamer quay at Burnham made no real difference, nor did the through service to France from Burnham via Poole, advertised in the mid-1860s. By 1870 the directors realised they had a railway that did not really go anywhere important and they decided to build a branch northwards from Evercreech to Bath and Bristol − a desperate last fling, bearing in mind the nature of the terrain that had to be crossed. This line was completed in 1874, its route marked by dramatic engineering. A number of tunnels, viaducts and cuttings were built but, to save money, these expensive constructions were kept to a minimum. Instead, the line was heavily graded, with long stretches of single track at

Below One of the Somerset & Dorset's best-loved and most enduring features was its elegant dark blue livery, shown here on an early twentieth-century postcard depicting a new 4–4–0 express locomotive

Somerset and Dorset Joint Railway – No. 77 Express Engine.

up to 1 in 50. The trains were compelled to struggle over the hills relying on double-heading and banking engines as a matter of course. From its early days this gave the Somerset & Dorset a particular appeal for train enthusiasts, who even in the nineteenth century gathered at certain spots to watch the locomotives grinding their way up the hills amid clouds of smoke. For the passengers, however, this aspect had a more limited appeal, and it was not long before the S&D initials acquired their more familiar meaning, Slow & Dirty.

In the event, the construction costs of this new line bankrupted the company. The railway's potential, however, was not lost on its larger neighbours, keen to exploit both its access to the coal fields and its possibilities as part of a long-distance route from the Midlands to the south coast. So the company was subsequently leased jointly by the Midland and the London & South Western Railways, who resurrected it in 1876 as the Somerset & Dorset Joint Railway. It remained firmly independent, left largely alone by its new owners who were content to enjoy the income their investment was now generating. Its characteristic dark blue locomotives were able to retain their colours even after the 1923 grouping, when ownership was taken over by the Southern Railway and the LMS.

The irony was, of course, that in the end the Somerset & Dorset became a very successful railway, handling huge quantities of both freight and passenger traffic despite its demanding route. Many of the stretches of single track were doubled, a process that involved cutting new tunnels and rebuilding viaducts, but even so some major sections remained as originally built. The result caused continuous bottlenecks and delays, particularly in the summer months when the line was at its busiest. From the 1920s the Somerset & Dorset became increasingly the holiday route *par excellence*, a vital link for the long trains taking holidaymakers from the Midlands and the North to Bournemouth and other south coast resorts. The best-known of these was the Pines Express, a holiday service that continued to run until the early 1960s. Just as demanding were the freight services, operated continuously over the line throughout the year and requiring the stable of powerful 2-8-0 and, later, 2-10-0 locomotives that were a famous feature of the route. In fact, it was these and the great variety of other locomotives working the line which gave the Somerset & Dorset its lasting appeal. The sight of a long, twelve-coach holiday express or a massive mixed freight being dragged up the steep gradients by two huge locomotives was something special to the Somerset & Dorset, and something not easily forgotten.

The through traffic which had brought such success, albeit rather belatedly, to the Somerset & Dorset began to disappear in the early 1960s and, after the severe winter of 1963/4, when

sections of the route were closed for long periods by snow drifts, the line was downgraded. From then on, only local services operated and the writing was on the wall. In March 1966 the Somerset & Dorset network, independent to the end and widely lamented, was closed.

Since then, much has happened. The Somerset & Dorset has retained its popularity among railway enthusiasts, its memory kept alive above all else by the remarkable and comprehensive series of photographs of the line taken by the late Ivo Peters. Even though large sections of the route have disappeared, many remains are still to be seen on the ground and these are apparently much visited. Anyone tracing the line today cannot fail to notice the well-trodden paths that lead to every surviving relic or site, paths that make their way with noticeable directness through barbed wire fences and other man-made barriers. Clearly, the Somerset & Dorset railway enthusiast is a particularly determined variety of the species, undeterred by conventional concepts of privacy or trespass. Some of these enthusiast routes are now so established that they are well on the way to becoming proper footpaths, and a serious temptation for an explorer who never knew the line in its railway days.

Above *In its latter years, the Somerset & Dorset's best-known train was the Pines Express. Double-headed near Prestleigh in July 1960 by class 2P No. 40564 and class 9F No. 92205, the long train is a typical heavy holiday working*

SOMERSET & DORSET J. RY. This Ticket is issued subject to the regulations & Conditions stated in the Time Tables & Bills of the Joint Line
FIRST CLASS.
BATH to
MIDFORD
FARE 9d.
Midford
FARE 9d.
Midford
4957

Right *On a summer's day in 1958 class 2P No. 40569 pulls the 1.10pm local to Templecombe out of the fine train shed at Bath Green Park*

Below *Still exciting, Bath's Green Park train shed now shelters visitors to Sainsbury's nearby supermarket*

BATH GREEN PARK TO EVERCREECH JUNCTION

I started my exploration of the S&D at Bath, on the site of the old Green Park station to the west of the city centre. Known originally as Queen Square, this was built by the Midland Railway in 1870, its grand classical façade making a significant Victorian contribution to the Georgian city. Behind the façade was a large and extravagantly glazed iron train shed, a big and handsome arched cover for the trains using this terminus. From 1874, and until closure in 1966, Somerset & Dorset trains also used the station, the through trains from the Midlands, the North and the south coast having to enter the platforms and then reverse out again with a different locomotive.

Finding Green Park is not difficult as the station building and the arched train shed both survive, now incorporated into a supermarket development. Cars and shopping trolleys now stand where the trains used to be and, disconcertingly, the entry to the complex is across the iron Midland Railway bridge built to take trains over the Avon. From here, trains ran along Midland rails for half a mile to Bath Junction, and the trackbed of this section can be glimpsed from time to time between the factories and industrial estates. The junction itself has disappeared, along with the bridge that carried the Somerset & Dorset over the old A4. It was at this point, swinging southwards away from the Midland line, that the S&D drivers met their first test, the sharp 1 in 50 gradient curving round to climb past Twerton and out of the city. Today, the steepness of this gradient is easily appreciated, for the section from just south of the former A4 crossing to the Devonshire tunnel is now the Bath Linear Park, a walkway and urban nature reserve. Houses that used to be shaken by blasting locomotives attacking the hill now enjoy more peaceful days watching over dog-walkers, courting couples and others with time on their hands. It is a pleasant and surprisingly rural walk, with nature encouraged to take over, and is interrupted only by the crossing over the Great Western main line to Bristol. The railway bridge is still there, firmly barricaded, inaccessible and overgrown, and walkers have to make a little detour over the adjacent road bridge. Other bridges are still there, except for one over a road that is now crossed on the level.

The path ends before the famous Devonshire tunnel, whose narrow bore and steep gradient gave locomotive crews a very unpleasant time. With only about a foot's clearance above the train, it must have been a smoke and noise-filled hell-hole. Today, the tunnel is sealed and inaccessible. There is not much to be seen either in Lyncombe Vale, a short stretch before the line plunged into the much longer Combe Down tunnel, which was also single-tracked and without ventilation and ran for nearly a mile through the hills that surround Bath to the south. The track is elusive in the folded hills around Combe, but it comes to life at Tucking Mill. From a footpath that runs parallel to the line, one of those well-trodden but unofficial paths leads along an overgrown cutting lined with fine brick arches to the southern portal of Combe Down tunnel. Damp and muddy in winter, it is none the less an eerily romantic spot and the sheet of iron that completely seals the tunnel records the long popularity of this secret place with local lovers. The names, scratched, scrawled and sometimes carefully inscribed, go back years, with many including the date and the word 'always'. Where are they all now, one wonders.

South of the tunnel is the line's first viaduct, Tucking Mill, striding tall and severe in black brick over the steep, wooded valley. The best approach to the viaduct is along a footpath that leaves the minor road which runs alongside the Midford Brook to the left of a pretty stone cottage with Gothic windows. This was the home of William Smith, popularly known as the father of British geology and a key figure in the industrial development of the region. He had a mill here at the beginning of the nineteenth century and was the surveyor for the Somerset Coal Canal, whose route ran beside the road across from the cottage. Keen eyes can still find traces of the canal, including the parapets of an infilled bridge near by. Smith also built a tramway to take stone to the canal. The much enlarged mill pool, owned along with the viaduct by Wessex Water, now stores water pumped up from the Avon at Limpley Stoke. Around it is a series of fishing platforms reserved for disabled anglers. The viaduct, whose gaunt brickwork now supports a number of

Right *With a halo of smoke and steam, class 9F No. 92210 blasts out of the narrow confines of the Devonshire tunnel south of Bath at the head of the 8.15am train to Bournemouth, in July 1962*

Below *The grey brick arches of Tucking Mill viaduct frame Wessex Water's fishing lake, reserved for people with disabilities*

line on the valleyside to carry coal from Radstock down to the canal at Midford. A footpath runs beside the trackbed for much of the way, making it easy to enjoy this rural stretch.

The next station is Wellow, approached by another hefty brick viaduct. The track here is now inaccessible, much having been subsumed into village gardens, but the abutments of the bridge that carried it over the road are still visible. The station, a simple building, survives as a private house and near by, at the end of a little lane, is a former signal box, now also taken over for domestic duties. A pleasing survival is the kissing gate formerly used by pedestrians crossing the line.

After Wellow the track has been ploughed up or filled in by farmers and only the dotted line on the map reveals that a railway was ever there. At one point there is one of those mysterious bridges that are a feature of long-lost railways, with parapets looking out over land that is now the same height as the road. The bridge is buried, and of the railway that once ran under it there is no trace.

This pattern continues. There is nothing much to be seen at Shoscombe, where the halt with its simple concrete platforms was not opened until 1929, and then the line makes its way, inaccessibly, into Radstock. Outside the town some travellers have made a base on the trackbed with their elderly caravans, taking advantage of the firm ground and the sense of no man's land that is often part of an old railway. Radstock was the heart

Above *Midford station on a quiet summer's day in July 1960. Today the platform survives, but little else*

Right *Looking like some ancient ruin, the S&D's Midford viaduct strides over the remains of the Great Western Camerton branch. It was on this typical GWR rural line that* The Titfield Thunderbolt *was filmed*

Far Right *British Railway's last steam locomotive, class 9F* Evening Star, *was nearly new in September 1962 when this picture of a double-headed express was taken near Midford*

young trees, looks magnificent across the water. There is no way on to it but a path to the left of the pond leads up into the trees beside it and on to the trackbed which curves away and down towards Midford.

At Midford, a long curving platform, which still has white paint along its edge, remains looking out over the steep valley, but there are no buildings. It is now on private land but can easily be examined from the car park of the Hope and Anchor pub, formerly the station forecourt. From the station the line went straight on to the big arches of Midford viaduct, which crossed the B3110 road, the Cam brook, the Somerset Coal Canal and the Great Western's Camerton branch. Today the broad arches of the Somerset & Dorset viaduct crossing high above the broken and overgrown brickwork of the old Great Western line are notably picturesque, with a definite Piranesian quality underlined by the tumbling waters of the river. Tall trees rise out of the Great Western trackbed, making it hard to believe that trains ever ran here, let alone as recently as the mid-1950s. From Midford, which was the end of the single track section from Bath, the line becomes a broad path sweeping along the Midford and Wellow valleys in a series of generous curves, in and out of cuttings, and above the river. The curving route followed that of an earlier tramway, built along a contour

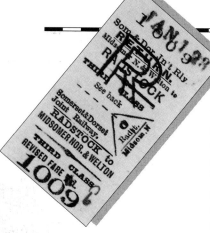

of the Somerset coal field with collieries all around connected to the once busy railway network. There were two stations, almost side by side, one on the S&D, and one on the Great Western Frome to Bristol line, and there were yards filled with sheds, wagons and shunting engines. Although they crossed, the two lines did not meet, running for a while side by side and having separate level crossings over the same road. Today, it is virtually impossible to imagine such a scene, so little remains to give any sense of historical reality. There is more sense of the past in the towns, with both Radstock and its neighbour Midsomer Norton having, despite their rural location, something of the atmosphere of the industrial north. Traditions and the way of life linger on, even though the industry itself is long gone. Only the lardy cakes in the baker's shops are firmly Somerset.

For the mile or so from Radstock to Midsomer Norton the steeply climbing track is a public walkway or linear park, as the preferred term seems to be. Raised on an embankment for much of the route, this gives good views and firm walking on a stony trackbed. The best feature is a big five-arch viaduct, handsomely built in skewed brick, carrying the S&D over the well-defined Great Western line, itself also a footpath, and still boasting a recognisable but severely rusty signal pole. The walk ends just to the east of Midsomer Norton town centre. The station, which year after year in the 1950s won the Best Kept Station award with its wonderful floral displays, is now used as study centre by a local school.

From here the climb up the Mendips continued, with heavy gradients all the way to test both the locomotives and their crews, but today one's imagination has to work overtime as there is little to see until the short Chilcompton tunnel. The two bores sit close together, one of them now housing the Midsomer Norton Shooting Club's range, and from here a footpath follows the grassy trackbed as it curves round to the south of the village, ending at a bridge over a minor road where some rather precarious steps lead down the embankment.

Right *Apparently issued in August 1947, this consignment note for the transport of pigeons, still an important railway cargo then, offers an insight into the workings of the S&DJR in the final months of its existence*

Far Right *Another view of the S&D survivor, No. 53807, this time hauling the 6.43am Birmingham to Bournemouth train out of Midsomer Norton station in July 1962*

Ahead is the rocky cutting that used to lead to the station, now an overgrown jungle filled with domestic rubbish.

South of Chilcompton, railway hunting becomes more problematic. Initially, sections have disappeared into back gardens and then there is a stretch of impenetrable jungle. Elsewhere, everything has been removed by farmers and the land turned back to fields. Large embankments remain either side of the big viaduct north of Binegar, but of the viaduct itself not a brick is to be seen. Binegar station survives as a private house, with the goods shed now in agricultural use, but there is no sense of the railway at all in this isolated region. There are clues if you look hard. Station Road still leads to the former station, and near by is a rather flashy new house called The Beechings. Beyond Binegar the track has either disappeared or is mostly impossible to follow, and it makes its way privately to the summit at Masbury, 811 feet above sea level. This was the moment that every south-bound engine driver longed for, the end of the punishing climb that had continued virtually without a break from Bath. For the first time the fireman could take a breather and a quick rest on the shovel. Masbury station is now a private house, hidden in the woods that have grown up since the closure. Near by the old bridge carries on its parapet a cast-iron maker's plate dated 1890.

In the stony Mendip heights the railway wound its way down a steep gradient between quarries, all of which originally had networks of sidings linked to the main line. Today the quarries are silent and the trains have gone from this remote region, but what they have left behind is Windsor Hill tunnel. A short walk from the site of a demolished bridge over a minor road to the south of the quarries, along one of those well-trodden but unofficial paths, leads to the mouth of the original 242-yard-long tunnel which, rather surprisingly, is open. The overgrown cutting with its carpet of late autumn leaves drew me on towards the brick arch, and the darkness beyond, and I walked through the tunnel, noting the steep gradient and gangers' shelters cut into the side walls. There is nothing like an abandoned tunnel to bring a

railway to life, and it was all too easy to imagine the pounding monster blasting through on waves of heat and noise. A second, shorter, tunnel built later when the track was doubled is hidden in the bushes to the west. I walked back and then carried on across the road and along a straight stretch of raised embankment over the surrounding fields. Bridges maintained the sense of reality engendered by the tunnel. This walk ended at Bath Road viaduct, the first of the two that carried the line round to the east of Shepton Mallet. Access was denied, as always for safety reasons, by impenetrable barriers topped by razor wire. Far down below was the B3136 winding its way up through Shepton's northern suburbs, lights twinkling in the deepening dusk. Later, driving along that same road under the viaduct, I noticed that two of its arches were completely encased in scaffolding, a reminder that expensive and difficult maintenance problems remain long after the railways have disappeared. No wonder British Rail tried to sell off some of its 'disused' viaducts a while ago for £1 each.

The next day I returned to Shepton Mallet. It was grey, damp and cold, depressing weather for railway hunting in muddy fields, and Shepton's suburbs and industrial estates were distinctly unwelcoming. On the north side of the town the line is largely inaccessible, but a number of local footpaths do cross it if addicts are really determined to see it. It all comes to life again by the A37, a former school marking the point where the great 27-arched Charlton viaduct strides off across the valley. Built on a curve, a soaring mass of dark stone and brick, this was the line's major engineering feature, and is still the high point for

Above *Arching trees screen the approach to Windsor Hill tunnel in autumn 1994*

Right *The same tunnel seen in its more active days, in the summer of 1962*

South Western & Midland Railway Companies'
Somerset & Dorset Joint Line.

(492)

INSURED.

(*No.* _____)

From _____

To _____

Train _____

Date _____   187

Above *An unexpected survivor thirty years on is Midsomer Norton station, still complete with platforms and a goods shed, now a study centre. All that is missing is the track*

any modern explorer. The dismal weather was soon forgotten as I turned off the A37 along a little white lane that led to a footpath passing under the viaduct's central arches. From below it was easy to see how it had been built initially as a single-track structure and then doubled in the 1880s. Plants now flourish in the cracked and dripping stonework, but the elegance of its curving line and towering arches, and its massive power, isolated in the fields, give it the excitement of a Mayan temple discovered in the jungles of Mexico. The footpath across the fields to the north give an excellent distant view, making clear the dip in the centre caused by the change in gradient. I could imagine the drivers of north-bound freight trains opening the regulator wide as they came on to the viaduct, making the most of the downward stretch before before hitting the start of the long, steep climb all the way up to Masbury summit. Shepton Mallet is the home of Gaymers, the drinks manufacturer (a large leaping Babysham deer stands on top of the factory), and it is they who own the viaduct and have surrounded part of it with a landscaped garden. At one time it was possible to walk across it, and the trackbed is still tarmaced, but safety concerns have now made it as impenetrable as all the others along the S&D.

This apart, there is not much to see in Shepton. The site of the station, and the bridge that carried the Great Western's

Wells line over the Somerset & Dorset, has vanished beneath factories and a business park. To the east, at Cranmore, the Great Western lives on in the form of David Shepherd's East Somerset Railway, a preserved line linked to the main network by the Merehead quarry freight route. In Shepton, only a mile away, it is hard to believe that either railway ever existed.

South of Shepton the story is the same. Farmers and natural attrition have driven the track back into the landscape, and there is precious little to be seen. By East Compton a muddy farm track was once the railway, but the only clues for the sharp-eyed are some distinctive concrete fence posts and an old railway gate buried in a hedge. A bit further south at Prestleigh there is at least an embankment, but there is a huge gap in the middle of it where the eleven arches of the Prestleigh viaduct once stood. The substantial bridge that used to carry the railway over the B3081 just north of Evercreech has also gone completely. The embankments survive, as they do at Prestleigh and elsewhere, but they are clearly private, and have plenty of barbed wire, warning notices and other devices to deter visiting S&D enthusiasts.

Evercreech is an emotive name in the history of the Somerset & Dorset. The original main line, from Highbridge to Wimborne, passed two miles to the south of the village where there was a remote and inconveniently placed station. The new line to Bath, which in time became the main line, started just by this station and then passed close to the village on its way north. A new station was therefore built here, called initially Evercreech Village, and then Evercreech New, the old station becoming known as Evercreech Junction. As the meeting point of the two arms of the S&D, this became a major centre of activity, with three goods yards, a turntable, sheds, a signal box and plenty of sidings for the lines of banking engines waiting their turn to help northbound trains climb over the Mendips. Everything stopped here, from the Pines Express to the regular freights, and for that reason Evercreech was well known as an enthusiast's mecca.

Evercreech today is a very different place. The track skirts the village on a low embankment and is generally visible, although parts are hidden by bushes. From time to time adjacent houses have allowed their gardens to encroach upon it, taking over the raised area as a kind of ready-made terrace, barbecue area or rockery. Elsewhere, particularly where the station used to be, new houses have sprung up right on the track. South of the village, at Pecking Mill, the line crossed the A371 on a big brick and stone viaduct. Curiously, and in contrast to the more usual situation, the viaduct remains but the embankment has gone. The result is like some Roman ruin, splendidly meaningless out of context. The hurtling lorries make it particularly hard to appreciate. Carry on down this road and you pass on the right a sprawling collection of buildings and sheds. This was Evercreech Junction. Pull off the road and then it all begins to make sense. The station itself is there, now a private house and extended. Beyond are buildings which fall into place as goods sheds, and yards which once were sidings now full of old vehicles and farmers' junk. By the road is a tall stone house helpfully called Evercreech Junction. Here was a level crossing, its site easily identified once you have stopped. Gone are the signal box, water tower and many other structures but at least enough survives of the complex to make it comprehensible in archaeological terms. Now go back up the A371 for a few hundred yards and take the first proper turning to the left. This leads past a pond to a DIY superstore and a huddle of old sheds housing various post-railway activities. A footpath leads down beyond the car park into and across a field. The trackbed is apparent for a while and then there is absolutely nothing, just a green field with distant sheep and a horizon formed by a hedge and two tall trees. Stand and wonder, for in the middle of this rural scene is the site of the actual junction. Over this grassy field pounded huge trains, swinging left for Highbridge and right for Bath. Across here came the double-headed Pines Express, its twelve coaches packed with holidaymakers returning home after their week on the south coast. Not a trace remains, recent history totally obliterated. At the far end of the field a shallow curving depression marks the

Above *Standard class 5 No. 73052 hauls a Bournemouth-bound train into Evercreech Junction station in July 1959. Despite major changes, this scene is still recognisable today, with a number of buildings surviving, mostly now in agricultural or industrial use*

Left *While the station at Evercreech Junction can still be seen, the site of the actual junction has vanished almost without trace, absorbed back into the green fields from which it was formed*

start of the line to Bath, and buried in the hedge are old bits of track, characteristic concrete fence posts and an old railway gate – scant clues to the existence of a major undertaking that ruled here for nearly a century.

The ability of an old railway to disappear back into the landscape is remarkable, considering the scale and the apparent permanence of all railway-associated works. I once took a trip in a hot air balloon in this area, and by chance the wind took us for a while along the the line of the Somerset & Dorset. From 500 feet up the route was quite clear, with curves and embankments, cuttings and bridges well defined against the fields. At some points the line of the track just stopped and became indistinguishable from the pattern of fields and then a little while later, by a hedge or some trees, it would suddenly appear again, marked as clearly on the ground as it is on the map. An aerial view of an old railway certainly gives a sense of both its permanence and its impermanence.

EVERCREECH JUNCTION TO TEMPLECOMBE

South from Evercreech the track is only occasionally visible and generally inaccessible, Some long sections have vanished completely. At Wyke Champflower a bridge on a minor road has one of its parapets level with a field, while from the other the trackbed, delightfully green and overgrown, stretches away. It was while I stood on this bridge that I heard, approaching out of the winter's gloom, the distinct roar of an oncoming train. The noise built up to a climax and then passed quickly away into the distance. It was, of course, all wrong, a modern high-speed diesel on the Great Western main line to the south, hidden by the mist, rather than some ghostly steam-hauled S&D freight, but it was, none the less, an exiting moment. At the next bridge, still standing over the road, the owners of the adjacent house have built a picnic area on the track. The bridge leads to nowhere, everything beyond it having been levelled back to the fields.

Below *Another surviving station is Cole, now a private house complete with platforms. In earlier days at Cole, the veteran class 4F locomotive No. 44422 draws the local Bath to Templecombe train to a steamy halt in the summer of 1959*

From here there is a good view of the 125s racing along the main line, bound for London or Taunton and Exeter.

It was just beyond here that the S&D crossed over the Great Western line, another spot well trodden by generations of train enthusiasts, but all that remains today is a series of grassy embankments that are home to hordes of rabbits. Gone are the railway bridge and the big five-arched viaduct, but Cole station survives as a private house, with old platforms that run away into the fields, and fine concrete railway gateposts. From the road bridge to the south there is a good view of Cole and its former sidings, one frequently photographed during its railway past. It was near here that the Dorset Central, pushing north, met the Somerset Central, pushing south, to form the Somerset & Dorset.

Immediately after Cole is Pitcombe, a village still completely dominated and divided by the railway. In the valley below the A359 the gaunt black viaduct strides above the houses, a silent and enduring memorial. What a noisy place it must have fifty years ago, and how quiet and attractive it must have been before the railway came. It is a good place to consider the impact of the railway upon the landscape. At the centre of the village is a lovely square seventeenth-century house whose windows, which must originally have looked out at fields, stare only at the blank wall formed by the railway embankment and viaduct. From Wyke to Pitcombe, and onwards towards Wincanton, the railway is easily followed and there are ample opportunities to think about the scale of its engineering, and its lasting effect upon the countryside.

A tall bridge near Shepton Montague gives a good view of the overgrown but well-defined trackbed, which then wanders away to make a private but unusually straight approach along the valley to Wincanton, visible but inaccessible, passing the racecourse and then swinging to the west of the town. The station has disappeared beneath new houses and other recent development, and the extensive industrial estates south of the town have obliterated the railway completely. It appears again just south of the A303 and then goes straight across the open landscape, remote among surrounding farmland. The best viewpoint is from a big double bridge on a minor road immediately north of Horsington. From here an embankment took the line towards Templecombe.

Today, trains running between Waterloo and Exeter along the old London & South Western main line stop at Templecombe, a station brought back from the dead by the efforts of a remarkably effective local support group. It is a fine place, as well cared for as stations used to be, with flower beds and hanging baskets, displays of old photographs and a striking sundial sculpture. The old 1930s streamlined signal box is now the ticket office, and there is a smartly restored old footbridge,

Above *A fine house at Pitcombe dwarfed by the old viaduct*
Left *The 7.45am Bradford to Bournemouth express climbs to Templecombe Upper in August 1962, the long holiday train double-headed from Bath by class 9F No. 92205 and the unrebuilt Bulleid West Country Pacific, Combe Martin, No. 34043*

Right *Two elderly locomotives come to a standstill at Templecombe in August 1954 having hauled their train there from Highbridge*

rescued from the depths of Sussex. Those who take time to study the photographs in the waiting room will realise that Templecombe used to be much more important. Not only was it a stopping place for grand trains such as the Atlantic Coast Express, but it was also the place where the Somerset & Dorset connected with Waterloo's main line to the west. Here, holiday trains from the North bound for resorts in Devon and Cornwall would leave the S&D to turn westwards towards Exeter and beyond. More than just a place where two railways crossed, it was the meeting point for trains from distant parts of Britain, where the maroon of the LMS met the dark green of the Southern. In those days Templecombe was a huge station, with engine sheds and massive sidings laid out around the embankments that led from one line to another. Train movements were constant and complicated, with trains on the S&D line being drawn backwards in and out of Templecombe station, before continuing southwards or northwards on their own line. There was a small S&D station down below, called Templecombe Lower, where the S&D line plunged under the Southern's metals, but few trains used it.

Trying to make sense of all this is very hard when so little survives today. The steep spur that took trains from the S&D line into Templecombe station has gone, along with much of the station and all its supporting buildings and yards. For travellers on South West Trains' modern turbo diesels the best view of the trackbed of the S&D passing beneath them, largely incorporated into someone's garden, is just east of the modern Templecombe station. They can also see another spur that used to link the two lines, now overgrown, piled with builder's rubble and often inhabited by goats. It is very hard to imagine the turmoil of activity that Templecombe represented a mere forty years ago.

It is worth continuing a mile or so south from Templecombe to Yenston, for in the fields to the east of the A357, like a dream, rails suddenly appear. Admittedly they are narrow gauge, but there are platforms, signals, passing loops and other signs of real railway activity. A short stretch has been brought back to life, about half a mile from Common Lane Farm to the site of the next road crossing, by a minor road that runs east from the centre of Yenston. This is the Gartell Light Railway, a private line and the fulfilment of a personal whim, but there are regular open days when passengers are carried to and fro. It may be small, and it may go nowhere, but at least it has brought trains back to the Somerset & Dorset Joint Railway.

Practical Information

OS Landrangers
172, 183

Information points
Bath Tourist Information Centre: Abbey Chambers, Abbey Church Yard, Bath BA1 1LY. Tel 01225 462831.
Shepton Mallet Tourist Information Centre: 2 Petticoat Lane, Shepton Mallet, Somerset BA4 5DA. Tel 01749 345258.

Official cycle/walkways
Bath Linear Park: from Bloomfield Road (access through playing field next to Wentworth House Hotel), Bath, to Lower Bristol Road (access in Bellotts Road), Bristol (approx. 1 mile)
The Bristol and Bath Railway Path: on the old Midland Railway track, between Brassmill Lane, off Newbridge Road, Bath, and Trinity Street, Bristol (12½ miles).
Radstock to Midsomer Norton: 1½ miles.

Cycle hire
Bath: Avon Valley Cyclery, Arch 37, Rear of Bath Spa Station. Tel 01225 461880. Open all year, daily except Christmas and New Year 9–6.

Nearby attractions
East Somerset Railway: Cranmore Railway Station (on A361), near Shepton Mallet. Tel 01749 880417. Nine steam locomotives, rolling stock, engine shed, workshops; David Shepherd art gallery, museum, restaurant. Open May–Aug, Wed–Sun 10–5.30; Sep, Wed–Sun 10–4; Mar, Apr, Oct–Dec, Sat; Sun 10–4. See timetable for Steam Days.
Gartell Light Railway: Common Lane, Yenston (on A357, 1 mile south of Templecombe). Tel 01963 370752. 2ft gauge system on old S&D trackbed. Open May–Sep on selected days only (phone for details).

Left *Open day, July 1994, at the private Gartell Light Railway, with trains running to and fro along the former S&D track near Templecombe*

TICKET TO RYDE

♦

Ryde to Ventnor and the Brading to Bembridge branch
Newport to Cowes
Newport to Freshwater
Newport to Smallbrook Junction

The timeless style of the Isle of Wight's railway network is shown by this June 1961 view of Ashey station, with the Ryde Pier Head to Cowes train at the platform

HISTORY

The first railways in the Isle of Wight were planned in the 1840s but nothing much happened until the 1860s. In June 1862 the line between Cowes and Newport was completed and the island's first passenger train service started. The success of this short line encouraged the building of others and the next twenty years witnessed the development of an extensive network in the eastern half of the island, linking the major ports with the main towns and villages and the growing resorts. Next came the line from Ryde St John's Road southwards towards Ventnor, completed in 1866, and at the same time the tramway service along Ryde pier came into use. In 1880 the line from Sandown to Newport was completed, along with the new railway pier at Ryde and the Pier Head and Esplanade stations. This was a joint development by the London & South Western and London, Brighton & South Coast Railways, keen to expand passenger traffic to and from the Isle of Wight. Owing to the high construction costs, initial fares between Pier Head and St John's Road were 1s 2d, and it was said at the time to be the most expensive railway journey in the world, for the distance of under a mile. Two years later the Bembridge branch was opened, linking the railways to the island's main commercial port, and from this point onwards the network played an increasingly important role in the local economy. Cement mills, brick works, quarries and dairies were among the local industries dependent upon their rail connections. From the late 1880s the network was further expanded, by the opening of the lines from Newport to Freshwater, and from Newport to Ventnor via Godshill, the latter being finally completed in 1900.

In many ways the Isle of Wight was a microcosm of Victorian Britain, and its railways were typical of the country lines being built all over the land. Initially the lines were constructed and operated by local companies, fiercely independent despite the small mileages and territories they controlled. The list of Isle of Wight railway companies includes the Cowes & Newport, the Ryde & Newport, the Isle of Wight (Newport Junction), the Freshwater, Yarmouth & Newport, the Newport, Godshill & St Lawrence and the Brading Harbour. Later, most of these were merged into two larger companies, the Isle of Wight and the Isle of Wight Central, which in turn were absorbed into the Southern Railway following the grouping of 1923. The Southern Railway invested heavily in the Isle of Wight network without significantly altering its individual character which was, already, part of its appeal.

Left *Locomotive W33* Bembridge *runs round its train at Freshwater in September 1853*

The system flourished through the interwar years. Then in 1948 the nationalised British Railways took over. Increased competition from roads, changing patterns of tourism, reduced freight traffic and the greater dependence upon outmoded equipment discarded by mainland railways brought about an inevitable and irreversible decline. The first closures came in 1952 and 1953 with the abandonment of the lines between Merstone Junction and Ventnor West, Newport and Freshwater, and Brading and Bembridge. Three years later the Newport to Sandown line was closed and then, in 1966, all other lines except the Ryde to Shanklin section of the Ventnor route went, along with the end of steam haulage. This surviving fragment was electrified, and brought back into service in 1967. In 1971 the Isle of Wight Steam Railway began to operate its restored trains between Wootton and Havenstreet, making available once again the distinctive flavour of the island's railways in their heyday. In 1991 this preserved line was expanded to meet the main Island Line at Smallbrook Junction, ensuring at least that a sizeable section of the original network remains alive.

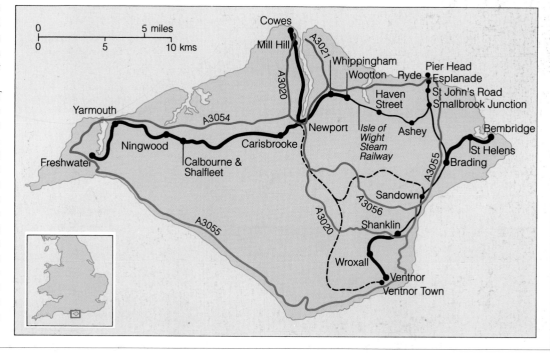

SOUTHERN RAILWAY

BEMBRIDGE

I HAVE TO admit right away that, despite numerous visits to the Isle of Wight from childhood onwards, my memories of train journeys on the island are very limited and mostly rather recent. The first visit was a day trip in the mid–1950s, organised by my grandmother and full of incident, as were all such outings under her control. I remember the train journey to Portsmouth from Surbiton, where she lived, and the crossing to Ryde on a paddle steamer, but beyond that it all fades. I suspect we took the train from the pierhead to Ryde, as that was the kind of novelty that appealed to her, and I am sure we stamped out our names on a metal strip on one of those machines that used to exist for that purpose on many stations. However, I suspect we ate our sandwiches in Ryde and went no further.

Later visits were generally associated with family holidays, and trains do not seem to have featured in these, nor in the various day trips I have made a couple of times a year since then

Below *The classic lost railway view is the overgrown bridge, crossing nothing. This example stands in the fields between Newport and Shalfleet*

for one reason or another. Definite memories of rail travel on the island are all associated with the superannuated London tube trains that operate the surviving Ryde to Shanklin services, or with the reincarnated steam railway.

My search for the tangible remains of the island's railways had, therefore, to start from scratch and involved primary research in the field, aided by published secondary sources and the essential Ordnance Survey map. Looking at this map, I was soon regretting deeply my lack of direct experience of this remarkable network, one which I could so easily have explored, if not in its prime then at least in its declining years, as one of the last bastions of British Rail steam. Self-contained, independent, quirky and delightfully old-fashioned without any of the self-conscious antiquarianism of the preserved line, it must have offered within its small world all those things that make railways so hard to resist.

The building of the network, so comprehensive in its routes and services by 1900 that the island really had no need for any other kind of public transport, reflected on a small scale all the fervour of the Victorian railway age. Beginning with one short line opened in 1866, and expanding to reach almost every corner by the end of the century, the island's railways were its commercial, economic and social backbone, and the perfect example of a system built to serve the local community. In the heyday of the railways, everything the islanders needed to import or export was carried by train, along with all their local commodities. Cattle and milk, cement and bricks, fish and fruit, letters and letterboxes, fabrics and saucepans were typical railway cargoes, as well as the thousands of passengers going to work, to school, and on shopping or social trips. During the holiday season, with many of the island's growing resorts being totally dependent upon the train, these numbers were hugely increased. The opening up of the island by its railways coincided precisely with its development as a popular holiday centre, and year by year more and more hotels and other facilities were created to match the demand. At busy times, tourist trains were sometimes double-headed, but generally the system coped very well.

Such was the island's popularity in the nineteenth century – built on foundations laid by Victoria and Albert with their life at Osborne House and fostered by famous local residents such as Alfred Lord Tennyson – that there were even schemes to dig a tunnel under the Solent to the mainland. The promoters of such schemes had visions of holiday expresses from London, the Midlands and the North travelling direct to the island's resorts. In the event, however, all these plans came to nothing, and it was left to the ferries and the island's own little trains to handle the holiday traffic.

Despite their comprehensive nature, the Isle of Wight's railways were always small-scale affairs, often kept running by outdated and outmoded equipment handed down from the mainland. Traditionally, the island became the last resting place for all sorts of things that had been discarded elsewhere, and it is satisfying to see this tradition maintained today by the elderly tube trains, long-suffering pit ponies enjoying the unexpected bonus of a seaside retirement. Even during the heydays of the Edwardian period and the interwar years, journeys on the island were short, speeds were slow and traffic demands were generally well within the powers of the fleets of elderly carriages and wagons, and the small Victorian tank locomotives that had either been built for the network years before or found their way to the island late in their working lives. These distinctive little engines – often designed or made by some of the great

names in British railway history such as Adams, Stroudley, Beyer Peacock, even Stephenson – usually carried the names of island towns and villages. The earliest dated from 1864; some came over with the contractors building the lines and then stayed. At least one of that generation, *Ryde*, kept going until 1940. Equally long-lived were locomotives such as *Ashey*, *Brading*, *Chale*, *Merstone* and *Shanklin*, dating from the 1920s and still at work in 1966 when steam haulage ceased and all the lines except Ryde to Shanklin were closed. Three other locomotives, *Newport*, *Freshwater* and *Calbourne*, along with a fine selection of the vintage carriages that had made the island their final resting place, were saved from the scrapyard and given a new lease of life by the preserved Isle of Wight Steam Railway.

Below *In the late 1920s Isle of Wight Railway's No. 18,* Bonchurch, *pauses to take on coal at Ventnor. The coaling stage, just outside the tunnel mouth, and signalman's hanging baskets seem to underline the leisurely nature of the Island's railways*

RYDE TO VENTNOR AND THE BRADING TO BEMBRIDGE BRANCH

There are very few places in Britain today where one can still enjoy that old Victorian practice of stepping straight from a ferry on to a train. It is possible at Folkestone Harbour, and just about at Newhaven Quay, but not at that grand and famous maritime terminus, Dover Marine (Western Docks), which is now no more. Another recent loss is Weymouth Quay, the best of all such stations in southern Britain, and the only one where trains were still running through the streets of the town on their way to and from the quayside into the late 1980s. Pembroke Dock and Tilbury Riverside are but fading memories, while Port Victoria has gone beyond recall. Curiously, the most romantic of all, Southampton's Ocean Terminal, still survives but is in effect accessible only to QE2 passengers and those taking certain cruises. A trip over to the Isle of Wight, however, continues to offer appealing opportunities for a taste of this old-fashioned pleasure.

On the mainland, at Lymington Pier, the end of a surprising branch line survivor, the train stops virtually in the sea, just a few yards from the ferry to Yarmouth. Even better is the Portsmouth to Ryde crossing of the Solent, where there are train and ferry connections at both ends. Portsmouth Harbour

Above *Ryde Pier today, with a superannuated London tube train now at work for the Island Line's service to Shanklin*

Right *Nearing the end of its life, and the end of the Island's railway network, locomotive W20,* Shanklin, *hauls its train for Ventnor along Ryde Pier in 1965*

station stands on piles above the sea, with the tide coming in and out underneath the trains, and the ferry waits at the quayside below. For traditional maritime excellence, however, Ryde has to be top of the list. The ferry docks at the end of a long old pier that stretches half a mile out to sea and there, waiting at the Pier Head station, is the train. Originally Pier Head was, of course, far busier, with trains departing for a variety of island destinations. There was even a separate tramway along the pier, running parallel to the main railway. That the Pier Head station survives at all, albeit in a much reduced form, is little short of miraculous, and its continued existence puts the small town of Ryde in that élite list of places which have three railway stations.

The tube train stock may seem particularly incongruous as the train rumbles slowly along the length of the pier on its way to the grandly named Ryde Esplanade station, but this is merely setting the scene for a line whose whole existence is incongruous. Closures of Isle of Wight lines began in the 1950s and came to a head in the Beeching era when the whole network seemed likely to disappear. At that point the routes that were still in operation were Ryde to Newport and Cowes, and Ryde to Ventnor, and complete closure must have seemed the obvious course of action. For some unfathomable reason the Beeching axe was halted in mid-swing, and the line from Ryde

to Shanklin was spared, electrified and left in isolation to make the best of what remained to it. With hindsight, this does seem to have been a most extraordinary decision, for the costs involved in modernising and maintaining a single, truncated line on an island several miles out to sea must not only have far outweighed any notional savings gained from the closing of the other routes, but would also have completely undermined the whole rationale of the Beeching programme. Be that as it may, since 1967 electric trains have continued to operate their distinctive service between Ryde Pier Head and Shanklin. Indeed, their popularity brought about the opening, in 1987, of Lake, a new station designed to serve the expanding Sandown and Shanklin conurbation. The Island line is very much a part of Wight life today, a hint of what might have been had the rest of the network been left alive as well.

The journey is short but enjoyable. A tunnel takes the line round to Ryde's third station, St John's Road, and then it cuts across a typical Wight landscape of farmland, woods and little streams to Brading. On the way it passes Smallbrook Junction, where the old tubes meet the old steam trains of the preserved Isle of Wight Railway. At Brading, a disused island platform was formerly the departure point for trains on the Bembridge branch, closed in 1953. Next is Sandown, with distant views of the sea and the cliffs at Culver as the train follows the valley of

Above *Trains on the Ryde to Ventnor service meet at Brading in 1964, hauled by* W18 Ningwood *and* W28 Ashey. *This scene lives on, thanks to the Island Line's electric trains*

Left *A timeless and characteristic Isle of Wight scene: taking the single line token at Ryde St John's Road, in this case in December 1966*

the Yar. Sandown and Shanklin have grown inexorably together, a pattern of growth greatly encouraged in the first place by the railway. Lake is right by the sea, and then the train runs inland to Shanklin, very much the end of the line, a sad station whose grand buildings resonate with echoes of the past. A set of buffers marks the abrupt end of a journey that once continued to Wroxall and Ventnor.

We started our search for the island's railway past in Brading, on a wet and windswept day. As railway hunting involves plenty of field work, literally, these conditions were far from ideal. Mud was to become a major feature of the next couple of days, spreading itself inexorably over boots and clothes and into the more obscure corners of the car. My companion, hoping in fact to see the Isle of Wight rather than the muddy relics of its railway past, did her best to remain cheerful while the rain and mist concealed the views and her car became filthier by the minute. Despite this, she stuck to her map-reading duties with dedication and entered bit by bit, and rather against her better judgement, into the spirit of the hunt.

The branch from Brading to Bembridge was opened in 1882 and enjoyed quite an active life, for the harbour at Bembridge was, until the late 1920s, the island's major commercial docks complex. There was also a cement works near by, as well as various other industrial enterprises dependent upon the railway. The needs of passengers were catered for by the generous stations at St Helens and Bembridge, handsome brick structures with decorative chimneys and barge boarding, and broad wooden platform canopies. Adjacent to Bembridge station was the tall Royal Spithead Hotel. Today, remarkably little survives. A footpath follows the trackbed from Brading to the site of the former cement works, and then continues

roughly parallel to the track across the marshlands of the Yar. The track itself becomes a farm lane, and then disappears for a while into the landscape. The most tangible relic is St Helens station, now a private house, but with chimneys and barge boarding intact and its platform canopy converted into a kind of conservatory. The building is, for reasons not entirely clear, dated 1877, in raised brickwork. The trackbed continues through the garden and then runs parallel to the B3395 as it skirts Bembridge harbour. The bridge that carried it over the Yar has gone, and from here on the route is inaccessible and often invisible. Of Bembridge station, its extensive sidings and the docks served by the railway nothing at all remains. A modern housing complex stands on the site of the station, and the quays are now given over to sailing and other leisure activities. The former character of the harbour is better captured by beach huts and houseboats, and all the attractive clutter that boating seems to engender. One houseboat, formerly a naval motor launch that took part in the D-Day landings, offers bed-and-breakfast. The town's best railway features require a detour back through St Helens and round to the north side of the harbour. Here, a narrow spit of land called the Duver stretches southwards into the harbour, almost closing its mouth. Scattered along the Duver, and in their final reincarnation as beach huts and store sheds, is a series of old wooden carriages, all of which finished their working life on the Isle of Wight after grander beginnings on the rails of more significant companies such as the Metropolitan and the London, Brighton & South Coast. The Isle of Wight is, indeed, a happy hunting ground for lovers of old railway rolling stock, now gone to ground, with over eighty examples recorded on the island.

From Bembridge we went on to Shanklin and stood on the platform by the buffers, looking down on to a road. The bridge that carried the line onwards towards Ventnor has long gone, along with much of the embankment beyond the road. What remains of the railway is now the access road to a new holiday village devoid of railway interest, but it is worth persevering for near the gate is the start of a footpath and bridleway that follows the trackbed to Wroxall. Climbing steadily all the way, passing under and over a series of brick bridges and through the long green-brown tunnels formed by the trackside trees and bushes, this is a pleasant three-mile walk with a firm and mud-free grass and gravel surface. Along the route are the lingering clues to former railway life, here some fence posts made out of old rails, there a broken gate still in faded Southern Region colours, and often the distinctive cast concrete boundary posts so typical of 1930s Southern Railway modernism. The path ends just short of Wroxall, in a rather tatty industrial estate that has grown up around the tall brick buildings of the old bacon factory. From the remaining parapet of the overbridge it is possible to look

Above *The St Helens viaduct in April 1953. Today it is gone and little of the line can be traced*

Far Right *Holidaymakers in 1947 watch as* Fishbourne *is swung on Bembridge's tiny turntable*

SOUTHERN RAILWAY.
FROM WATERLOO TO
BRADING
Via PORTSMOUTH.
(2/37)
(787 G)

down on this scene of decay and imagine the sidings filled with wagons, the smell of steam and hot oil pervading the air. Wroxall station has vanished completely beneath new development, along with the course of the railway, but the former railway hotel, whose bar had a direct access to the platform, survives, converted to flats.

South of Wroxall, things are more mysterious. Bits of trackbed, overgrown and impenetrable, can be glimpsed beside the minor lane that leads to Wroxall Manor Farm. A pause to examine one of these bits more closely brought a new layer of particularly glutinous mud well above the ankle and over the car's floor. A former bridge, now crossing nothing but jungle and mud, takes this lane over the trackbed which then disappears into someone's paddock, just recognisable by its shape as the cutting leading to the great tunnel that took the line beneath St Boniface Down. Cut in 1866 with great difficulty and expense owing to the presence of vast quantities of spring water, this 1,313-yard tunnel was closed a century later, maintenance costs being given as the justification for depriving one of the island's most popular resorts of its railway lifeline to Ryde. Ventnor has never really been the same since.

The other end of the tunnel opened directly through the cliff-face into Ventnor's extensive station complex, built on the site of a former quarry. Here were two platforms, a range of buildings and goods sheds, a network of sidings, some serving the series of caves in the cliff-face that were used for storage, and a large signal box to control all the comings and goings. Set high above the town, with fine views down over the roof tops to the sea 294 feet below, Ventnor station must have been a fine introduction to its town, even if it meant a rather laborious walk for those carrying heavy suitcases to their seafront hotels. Today, the tunnel mouth is firmly boarded up and all the station buildings have gone, replaced by the anonymous sheds of a modern industrial estate. An image of a train emerging from the tunnel decorates the estate's name board, but that is it. The only other clue to the estate's previous life is the Terminus Hotel, a large brick building on the corner by the road whose polychrome window arches provide a clear link with Isle of Wight railway architecture. Next door is another handsome Victorian survivor, the highly decorative building of the Ventnor Gas and Water Company, proudly dated 1888.

Ventnor did, of course, have two stations. Ventnor Town, known later, and more realistically considering its suburban location, as Ventnor West, was opened in 1900, the terminus of the line southwards from Newport via Merstone, Godshill and

Left *A young trainspotter in the 1930s watches a train emerge from the tunnel at Ventnor*

Right *The tunnel at Ventnor survives today, but little else*

St Lawrence. Arriving on the scene rather late, and well away from the town centre, neither this station nor its route ever enjoyed much success and this was the first of the island's lines to be closed, in 1952.

Ventnor provided a welcome break, for lunch, for a tour of the book and junk shops and for a walk by the beach, the rain having stopped for a bit. In one bookshop there was a stack of pamphlets making the case for the reopening of the line from Shanklin to Ventnor, tired and rather dog-eared foot soldiers in a futile but remorseless campaign that has been going on now for nearly thirty years, without any real sign of success.

NEWPORT TO COWES

Newport was the heart of the Isle of Wight's railway network. Here was the meeting point of all the lines, the Clapham Junction through which most trains had to pass, its importance underlined by its presence in the names of all those fiercely independent companies that built the lines, the Cowes & Newport, the Ryde & Newport, the Isle of Wight (Newport Junction), the Freshwater, Yarmouth & Newport and the Newport, Godshill & St Lawrence. In the years before World War I, Newport must have been a busy and colourful place, serving the needs of the various companies whose trains met here. Originally there were several stations, as each company made its way into the town, but by a process of logic, mergers and organic growth they all gradually came together in a huge complex of lines and sidings that spread out northwards from the Medina.

It is, therefore, extraordinary to find today that there is virtually no trace of Newport station. This massive centre of railway activity has been obliterated as effectively as those early Communist party officials who fell foul of Stalin, with the result that railway hunting in Newport is rather a waste of time. No doubt the dedicated enthusiast with hours of time and nothing else to do could find the occasional fragment of brickwork or some original structure hiding beneath layers of later rebuilding, but for the casual visitor there is really nothing to see. Road building schemes and industrial estates have made sure of that. Newport is an attractive town, with plenty to see from the various centuries of its history. All the more curious, therefore, is the thought that archaeologists, picking over the ruins at some point centuries hence, will never know that Newport was a major railway town.

The trackbed from Newport to Cowes is now a cycleway whose firm and well-made surface runs through

SOUTHERN RAILWAY. (787 L.A.)
(2/46) FROM WATERLOO TO
COWES
Via PORTSMOUTH & RYDE.

Right *Trains crossing the Medina bridge at Newport were always a popular sight. Here W24* Calbourne, *now preserved on the Isle of Wight Steam Railway, hauls the 1.31 train from Cowes to Ryde across the bridge in February 1966*

Far Right *Cowes station has now completely vanished, but in 1957 it was still a busy terminus. Here a spotless W35* Freshwater *drifts into the curving platform*

attractive and undeveloped land parallel to the River Medina. It is the best, and indeed the only, way to see this rather inaccessible region. The start of the cycleway at the Newport end is inauspicious, hidden away as it is in an industrial estate, but it soon gets into its stride and comes quickly to one of the highpoints of the journey, the crossing of the old iron railway viaduct that was built in 1875 to carry the line over the Mill Pond, a wide tributary of the Medina that is now the centre of a nature reserve. Riding between high and untrimmed hedges through a landscape that is notably rural, it is hard to believe that this was once an area of considerable industry, served by the railway. The huge cement works, which had its own single platform halt, has long gone, along with its branch line. Nor does any trace remain of the large freight yards built for Medina Wharf. From the late 1920s, when the Medina took over from Bembridge as the island's major commercial port, these, with their network of sidings, handled all the cargoes imported into the Isle of Wight, from coal and household goods to locomotives and rolling stock for the railway. Today, the wharf is still busy, but nothing remains to indicate its place in the island's railway history. The little timber halt used by people working at the wharf has vanished into the burgeoning undergrowth that lines the trackbed. As you approach Cowes, the sense of isolation is gradually diminished by the encroaching signs of industry and

urban life, and the cycleway ends to the south of the town. Beyond is the site of Mill Hill station. There is no trace of the station, but the 208-yard Mill Hill tunnel remains, firmly sealed and now used as a range by the local shooting club, a not uncommon role for redundant tunnels. From this point on, there is nothing to see, Cowes having been as effective as Newport in the complete obliteration of its railway past.

NEWPORT TO FRESHWATER

From Cowes we returned to Newport, refreshed by the easily followed and mudfree qualities of the cycleway, and ready for a far more demanding challenge. This was the line from Newport to Freshwater which even on the map appeared to be erratic and often invisible. Closed in 1953, the line had had plenty of time to return to nature. Again, there is not much to be seen at the Newport end and trying to track the line's route through Newport's western suburbs is pretty futile. Modern expansion has linked these suburbs to Carisbrooke where the station was once one of the island's busiest. Today, absolutely nothing remains of buildings or track and only a very well-trained eye can identify a small patch of raised ground in a school playing field as the site of Carisbrooke station. Equally, there was nothing to be seen at Gunville, where a modern housing estate

HOLIDAY
RUNABOUT TICKETS
SIX DAYS' UNLIMITED TRAVEL
IN THE
ISLE OF WIGHT

During 1959 Holiday Runabout Tickets will be issued from 26th April to 30th October.

These tickets are valid for six days from Sunday to the following Friday and can be obtained at stations in the Island for travel on any train between stations on the above map.

For details of train services during the summer months, please ask for Isle of Wight Runabout Ticket Folder.

10/-
SECOND CLASS

15/- FIRST CLASS

CHILDREN HALF PRICE
(3 years and under 14)

Tickets at reduced rates are also issued for the conveyance of accompanied bicycles, dogs, perambulators (not folded), etc.

Above *Destination board for 'The Tourist', the cross-island Ventnor to Freshwater summer special in August 1952*

Far Right *Approaching Freshwater, the trackbed cycleway runs along the estuary shore*

Inset Far Right *In 1953, not long before this route was closed, W33 Bembridge rests between duties at the end of the line at Freshwater. Today the site is occupied by a supermarket, garden centre and the End of the Line café, whose walls are lined with similar scenes*

hedges, is Watchingwell station, now a private house. The station was itself virtually private, for it was built in this remote spot to serve the needs of Sir John Barrington Simeon, the Member of Parliament for Southampton and the owner of the Swainston estate, which lies just to the south.

Beyond the battered bridge the trackbed disappears again, and from here to Yarmouth there are only occasional glimpses. A crossing-keeper's cottage stands on a minor road, with the trackbed clearly running through the garden and just to the west is the site of Calbourne station, sometimes called Calbourne and Shalfleet and equally remote from both the villages it claimed to serve. A new house stands on the station site and, but for the map, there would be nothing to suggest that trains ever passed this way. Also long gone is the iron viaduct that carried the line over the Caul Bourne. More recognisable is Ningwood, where the station building is now a private house and other relics, such as a station lamp, can be identified. Realignment of what is still called Station Road has removed the brick bridge that used to be here, but the trackbed is well defined, even though parts of it are now covered by stables.

West of Ningwood there is little to be seen except muddy fields and woodland, much of which is private and inaccessible. The best place to start again is just east of Yarmouth, where the B3401 crossed the line. This is the beginning of the path that follows the trackbed virtually to Freshwater. Initially this runs beside Thorley Brook to Yarmouth station, well preserved, complete with platform with white-painted edge, and in use as a youth club. It then turns south, crosses Thorley Brook, passes the old tide mill, and continues on a raised embankment alongside the tidal creeks and mudflats that flank the River Yar. Plenty of boating and wildlife interest and a firm path make this a delightful journey, even in the rain. There are seats from time to time to enjoy the view, and there are patches of woodland to vary the estuary scenery. Just outside Freshwater the trackbed runs right beside the river on a raised causeway and then crosses a minor road, with the crossing-keeper's cottage still in place. The path then branches away from the trackbed, to its end near the town centre. From here the railway's route to its terminus is hard to trace. There are clues in back gardens, but they do not reveal much. New industrial buildings, a supermarket and a garden centre have taken over the station site and there is nothing to be seen. Behind the garden centre is a wooden café, suitably named 'The End of the Line'. With its homemade food, and its collection of photographs and Isle of Wight railway relics, this proved to be the perfect escape from the rain, and a fitting end to our muddy exploration of the island's most forgotten line. My only complaint was that the café uses as its logotype a drawing of a locomotive that is clearly American, and in no way native to the Isle of Wight.

covers completely the site of the brick and tile works, faithfully served by the railway until the 1940s. From this point, mud was once again in the ascendant, as forays down obscure lanes and tracks running south from the A3054 revealed various traces of the railway, sometimes a raised hump running through a grassy field, now the province of horses rather than trains, sometimes just a noticeably straight hedge or line of trees. As ever, it was astonishing to find that something apparently so durable could vanish completely into the landscape from which it had been so laboriously carved. Archaeologists may be able to piece together the timber huts of Stone Age villages, but they will not have much joy with the forgotten corners of Britain's railway network. A good place to consider this phenomenon is the evocatively named Betty Haunt Lane bridge, near Newpark Farm, on a minor road linking the A3054 with the B3401. It is a fine brick structure, attractively covered with lichen. From the eastern parapet there is the familiar view of a muddy and overgrown jungle filling the approach cutting, and the distant view of the vaguely discernible trackbed vanishing into the distance. From the western parapet there is absolutely nothing to be seen, just the even expanse of a ploughed field with no more than a slight depression to suggest where the railway might have been. Further west, on another track running betwen the A3054 and the B3401, a little north of Swainston, a battered and ivy-covered bridge crosses little more than a pile of builder's rubble, but in between these two extremes there is a stretch of well-defined trackbed, serving as a farm access lane. Near by, well hidden by

NEWPORT TO SMALLBROOK JUNCTION

Our final task was to seek out the line from Newport to Ryde. Much of this, from Wootton to Smallbrook Junction, is not difficult, being the province of the Isle of Wight Steam Railway. The remaining section, from Newport to Wootton, proved in the event to be quite easy to follow, and as varied as any of the island's former lines. This time, the starting point in Newport was easily found, and even more easily identified as a former railway, mainly because of the short tunnel that still survives under the A3054 Ryde road. Just south of the tunnel is the start of a well-defined footpath that follows the wooded trackbed beside the road to Fairlee. Here it ends, and a familiar wilderness of mud and bushes takes over and continues for about a mile to the next bridge. The bridge itself, an iron structure, is uncrossable, having had its floor removed along with the rails, but just beyond it the footpath starts again, with a set of access steps cut into the embankment beside the road. This leads on for another mile, passing the former Whippingham station, now a private house. Like a number of the island's stations, this was remarkably remote and so can never have attracted much traffic, even though it boasted two platforms, double track and a siding. Not surprisingly, it was one of the first to be closed, in 1953. The path ends at a minor road, after leaving the woods and crossing Wootton Common. Beyond the road the trackbed disappears, a barely visible area of muddy clay filled by impenetrable woodland. Wootton station, another early closure, was just to the west of the road that leads south from the village, under the shadow of the a large multi-arched brick bridge. Today, there is nothing at all to be seen of the station, and the bridge has been filled in to form an embankment. However, to the east of the road there is a miraculous and unexpected sight. Here is a new Wootton station, complete with name board, ticket office, signal box and a signal. There is a passing loop and sidings full of elderly goods wagons in various states of repair and, best of all, there is track stretching away into the distance. This is the western terminus of the Isle of Wight Steam Railway, which since 1971 has been running trains and carefully bringing back to life the branch line atmosphere of the island's railways in their heyday. At the beginning, trains ran between Wootton and Havenstreet, but in 1991 the line was reopened all the way to Smallbrook Junction via Ashey, and so the traditional steam trains now connect with the Island Line's electric trains.

In failing light and with the rain now lashing down, we made our way to Havenstreet, the steam railway's operational centre, in time to see the last departure of the day for Smallbrook. A surprising number of people were sitting in the three old Isle of Wight carriages; in one a childrens' birthday party was in full swing. Other people waited on the platform, taking photographs and soaking up the atmosphere. It was a scene typical of preserved railways all over Britain, but somehow better than most, partly because of the harsh reality of a wet October afternoon and partly because the train, the station and all the surroundings seemed to fit so well in their Isle of Wight setting. The lady guard looked at her watch, waved her flag and leapt back into the shelter of her compartment. The driver gave the whistle a long pull, released the brakes and opened the regulator. With satisfying sounds and clouds of steam the saddle tank locomotive, enjoying an honourable retirement after years of service with the War Office, clanked slowly away and the train disappeared gently into the gloom. Happy with this re-created vision of the island trains I should have seen, but somehow never did, we walked back to the car and drove to Fishbourne, to fight our way on to a ferry.

Left In June 1961 the 11.18 Ryde Pier Head to Cowes train passes through a typical Isle of Wight landscape near Whippingham

Right A veteran Stroudley Terrier tank engine working on the Isle of Wight Steam Railway in 1994

PRACTICAL INFORMATION

OS Landranger
196

Information points
Cowes Tourist Information Centre: The Arcade, Fountain Quay, Cowes, Isle of Wight PO31 3AR. Tel 01983 291914.
Newport Tourist Information Centre: The Car Park, Church Litten, South Street, Newport, Isle of Wight PO30 1JU. Tel 01983 525450.
Ryde Tourist Information Centre: 81–83 High Street, Ryde, Isle of Wight PO33 2LW. Tel 01983 562905, fax 01983 56710.
Sandown Tourist Information Centre: 8 High Street, Sandown, Isle of Wight PO36 8DG. Tel 01983 403886.
Shanklin Tourist Information Centre: 67 High Street, Shanklin, Isle of Wight PO37 6JJ. Tel 01983 862942, fax 01983 863047.
Ventnor Tourist Information Centre:34 High Street, Ventnor, Isle of Wight PO38 1RZ. Tel 01983 853625.
Yarmouth Tourist Information Centre: The Quay, Yarmouth, Isle of Wight PO 41 4PQ. Tel 01983 760015.

Official cycle/walkways
Newport to Cowes (5 miles).
Yarmouth to Freshwater (approx 3 miles).
Shanklin to Wroxall (3 miles).

Cycle hire
Cowes: Offshore Sports, Birmingham Road. Tel 01983 290514. Open Jun–Sep, daily 9–5.30; Oct–May, Mon–Sat 9–5.30.

Nearby attractions
Isle of Wight Steam Railway: Wootton to Havenstreet, Ashey and Smallbrook Junction; direct connection with Ryde to Shanklin Island Line at Smallbrook Junction (5 miles). Tel 01983 882204. Open late Mar–end Oct, Christmas Specials (talking timetable: 01983 884343).

In and Around The Potteries

♦

The North Staffordshire Railway
from Uttoxeter to North Rode
and from Stoke-on-Trent to Cauldon
The Leek & Manifold Valley Light Railway

Wetton Mill Station, Manifold Valley, North Stafford Railway.

This 1904 postcard view of Wetton Mill station shows the distinctive locomotives and rolling stock of the Leek & Manifold Valley Light Railway

HISTORY

Authorised in June 1846, the North Staffordshire Railway was from the start a company catering for local needs. Over the next sixty years it constructed and operated a complex network of routes that radiated outwards in all directions from Stoke-on-Trent, the heart of its empire, to make valuable connections with surrounding companies. It rarely left the county of Staffordshire, however. Famous for its independent attitude and its distinctive colour schemes, it remained one of the most successful, and the most popular, of England's local railway companies until its absorbtion into the LMS in 1923.

The original act of authorisation was actually for three nominally separate companies, the Potteries Railway, which was to build the network's backbone, the line from Colwich to Macclesfield via Stoke, the Harecastle & Sandbach Railway, and the Churnet Valley Railway, responsible for the line from Burton-on-Trent and Uttoxeter to Macclesfield via Leek. The Churnet Valley line, the most attractive in scenic terms of the North Staffordshire's routes, was completed in 1849. Its structures and buildings, made from the local dark red sandstone, were particularly handsome and its stations maintained the general Tudor Revival or domestic Gothic style that was characteristic of the North Staffordshire Railway as a whole. By the early 1850s the three primary routes were complete but from this date many other lines and branches were added to the North Staffordshire's network. Some, such as the Potteries, Biddulph & Congleton Railway, were purely local, often serving collieries and other industries, while others, such as the extensions westwards to Market Drayton and eastwards to Ashbourne, greatly extended the network.

This pattern of development continued through the nineteenth century, with the Potteries Loop line, an early example of a line built for commuters and other local traffic, opening in 1875. Another late addition was the direct line to Leek via Stockton Brook, while one of the last was the extension of this eastwards to Cauldon Low and Waterhouses, completed in 1905. Climbing high into the hills of the Staffordshire and Derbyshire borders, this served the stone quarries at Cauldon. However, more important was its role as a link to the Leek & Manifold Valley Light Railway, a narrow gauge line aimed largely at the growing tourist market that was opened in 1904. Although an independent company until it became a part of the LMS in 1923, the L&MVLR always had close links with the North Staffordshire company, who operated the line. In fact, the Leek to Waterhouses standard gauge line and the narrow gauge L&MVLR were all part of the same proposal, authorised in March 1899. Although its route along the river valleys was delightful, the narrow gauge line never carried enough passenger traffic to remain in business and it was closed in March 1934. The rest of the North Staffordshire network, operated first by LMS and then by British Railways, survived until the the early 1960s, but closures then came thick and fast and included the Churnet Valley line south of Oakamoor, and from Leekbrook to Macclesfield. The remaining section, from Oakamoor to Leekbrook, and the line from Stoke to Cauldon Low stayed open as mineral lines until the early 1990s.

Above *Cheddleton station, a delightful building in the Gothic style favoured by the railway in 1849. The station is now the home of the Cheddleton Railway Centre, whose aim is to reopen the Churnet Valley line to Oakamoor*

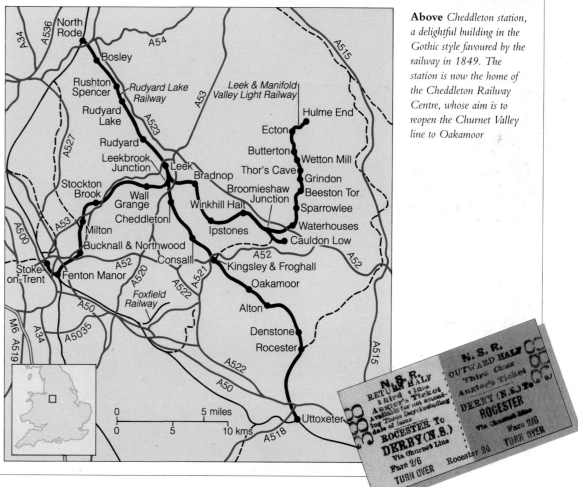

IN OCTOBER 1963 I took a train from Euston to Stoke-on-Trent. Although I did not know it at the time, this was the first of the hundreds of journeys I was to make along this route over the next thirty years, as the Potteries came to play an increasingly significant part in my life. It was then a long and rather slow journey, steam-hauled all the way – the kind that today would be a popular and high-priced outing, taken in considerable comfort behind some beautifully restored locomotive. In retrospect it was boring and all rather grimy. I doubt I even looked at the locomotive, but it would certainly have been dirty and the old maroon compartment carriages into which we were all packed had certainly seen better days. Stoke station, almost splendid in the gloom, was even dirtier, setting the scene for a city whose skylines of pithead winding gear, bottle ovens and blackened church towers rose above old terraces half hidden in smoke. I could taste the smoke as soon as I left the station, and the taste never went away. Today, museums and theme parks spend millions trying to recreate such visions of the past, but they always ignore the dirt and the smell. Nostalgia is curiously selective. In those days Stoke was still a coal-based city. Coal came out of the ground virtually in the city centre, and it was burned continuously in pottery ovens, in thousands of domestic fireplaces and in the fireboxes of the old locomotives that still banged their way around the Potteries loop line, that integrated local transport system which, had it survived, would now be the basis for a much-admired modern urban tramway network. In 1963 it was all still there but the writing was on the wall, and over the next decade or so Stoke dragged itself into the twentieth century. I am glad I saw it just in time; at least I know that those postcards of smoky views on sale in the museum and the souvenir shops show the real thing.

My first view of Stoke station did not really stick in the mind, but it was not long before I came to appreciate the qualities of this remarkable building. Together with the North Stafford Hotel across the road it forms a powerful and cohesive pairing, richly decorated in patterned brickwork and Jacobean-style detailing. Built in the late 1840s to the designs of H A Hunt, the architect of the North Staffordshire Railway, it is still the best architectural set piece in the whole of Stoke. It is also a fitting reflection of the dynamic individuality of Stoke's own railway, the North Staffordshire. Incorporated in 1846, this company created a network of predominantly local lines over the next few years, spreading outwards from Stoke to Macclesfield and Colwich, to Sandbach and Crewe, to Leek, Uttoxeter, Burton-on-Trent and Ashbourne, and to many other lesser places. On the map these routes looked like tentacles, reaching out into other companies' territory. Indeed, from quite early days the railway was known as 'the small octopus'. Firmly independent, the North Staffordshire spent the rest of the nineteenth century successfully fighting off the attentions of its powerful neighbour, the London & North Western. Its reddy-brown locomotives and carriages, decorated with the Staffordshire Knot emblem, went on running until 1923, when the company was finally absorbed into the LMS.

In 1963 much of the North Staffordshire's former network was still intact and I should like to be able to say that I immediately rushed off to explore it. In fact, I did not pay it any attention at all, getting to know the area instead on an elderly but willing BSA Bantam motorcycle bought for £16 in a local scrap yard. Over the next decade, the North Staffordshire's tentacles were lopped off one by one and all that remains today is the main line between Colwich and Macclesfield, with the link lines to Crewe, Norton Bridge and Uttoxeter. One or two other routes survived for a while as freight and mineral lines, but these too have now gone. Particularly hard hit were the lines that spread eastwards from Stoke, notable victims being Leek, a town that was once a major railway crossroads but now has no trains at all, and the scenic lines that served the Churnet Valley and reached out towards the hills and dales of Derbyshire.

During the ensuing years of fairly detailed and sometimes intimate association with Stoke and its surroundings, I came to know well both the railway routes and the towns and villages they used to serve. In some cases I watched, with an interest tinged with sadness, the pattern of decline from active line to closure and abandonment, and then the slow but inexorable return to nature. I explored the line that ran westwards from Stoke to Madeley, via Newcastle-under-Lyme and Silverdale, and its branch that swung northwards towards Alsager and

Below *For a small independent company with a largely industrial network, the North Staffordshire Railway had a surprisingly well-developed interest in tourism. Many postcard views were published early in the century, featuring popular spots such as Rudyard Lake*

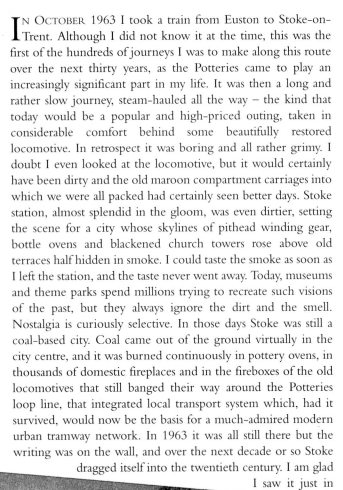

Sunset over Rudyard Lake, North Stafford Railway.

Kidsgrove. Passenger services had long gone, but the lines lingered to serve the local collieries. At that time these were closing down fast and taking the railways with them. Early one morning a friend and I drove up to Leycett, a former colliery village steeped in its history, where nothing had changed since the 1920s. The railway had gone, but the station was still there virtually complete, a delightful illusion of time suspended. It was one of those magic moments always to be treasured, and certainly one of those that turned me on to the particular appeal of the abandoned railway.

Over the years that followed, the tangible remains of the railways that had been closed were gradually swept away. Most of the Potteries loop line just vanished, but one section became a walkway, its route curiously scattered with fragments of locomotives and other pieces of machinery while trees softened the edges of the waste tips. The bottle ovens disappeared with speed until the handful that had by chance survived suddenly achieved a new and unexpected status as treasures of industrial heritage, and were painstakingly restored. Outside the city, the closed lines were left to moulder away more quietly, generally safe from the pressures of urban regeneration, and so, thirty years on, I was pleased to find that there was still much to see and enjoy.

THE CHURNET VALLEY LINE FROM UTTOXETER TO NORTH RODE

It was a very wet morning at Uttoxeter, the start of a day during which my railway hunting was to take place against a background of rain, mud and the grey light of misty horizons. The starting point was Uttoxeter station, still served by trains on the Stoke to Derby line and therefore easy to find. Not so apparent is Uttoxeter's other role, as the original southern terminus of the North Staffordshire's Churnet Valley line. Railways came surprisingly early to this rural and rather hilly region and the Churnet Valley Railway, incorporated as an independent company in June 1846, was to be one of the first, and the most important, of the North Staffordshire Railway's many routes. It was completed in 1849 as part of the company's backbone, its main line from Uttoxeter to Macclesfield later being extended to Burton-on-Trent.

The route of the Churnet Valley line is remarkable for the variety and quality of its landscape. Although some sections have vanished, it is an easy line to follow and explore, and offers the visitor everything from complete dereliction to active railway life, with all stages in between. It is also a line with an unusual history, for a large part of its route was built along the bed of an old canal. In 1811 a long branch canal was completed from the terminus of the Caldon Canal at Froghall to Uttoxeter.

Never a particularly busy waterway, the Uttoxeter branch was destined to have an unexpectedly short life. In 1846 the Caldon Canal and its branches were bought by the North Staffordshire Railway. Most of it survived, and indeed is still there today, but the Uttoxeter branch was immediately closed in order that the new railway could be built on top of it. The canal therefore disappeared. Those with keen eyes and great dedication can find a few traces, particularly in the river valley north and east of Alton, but in general terms the whole canal was obliterated.

The railway is on the whole much easier to find. From Uttoxeter station an unofficial path, used mainly by dog-walkers, follows the track for a short while to the site of the level crossing on the A518. Hidden in the bushes are the remains of a crossing-gate, but otherwise there is little to see. North of the A50 the line becomes a private and barely discernible route as it heads north towards Rocester across the fields. South of Rocester much of the line has been eliminated by the combined assaults of new roads and a massive JCB factory complex. The railway's route here used to lie alongside a lake that was originally within the grounds of a large country house called Woodseat, an ornamental feature on the old canal's route towards its Uttoxeter terminus. Much enlarged and used by the JCB Angling Club, the lake now forms part of the extensive landscaping that has changed the whole area. Late in the nineteenth century Woodseat was the home of Colin Minton Campbell, the owner of the Minton china works in Stoke.

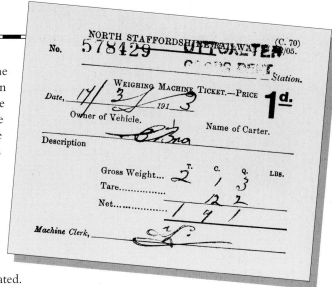

Above A weighing machine ticket issued by the North Staffordshire Railway at Uttoxeter in 1913

Below The staff of Rocester station pose for the camera, probably some time early this century. Not a brick remains today of this station or any of its associated structures, and the trackbed has completely disappeared

A typically ambitious Victorian entrepreneur, Campbell was also a director the North Staffordshire Railway. One of the benefits he enjoyed was a private railway saloon in which he would commute daily between Rocester and his factory in Stoke, hauled by a gleaming brown and red locomotive. Today, the area around Woodseat bears the stamp of a later transport revolution, and is a fitting memorial to the ubiquitous power of the JCB excavator. There is a splendid sculpture made out of excavator parts, an exciting and rather sinister blend of *Jurassic Park* and *The Planet of the Apes*, and a more than adequate replacement for a stretch of old railway trackbed.

The railway itself reappears north of Rocester, but there is little to be seen in the muddy fields either of its route or of the old junction at which the line to Ashbourne used to swing away to the northeast, along the valley of the Dove. The best place to start the hunt again is Denstone, on the site of a former level crossing in the middle of the village. On one side of the road is a building decorated with patterned brick in typical NSR style and conveniently named Station House. The track ran to the side of this, underneath a large modern house. On the other side of the road there is the old platform and a gate that marks the start of an official walkway. From here to Oakamoor the trackbed has become part of the Staffordshire Way, a broad and level path much used by walkers and cyclists. The surface is grass, gravel and, when I was there, mud with plenty of large puddles. Immediately north of Denstone the large and handsome bridge which carries the B5032, built from rough-cut lumps of red sandstone, is typical in material and style of the railway structures along this route. The pathway makes an excellent walk, along the steepening valley beside the Churnet and into the woods that surround Alton, and it is really the only way to see the old railway, which is otherwise inaccessible as far as Alton. Between Crumpwood and Abbey Wood there is also the chance of picking out some relics of the former canal, for the railway builders deviated briefly here from the line of the waterway. Turning to the west, the track crosses to the north bank of the river and then enters a narrow and dramatic valley whose tree-lined and rocky walls have a picturesque echo of the Alps or parts of southern Germany. Crowning the southern escarpment and rising above the trees are the equally Germanic towers and battlements of a mighty castle. This extravagant spectacle was the creation of the great Victorian architect and designer A W N Pugin. It was built in the late 1840s for Pugin's patron, John Talbot, the 16th Earl of Shrewsbury, whose great seat, Alton Towers, is beyond the trees that frame the valley's northern slopes. Today, of course, Alton Towers is something rather different and walkers enjoying the quiet of the Churnet Valley are likely to be disturbed by the sounds of machinery and the screams of visitors experiencing the various delights of the theme park.

Pugin built a convent and church at Alton, too. He also spent much of his life remodelling Alton Towers and its associated buildings. However, he definitely did not build Alton railway station, and no one really knows why. The line was being constructed at exactly the same time as Alton Castle, and he certainly designed the Tudor-style gatehouse across the road from the station. This was the way the Earl, and his guests, would enter the park when they arrived at Alton by train. An inveterate railway traveller, Pugin would have come to Alton many times by train during the last years of his life, and it must have irked him on every occasion to step out on to the platform of an Italianate station in the heart of his, and Shrewsbury's, Gothic empire. The architect of this curiosity is apparently not known. It is quite out of keeping not only with Alton Gothic but also with all the other buildings of the North Staffordshire Railway, which are marked by their adherence to a distinct Tudor/Jacobean style. The station remains intact and has been well restored, standing guard over its platforms as a permanent reminder of some distant and long-forgotten architectural dispute. The bridge that carries the road above the station has fine iron railings with Gothic finials – boundary markers, perhaps, in this early skirmish of the great Victorian battle of the styles.

From Alton a narrow road runs along the valley, just to the south of the Churnet, and this is a good route for those who do not want to walk. The track of the railway can often be glimpsed in the trees on the other side of the river. There is a

Below and Far Right *This early postcard view of Alton station shows how little has changed today. Carefully restored, along with the privately owned Italianate station house, this now stands beside the Staffordshire Way, in the shadow of Alton Towers*

Above *This postcard shows the line's dramatic route through the wooded hills of Oakamoor, and into the tunnel beneath the photographer's feet. Today the trackbed is an access road to the local sports ground, while the wagon-filled siding is part of the Staffordshire Way*

Right *The Caldon Canal and the railway ran side by side through Consall. This scene is one that the preserved railway aims to recreate*

Far Right *Leekbrook Junction today, a scene of romantic decay, awaits its resurrection as part of the preserved line to Oakamoor*

Leek to Oakamoor remained open for mineral traffic, notably sand. This traffic stopped some years ago but the track was left in place, partly at the instigation of the new Churnet Valley Railway, who have long cherished the dream of restoring the route and running steam trains over the seven-mile route. While this railway tries to raise the money, the track, its signs and its infrastructure slowly slip back into nature. Clearance and maintenance work is being undertaken, so perhaps the dream will one day become reality. In the meantime, the old rails and sleepers see nothing but the occasional walker. Gone for ever is the old branch line that ran eastwards from Froghall to the quarries at Cauldon Low, but much of its route can be followed.

Some years ago the Caldon Canal was rescued from dereliction and reopened to Froghall; how satisfactory it would be if the railway could follow suit and bring visitors to this most remote and delightful of Staffordshire's river valleys. From Froghall, canal, railway and river run tightly together along the narrow valley, a delightful if rather inaccessible stretch that continues past Consall to Cheddleton. Here the railway really comes to life, for the fine 1849 Tudor-style station is the headquarters of the Churnet Valley Railway. The lines and sidings are packed with carriages in various states of repair, and there is a big new shed housing the locomotives and rolling stock that operate over the short section of line that has been brought back into use. It is a tantalising glimpse of the possible future of the Churnet Valley line.

After Cheddleton the line leaves the river valley and plunges into the tunnel that leads to Leekbrook Junction. Here the Churnet Valley line met and crossed on the level the Stoke to Cauldon and Waterhouses line in a complex mass of intersections, points, crossings and sidings, all under the control of a towering signal box. Astonishingly, everything is still there,

path from this road that crosses first the river, on a fine old bridge, and then the railway, making this a good place for those wanting only a short walk to join or leave the path. The road, and the path, continue to Oakamoor, to the point just outside the town where the station used to be. Here the line crossed the river on a big girder bridge which now carries an access road for the local sports ground. Just before the bridge, the Staffordshire Way leaves the railway and skirts to the east of Oakamoor. Across the bridge a splendidly decorative half-timbered building stands at the site of the level crossing and the station. There is an inaccessible platform, and then the overgrown track disappears from view into the black mouth of a long tunnel beneath Oakamoor village.

It is hard to reach the tunnel's western mouth and the track remains fairly inaccessible as it makes its way along the river valley towards Froghall. Dedicated explorers can follow farm tracks and footpaths down into the valley, notably from Whiston, but most people will be content to go straight to Froghall. Here, surrounded by the traces and memories of the old iron and stone industries, the A524 (A52) crosses the Churnet and the railway. To the east of the bridge is the site of the station. The view from the bridge shows a long and rather battered platform, a solitary old British Railways notice board and, most surprising, a single line of railway track, rusty and overgrown, stretching away into the distance in both directions. Long after regular services had ceased, the Churnet Valley line from

Above *Seen from The Cloud, the old embankment cuts across the green Cheshire landscape*

the little 1ft gauge track, enjoying the views across the lake and following in the footsteps of the pottery workers of the 1920s and 1930s with whom the line was so popular. In those days, Rudyard Lake station was a grand and frequently busy place, with a big hotel near by.

The trackbed continues as a footpath to the end of the lake and then runs along the valley to Rushton Spencer, where it makes a brief detour around the fine station built in typical North Staffordshire style. This is now a private house, with a complicated garden planted between the old stone-edged platforms, and the former wooden goods shed now taken over for domestic or horticultural duties. The current owners have entered into the spirit of the thing by putting up a big cast iron 'Beware of the Trains' sign.

Near the Staffordshire/Cheshire border the footpath leaves the trackbed, which now makes a more private way above the River Dane, beneath the towering pinnacle of The Cloud. At Bosley the line has been taken over by a small factory complex, and there is little to be seen of the station. However, just beyond Bosley's big modern mill there is a wonderful stretch with the trackbed of even, green grass carried on a high embankment with the winding River Dane far below. This leads on to the Macclesfield Canal and the bottom locks of the delightfully remote Bosley flight that carry it up the rolling green hills. As embankment gives way to cutting, the track, now largely private and inaccessible, and in one place taken over by gardens and chicken coops, swings north to join the main Stoke to Manchester line at North Rode. High-speed electric trains thunder past the site of the former junction, rumbling the lingering ghosts of the North Staffordshire Railway.

a bit battered and overgrown, and a romantic mecca for the connoisseur of abandoned railways. Signals stand over rusting rails, waiting for trains that now will never come, and bit by bit the saplings and the rampant plants are taking over. The platform stays empty and distant figures walk their dogs along the tracks while young enthusiasts explore and try to make sense of it all. Chalked on the brick basewall of the signal box, a polite notice asks vandals not to wreck it, as it has been saved for restoration.

The rails stop just north of the junction, and then a long, low embankment marks the line of the railway's former approach to Leek. It all ends ingloriously in the Safeway car park, where the bridge that used to span the platforms now forms the entrance to the petrol station. The railway's route from here through Leek is of little interest, and the former tunnel on the northwestern outskirts is well hidden. However, the line soon appears again as Leek's northern suburbs are left behind and from here it becomes a local footpath that leads across the fields for a couple of miles towards Rudyard. A good place to pick it up is by the bridge that carries it over the B5331 at Harper's Gate, near the southern end of Rudyard Reservoir. Here there is a car park, picnic site and the northern terminus of the miniature Rudyard Lake Railway, whose brown and cream wagons bumble along beside the lake for a mile or so. A pleasant outing in summer is to walk one way and then ride back along

STOKE-ON-TRENT TO CAULDON

During my early years in Stoke, I was drawn increasingly to the canals of the region, and I had explored them all fairly thoroughly by the late 1960s. A particular favourite was the Caldon, then only partially navigable and awaiting the full restoration that has made it so popular since then. Its route from the Trent & Mersey near Etruria and up through Hanley was a favourite walk, sometimes enlivened by the sight of one of the special barges built to carry pottery between two canalside factories operated by the same company. Otherwise it was a forgotten paradise, the haunt of fishermen and wandering dogs. Between Hanley and Bucknall, one of Stoke's eastern outposts, it was joined by a railway line which, as I soon discovered, then followed it closely all the way to its terminus near Leek. Little-used when I first knew it, this line was soon carrying only the stone traffic from the quarries at Cauldon Low, a twilight existence that continued over many years. Inevitably, I became curious about this line and found that its history was closely bound in with the developing network of the North Staffordshire Railway, a complex story that continued to unfold throughout the nineteenth century. While much of this network was complete by the early 1850s, there were a number of additions in the latter years of the century. Typical among these was the grandly named Potteries, Biddulph & Congleton Railway, a line opened in 1860 primarily for the coal mines ranged along the Biddulph Valley. Passengers followed, in 1864, but the mineral traffic was always more important. Later, a branch was built to link this route with the Churnet Valley line south of Leek, thus opening a more direct route from Stoke to Leek, and it was this that followed the Caldon Canal so closely.

Although the stone traffic has ceased – and hundreds of extra lorries have thereby been thrown on to the small roads of Staffordshire and Derbyshire – the track remains in place, increasingly overgrown but easily followed. The first few miles from Stoke, mostly through suburbs, industrial estates and the remains of long-closed coal mines, are not particularly interesting and the best place to start an exploration is Stockton Brook, where the A53 crosses canal and railway side by side. Standing by the road is a timber building that was originally the station and is now a newsagent called, appropriately, Station News. The platforms have gone and the track is now the province of local dog-walkers, there in quantity on the day of my visit. It is remarkable how quickly a closed railway becomes an unofficial footpath, initially as a short cut and then as an easy place to go for a walk. The appeal is immediate and understandable, even if the tracks are still in place.

The next station was Endon and curiously this is now another newsagent. Platform, signs and the level crossing are all still there, if rather battered, and the dog-walkers were once again in evidence. One old labrador sat stubbornly on the platform as though content to wait indefinitely for a train, ignoring steadfastly its owner's repeated instructions to come down. From Endon the overgrown tracks stretched away into the distance and then swung eastwards towards Leek. This is an exciting stretch, with old farms and cottages folded into the wooded hills. At Denford the Caldon Canal splits into two, one arm dropping down through locks to pass under the other and then turn south towards Cheddleton and Froghall, while the other crosses over in flyover style before carrying on towards Leek. The railway is close by and after the canal junction it passes under the Leek arm where an aqueduct enabled boats to sail above the trains. Boats, of course can still be seen doing this, but the trains have to be imagined. The line then runs for a while between the two waterways, the towpaths providing a continuous series of good views. A long platform, disappearing under rampant nature, and a railway house now in private

ownership mark the site of Wall Grange station, a quiet stop for trains that served many villages and hamlets, without being close to any one in particular. The line then joins the valley of the Churnet and twists and turns through woodland to Leekbrook Junction, when it meets the Churnet Valley line in the complex of points and cross-overs just described.

For a long time this was the end of the story, with the trains from Stoke simply following the Churnet line into Leek's large and busy station. However, at the very end of the nineteenth century the North Staffordshire Railway decided to extend the line eastwards from Leekbrook Junction to Cauldon Low. The reasons for this were twofold. First, the expanding quarries there demanded a more direct route than the old narrow gauge mineral line to Froghall, and more traffic than this line could handle. Secondly, and more importantly, there was the plan to build a narrow gauge tourist line along the valleys of the Hamps and the Manifold. This was given the go-ahead in 1897 and part of the scheme was that the North Staffordshire company should build a new standard gauge line from Leek to Waterhouses, where it would meet the narrow gauge line at a shared terminus, and thus provide direct links with Leek, Stoke and other parts of the North Staffordshire network. Work proceeded fairly slowly and the line to Cauldon Low was finished in 1904, with the short link line to Waterhouses following in July 1905, by which time the narrow

Above and Below *In the 1950s Stockton Brook station was a quiet oasis during the day, busy only in the morning and evening rush hours. Today the line lingers on, although disused except by local dog-walkers*

gauge line had been in operation for over a year. Although tourist traffic on the two lines was considerable, particularly before World War I, it is hard to escape the feeling that the North Staffordshire company was rather half-hearted about the joint arrangement. For a while, for example, it refused to run Sunday trains from Leek to Waterhouses, even though this was the busiest day for outings along the Manifold Valley. In the event, the two lines existed in a rather uneasy relationship until 1923, when they both became part of the LMS.

From Leekbrook Junction the line swings on to a high embankment and then crosses the A520 on a grand bridge whose scale and style reveals the lateness of its construction. It was a line that demanded heavy engineering as it made its way across the hills of the Staffordshire/Derbyshire borders and its route is marked by long embankments and deep cuttings. Typical is the cutting at Bradnop, where the line runs far below the bridge that carries a minor road over it. There is little to be seen of the station that used to be here, but a mile further on a level crossing is still intact, if rather the worse for wear. The only other intermediate station was Ipstones, an isolated halt a long

way north of its village. The platform is still there, just to the west of the bridge that carries the B5053. With everything still in place but overgrown and quietly decaying, this captures well the ghostly atmosphere of this line. Saplings rise between the sleepers and the lineside bushes quietly encroach on the tracks, and yet there is the feeling that at any moment some much-delayed train could come creeping along. Another long cutting follows, and then Cauldon comes into view, a great scar of quarry-working standing out against the background of the Derbyshire hills. Climbing steadily, and passing the site of the junction with the short Waterhouses branch at Broomyshaw, the line runs up to the quarry, spreading into a series of sidings as it reaches its terminus beside the new lorry park. As dereliction and decay take over, it makes a sad sight, an incomprehensible victory for road transport in a field where railways are the natural carriers. Knowing that the line is still there and could so easily be brought back to life makes it all seem even worse. Perhaps at some point in the future common sense will be allowed to prevail again, and the long mineral trains will once more be rattling down to Leekbrook and Stoke, and out on to the national railway network.

Below *Waterhouses was the interchange station for the Leek & Manifold Valley Light Railway. This early postcard view shows the standard gauge North Staffordshire Railway shuttle that linked Waterhouses with Cauldon and Leek. The wooden goods shed survives today, now housing the Peak National Park Cycle Hire Centre*

THE LEEK & MANIFOLD VALLEY LIGHT RAILWAY, FROM WATERHOUSES TO HULME END

Delightfully eccentric and rather short-lived, the Leek & Manifold Valley Light Railway was born out of the kind of nineteenth-century railway mania that instilled in people who lived in remote regions of Britain a determination to be joined to the national railway network, at almost any cost. One such region was the peaks and moorlands spanning the borders of Staffordshire and Derbyshire, whose isolation was finally ended in 1899 by the opening of a railway that linked Buxton and Ashbourne. This line, a late arrival in railway terms, inspired many other schemes, notably among the residents of Dove Dale and the Manifold Valley. The latter were particularly vociferous and a group of local landowners and politicians finally persuaded the North Staffordshire Railway to support two linked proposals, first for a standard gauge line eastwards from Leek to Waterhouses, and secondly for a narrow gauge line from Waterhouses to Hulme End, near Hartington, to be built under the provisions of the recently established Light Railway Act. Despite various setbacks, these proposals were authorised in 1897 and contruction of the Leek & Manifold Valley Light Railway finally started in 1902. Two years later the trains began to run along the 2ft 6ins gauge line, even though they had to wait another year before the North Staffordshire Railway was able to complete its linking line from Leek to Waterhouses.

Although it served a popular tourist area, the L&MVLR never achieved the success it hoped for. Its delightful line followed closely the twisting valleys of the Hamps and the Manifold, and its well-built and generously sized trains were

Above *Two elegant Edwardian ladies wait for a train at Beeston Tor station on the L&MVLR*

Below *Both the L&MVLR's locomotives and almost all its rolling stock were used for this packed Bank Holiday train, just before World War I*

known for their comfort. It made accessible the hidden corners of some particularly attractive countryside, and enabled those who lived in these remote regions to travel to the outside world with relative ease. It carried plenty of passengers, especially during the tourist season, but not nearly enough freight, milk being the only bulk commodity that it could attract. It continually lost money, never even coming close to repaying the costs of construction or fulfilling the hopes of its shareholders. Its partnership with the North Staffordshire Railway, on which it depended, was always uneasy. The LMS took over in 1923 but was never prepared to invest in it in the face of increasing road competition. No one was really surprised, therefore, when it closed for ever in March 1934. Throughout its thirty year's life the railway was always operated by the same two locomotives, four passenger carriages and eight freight vehicles that made up its total rolling stock, the little trains running slowly to and fro in an unchanging pattern that was part of the railway's appeal.

Also endearing were the L&MVLR's peculiarities. Despite its ambitions and its grand title, it was a railway that went from nowhere to nowhere via some beautiful scenery. Its sturdy locomotives with their huge headlamps, and its carriages with their open verandahs would not have looked out of place in India, and were in fact inspired by the rolling stock of that country's Barsi Railway. Most of its freight vehicles were novel transporter cars, designed to carry standard gauge goods wagons and thus avoid costly and time-wasting trans-shipment operations, a practical idea that none the less never really caught

BEESTON TOR STATION.

On the Manifold Valley Light Railway, Derbyshire, near Beeston Tor.   (North Staffordshire Railway).

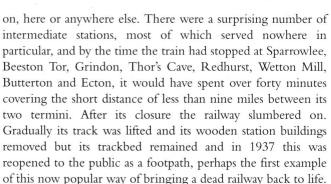

Left *The winding trackbed of the Leek & Manifold Valley Light Railway is now a popular cycle trail, seen here from Thor's Cave*

Inset Left *An early twentieth-century postcard view of a L&MVLR train near Beeston Tor*

Right *J B Earle, one of the L&MVLR's two locomotives, receiving attention at Hulme End in September 1933, shortly before the line's closure. The wooden station building has recently been restored for a new life as a tourist information centre*

PRACTICAL INFORMATION

OS Landrangers
118, 119, 128

Information points
Congleton Tourist Information Centre: Town Hall, High Street, Congleton, Cheshire CW12 1BN. Tel 01260 271095.
Leek Tourist Information Centre; Market Place, Leek, Staffordshire ST13 5HH. Tel 01538 381000.
Stoke-on-Trent Tourist Information Centres: The Potteries Shopping Centre, Quadrant Road, Hanley, Stoke-on-Trent, Staffordshire ST1 1RZ. Tel 01785 40204

Official cycle/walkways
Denstone to Oakamoor, part of the Staffordshire Way (4 miles)
The Manifold Trail: Waterhouses to Hulme End (8½ miles)

Cycle hire
Booking is advisable in summer months.
Peak National Park Cycle Hire Centre: Old Station, Waterhouses. Tel 01538 308609. Open Feb–Nov daily, Dec–Jan Sun only, 9.30–6.

Nearby attractions
Cheddleton Railway Centre: Cheddleton Station, near Leek, Staffordshire ST13 7EE. Tel 01538 360522. Rolling stock, engine shed, steam locomotives operating on a short length of track. Open Easter–Sep, Sun and Bank Holidays 11–5.30. Phone for details of special events.
Foxfield Light Railway: Blythe Bridge, Caverswall Road Station, near Stoke-on-Trent ST11 9EA. Tel 01782 396210/01270 874959. 5-mile round trip on former colliery railway; museum with a small collection of locos, rolling stock and relics. Open for special events Easter–Sep. Phone for details.
Rudyard Lake Railway: Rudyard Old Station, near Leek, Staffordshire ST13 8PF. Tel 01260 272862. Miniature railway running on 1ft gauge track along the western shore of the lake (1 1/2 miles). Open Jan–Nov, Sat, Sun plus fine days in school holidays. Phone for details.

on, here or anywhere else. There were a surprising number of intermediate stations, most of which served nowhere in particular, and by the time the train had stopped at Sparrowlee, Beeston Tor, Grindon, Thor's Cave, Redhurst, Wetton Mill, Butterton and Ecton, it would have spent over forty minutes covering the short distance of less than nine miles between its two termini. After its closure the railway slumbered on. Gradually its track was lifted and its wooden station buildings removed but its trackbed remained and in 1937 this was reopened to the public as a footpath, perhaps the first example of this now popular way of bringing a dead railway back to life.

Although I had always known about the Leek & Manifold and its curious history, I had never seen it. On the map its route looked isolated and inaccessible, rarely crossed by roads of any significance and I was still wondering how to attack it as I followed the route of the former branch to Waterhouses from Cauldon. This could be traced along an embankment and across a massive bridge over a minor road before it reached the site of Waterhouses station. This was now a car park and picnic site, surprisingly busy in the cold sunshine of a February Sunday. At the centre was the old station goods shed, a fine timber building with cast-iron detailing, and now the home of one of the Peak National Park Cycle Hire Centres. The decision was quickly made and I was soon equipped with a fine mountain bike, the ideal way to explore the Leek & Manifold.

In its heyday, Waterhouses must have been an interesting station, with the brown-painted standard gauge North Staffordshire trains standing side by side with the colourful and exotic-looking rolling stock of the L&MVLR. When it left this shared terminus, the little train set off down a steep slope,

crossed what is now the A52 (A523) with whistle blowing, and then immediately entered the twisting valley of the River Hamps and as I set off on the bicycle, I thought of what it must have been like in railway days. This was just the start of a delightful hour or two spent following the track's winding course northwards, criss-crossing the river and dropping down into the grander, rock-lined valley of the Manifold. The going was even and firm and the route was one continuous stream of walkers, joggers, dogs and cyclists, including many family groups with small children pedalling away. There were plenty of places to stop and watch the world go by and the old farm at Wetton Mill served teas and snacks. From Wetton the track has been taken over by a minor road and this continues to the far end of the short tunnel, the line's major engineering feature and a tangible link with the railway past. There was a fair amount of traffic on this part and although there was plenty of room in February it couldbe less appealing on a busy summer weekend. After the tunnel the line left the steep-walled valley and crossed a more open landscape to its terminus at Hulme End. Here, some of the station buildings survive, including the old timber ticket office and passenger shelter, now in use as an information centre. As the terminus of the L&MVLR, Hulme End can never have offered much and I am sure I did the same as everyone has always done there when I just had a quick look, turned round, and set off back up the line, now uphill and against the wind, enjoying once more those sweeping curves, the first flowers of an early spring and the rivers in full spate. How fortunate we are that those ambitious late Victorians spent so much money building an eccentric little railway whose lasting legacy is one of England's most enjoyable trackbed paths.

NORFOLK HORIZONS

◆

The Midland & Great Northern Joint Railway
from Norwich to Cromer via Melton Constable
and from Melton Constable to Yarmouth Beach

The M&GNJR built classically elegant locomotives, and some enjoyed a long working life. One such veteran is class A No. 35, making plenty of smoke during shunting operations at Cromer Beach in about 1930

HISTORY

On an old map, Norfolk is a mass of railway lines, criss-crossing and winding across the landscape to serve practically every corner of the county. This was one of the best rural networks in Britain, and particularly well covered was the northern half of the county. Today, apart from the line from Norwich up to Cromer and Sheringham and a couple of preserved lines, the North Norfolk and the Bure Valley, there is nothing left.

The creation of this complex network was the work of an extraordinary number of small and independent companies between the 1840s and the turn of the century, initially for largely local reasons. In a somewhat unplanned way these small railways gradually merged together, to form larger and more ambitious units and then, in 1862, the Great Eastern Railway was formed to take over most of the lines in East Anglia. This company continued to run the great variety of services the region required with considerable efficiency until the grouping of 1923 when it all became part of the LNER. However, the existence of the Great Eastern did not stop railway building in the region, and a whole network of new lines began to snake across north Norfolk, encouraged and actively supported by other major companies with their eye on East Anglian traffic, notably the Great Northern and the Midland.

In 1893 they revealed their hand, with the formation of a company known as the Midland & Great Northern Joint Railway to take over a network of 182 miles of predominantly rural and single-track railway spread between Peterborough, King's Lynn, Fakenham, Cromer, Norwich and Yarmouth. This network had been assembled in a rather piecemeal fashion by a number of small companies from the 1870s, the most important of which were the Lynn & Fakenham Railway and the Great Yarmouth & Stalham Light Railway and its successors. In 1883 these all merged together to form the Eastern & Midlands Railway, and this company completed the main line from King's Lynn to Yarmouth, and the branches from Melton Constable to Norwich and Cromer. Melton Constable, a remote Norfolk village chosen by the Lynn & Fakenham as the site for its railway and engineering works, became the hub of the network and was for fifty years a centre of industry before sinking back into the clay from which it had arisen.

The spirit of independence that had brought the network into being was maintained during the long period of ownership by the Midland & Great Northern Joint Railway, which also enlarged it, adding, via its

Left *Another class A veteran, No. 80, prepares to leave Norwich City station in February 1929 with the 5.20pm train to Melton Constable. Despite its imposing façade, Norwich City was a rather insubstantial station and, towards the end of its life, it looked more like a small town halt than a city terminus*

subsidiary the Norfolk & Suffolk Joint Railway, the coastal routes between Cromer and North Walsham and Yarmouth and Lowestoft. Although it was absorbed into the LNER in 1923, it still retained much of its original independence, and it lived on in this way into the era of British Railways. However, faced by increasing financial difficulties, the M&GN network began to be cut back in the 1950s. Many of its routes in any case were considered to be unnecessarily complicated duplications of existing lines. This pattern of closures continued steadily and by the end of the 1960s all passenger services had gone. Freight followed more slowly but by 1983 the whole network had gone, after an active life of little more than a century.

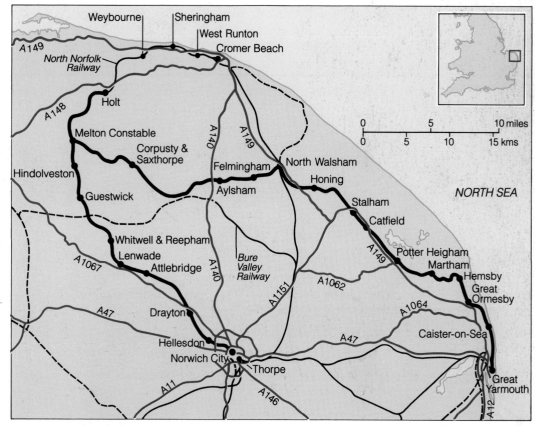

Below *This early twentieth-century postcard of a M&GN 4–4–0 locomotive shows the railway's smart livery*

ALTHOUGH a Londoner by birth and by habit, I have always been drawn to East Anglia. Long before I was around, my grandparents lived near Dedham and spent their summer holidays in a camping coach at Hopton-on-Sea, a station between Yarmouth and Lowestoft that was then so remote that a locomotive would arrive each morning with their daily supplies of water, milk and bread. As a child I was introduced by my father to the pleasures and perils of boating on the rivers and estuaries of Essex and Suffolk. Later, with a group of friends, I rented a weekend cottage for a while near Stowmarket and so became accustomed to both the (then) somewhat erratic train service to Norwich from Liverpool Street and the architectural delights of Stowmarket's magnificent 1849 Jacobean-style station. Standing on the platform there one Sunday evening, I was surprised and pleased to see the Flying Scotsman steam slowly through, at the head of an enthusiasts' special. However, it was my three years as a university student at Norwich that really established my appreciation of East Anglia. In retrospect, I seem to have spent much of my time there exploring the county, generally by car, but sometimes by train or even boat, and my old Ordnance Survey map is covered with circles and scribbles whose significance is long forgotten. Some of them are on or near railway lines, a number of which were then still on the map, even if they were rarely used. I remember the difficulties of coming to grips with the railway history of East Anglia, surely one of the most complex and convoluted in Britain. The whole place seemed to be a mass of lines and a mass of initials, the M&GNJR, the E&MR, the ECR, the EUR, the Y&NNR, the N&SJR, the L&FR, the W&FR, the LJR and many, many more. I gave up trying to sort it all out, and just enjoyed what was still there to be seen. A friend was involved in the setting-up of the North Norfolk Railway and so I made a number of visits to Sheringham and Weybourne to look at what was then a collection of decaying rolling stock and locomotives that had seen better days.

I travelled frequently to and from Norwich's grandiose Thorpe station, then, as now, a busy place but nothing like it must have been in earlier years when Norwich was the hub of a huge railway network. There had, of course, been two other Norwich stations, Victoria and City, and when I was there they were still just existing, if not actively.

Victoria dated from the late 1840s, when it was used as a terminus for the Eastern Union Railway's line from Colchester and Ipswich. In the 1860s, through a complicated series of amalgamations, it came under the control of the newly formed Great Eastern Railway, along with Thorpe. Not really needing two Norwich termini, the GER concentrated its efforts at Thorpe and created the present French château-style station in 1886. Victoria was quietly run down, and all its passenger services ceased in 1916. However, it lived on as a goods depot into the 1960s. Norwich City, no more centrally placed than the other two despite its name, was a small-scale affair and a relatively late arrival, opening in 1882 as the terminus of the Eastern & Midlands Railway, a company formed from a handful of small and predominantly local lines, one of which, confusingly, was called the Midland & Eastern.

A little over ten years later this was in turn absorbed into another new company, the grandly named Midland & Great Northern Joint Railway. As its title suggests, this was a venture backed by the Midland and Great Northern Railways, and a clear attempt by them to break into Great Eastern territory. A highly individual and completely East Anglian operation, the M&GNJR ran trains over 182 miles of track, mostly covering the rural heart of Norfolk. Its backbone was the line from Peterborough to Yarmouth via King's Lynn, Fakenham and North Walsham, with branches to Spalding and Bourne, Cromer and Norwich. After the 1923 grouping, it remained a joint venture shared by the LMS and the LNER, and it then lived on into the era of British Railways, retaining much of its local flavour but declining steadily in revenue terms. In the 1960s it was completely obliterated. By the time I came across it, the M&GNJR had largely disappeared into history, and the only section of any significance that remained was the line from Norwich to Reepham, then still open for freight traffic.

NORWICH TO CROMER VIA MELTON CONSTABLE

It was with these early memories very much in mind that I returned to Norwich recently to seek out what remained of the Midland & Great Northern Joint Railway. I started by looking for Norwich Victoria station but it had disappeared beneath new and interminable industrial estates, along with all its associated structures and goods yards. Coming into Norwich so late, the railway took the economical and the easy option and so its route followed the River Wensum on its way towards the city centre. Today, much of the trackbed survives as a footpath and it is a pleasant way to enter or leave Norwich, with the river never far away. The surroundings are initially unexciting but the Wensum and its surrounding parkland offer some relief from housing estates and hurtling traffic. The first two, essentially suburban stations were at Hellesdon and Drayton, and it is at the latter that the rather low-key trackbed footpath from Norwich turns into something more substantial. Just north of the station, where the railway left the river, is the start of Marriott's Way, a 21-mile cycletrack and bridle path to Aylsham via the trackbeds of two railways, the M&GN and the GER. It is a well-made and well-maintained path through a varied landscape, with plenty of reminders of railway days along the route.

From Drayton, the last outposts of Norwich are quickly left behind as the track crosses a mixture of open heathland and woods. The next station was Attlebridge and then the line crosses the Wensum, the river's meanders bringing it back beside the track for the couple of miles to Lenwade. The M&GN had a very distinctive architectural style and most of the stations conform to a pattern, along with the lesser buildings such as crossing-keeper's cottages. This makes surviving structures easy to identify, but their appeal is more than mere convenience. The single-storey two-bay stations are simple but satisfactory buildings within a recognised local tradition, and their decorative details, notably the barge-boarding, link them firmly with East Anglia. Dating mostly from the 1880s, they reflect in a gentle way the vernacular enthusiasms of Arts & Crafts designers.

The station at Lenwade is typical but enjoyment is hampered by the high wire fences erected round it by the current owner and the ranting Alsatian racing up and down behind them. Here, the old crossing gates are still in place, rather decayed and covered with 'Keep Out' notices. These can safely be ignored, however, for the path follows the trackbed past the platform, crosses the road and then crosses the river on a low iron bridge to enter a broad undulating landscape of large fields broken by little clumps of woodland. In one such wooded area is the next station, Whitwell and Reepham. The platforms, beautifully edged with patterned black brick and overgrown with

primroses and shrubby bushes, stand guard over the track, and on one there is the brick station building, intact, but well boarded-up. The former goods yard is now a large car park and picnic site. This area is a popular starting point for walkers and cyclists and there are also good access points at the next three bridges. From here the trackbed swings to the west and then curves north again towards Themelthorpe.

A gloomy-looking but original keeper's cottage stands by the site of the former level crossing and across the road in the adjacent field there is the remains of a low embankment that curves away to the east. Marriott's Way follows this, to leave the M&GN and join the old East Norfolk, later Great Eastern, line from County School to Wroxham via Aylsham. County School was an important junction in earlier days, and the line south from here to Dereham and Wymondham is now the subject of an ambitious preservation scheme. The footpath continues as far as Aylsham but it has to stop there for Aylsham South station is now the headquarters of the narrow gauge Bure Valley Railway, which operates steam trains along the remaining nine miles to Wroxham.

Above *Cromer and Norwich-bound diesel railcars meet at Whitwell and Reepham station in the summer of 1958, with plenty of passengers to keep the service running. Today, the platforms and the main station buildings survive, but the scene has been radically altered by the encroaching woodland and by the Marriott's Way footpath and cycleway that has taken over the trackbed*

(18 V19)

MIDLAND & GREAT NORTHERN RAILWAYS JOINT COMMITTEE.

TO

LENWADE

The low embankment, known as the Themelthorpe Curve, which looks as though it has not seen a train for a hundred years, was actually built in 1964. At the time, closures were going on all around but for some reason British Railways decided to create a new route from Norwich City to Wroxham via Aylsham by linking together the M&GN and the GER lines at a point where they had previously crossed without any connection. Not surprisingly, the new line saw little traffic, but it lingered on until 1983 when the remaining section, from Lenwade to Wroxham, was finally closed.

After the Themelthorpe level crossing, the M&GN went straight on, to cross over the GER line on a bridge which has since disappeared, leaving truncated embankments standing back in the fields, and easily seen from the bridge on the minor road just to the west. From here the trackbed makes its own way across the fields, often invisible in the flat landscape although well marked on the map. It is most easily seen near stations, which have often survived remarkably well. The next one was Guestwick, but first of all there was another crossing-keeper's cottage, in good original condition and with a very pretty garden that incorporates railway relics among the plants. A quarter of a mile further on the station also survives, now in private use but complete with platform and signal box and called, not surprisingly, Station House.

Guestwick had one further treat in store. Just beyond the station there are a few houses and among them is the village post office and general store, housed in an old wooden goods wagon, parked by the roadside and painted blue.

From here the line runs close to the road for a mile or so, but there is little to be seen in the fields as the farmers have efficiently ploughed it out. In this flat landscape this is a common fate for old railway lines . After a while it reappears as an embankment raised above the fields, and the trackbed becomes a straight line against the open sky before curving away into a wood. Beyond the wood is Hindolveston, and an even better group of buildings. First, the familiar crossing-keeper's cottage, white-painted and with a signal box in the garden. On the other side of the crossing there is a long, silent line of wooden goods wagons which look as though they were shunted on to a siding thirty years ago and then forgotten. Cows were living in some of them, along with a huge but rather placid-looking bull that stared at me mournfully as I walked past, along the muddy lane that leads to the station. This stands amongst the trees, white-painted and looking very decorative on its long platform while ducks splashed about in a large puddle on the trackbed. Instead of 'Beware of the Trains' a sign said 'Look Out for the Geese'. It must have been a pretty place to wait for a train. North of Hindolveston the line follows a private route across the fields and through the woods for a couple of miles,

out of sight and largely inaccessible until it comes to Melton Constable.

One of the most unusual and unexpected villages in Norfolk, Melton Constable was created entirely by the railway. Until 1881 there was nothing here at all – just a few cottages and a ruined medieval church, all dependent upon, but detached from, Melton Hall. Then in 1882 the Lynn & Fakenham Railway arrived and decided to build its railway works here, before merging with the Yarmouth & North Norfolk and the Yarmouth Union to form the Eastern & Midland Railway. As the works with its great engineering sheds rose up out of the Norfolk soil, so it brought in its wake rows of workers' terrace houses, pubs and shops and a corrugated iron church, a small industrial town in the heart of rural Norfolk. Locomotives were built here, along with all the paraphernalia the railway required. Initially, Melton Constable was just a stop on the line between King's Lynn and Yarmouth, but as other routes opened it soon became a major junction, and the hub of the Eastern &

Above *The railways of Norfolk were early victims of the closure programme. Posters like these, announcing the withdrawal of passenger services on the Melton Constable to Norwich City route, were soon to be a common sight all over the county*

Far Left *South of Guestwick, the old embankment strides across the fields, its growth of trees silhouetted against the evening sky*

elusive again and generally inaccessible to Holt. South of the town a long stretch has disappeared beneath the new ring road and there is really nothing to be seen until the site of the bridge that carried the A148 over it, well to the east. Here, there is a dramatic change for, although the bridge has gone, the railway has returned to life. In the woods by Kelling and just off the old road there is a simple platform, a temporary ticket office, and a set of buffers that mark the start of the North Norfolk Railway, the preserved line that has brought steam back to Norfolk, and the M&GN back to life. Trains run from here to Sheringham via Weybourne, where the railway has its depot and workshops.

Sheringham's fine station is the end of the line but just across the road is the little platform used by British Rail's modern diesels for the service to and from Norwich. These trains run over former M&GN metals to West Runton and into Cromer's terminus station. They then reverse back to Newstead Lane Junction to swing southwards on to the old East Norfolk line to Norwich via North Walsham and Wroxham. Cromer's railway history is extraordinarily complex for a relatively small town, and it had at one time two stations and three railways. First to

Left *One of the few memorials to Melton Constable's days as a railway town is the huge cast-iron water tower that served the engine works*

Below *Class C No. 53, shown on the postcard on page 88, enjoyed a long life. Here, in 1935, it still looks smart as it leaves Cromer Beach*

Midland's network. First came the line south to Norwich City, opened in December 1882, and then, five years later, the line northwards to Cromer. In 1893 the Midland & Great Northern Joint Railway took it all over, including the railway works, which then continued to operate well into this century.

Today, Melton Constable is a strange and rather sad place. It has no railways of any kind and no station, but there are plenty of clues to its more glorious past. In the centre is a bus shelter which incorporates some decorative cast-iron canopy brackets, and a panel depicting a Melton-built locomotive. Parts of the works survive in the industrial estate, but most impressive of all is a huge water tower behind the works, a gaunt structure in fading British Railways cream and green paint with the M&GN initials cast on to the side panels of the great water tank.

The line to Cromer branched away to the north just outside the station, but little has survived the combined assaults of road builders and farmers. In Briningham the site of the level crossing is just discernible and there are glimpses hereabouts of bits of embankment against the horizon. The best place to find the old railway is between Thornage and Hunworth, where it crosses a minor road and the River Glaven on sturdy brick arches. To the west of the bridge the well-defined embankment now carries a farm track, and to the east it curves away into bluebell woods, accessible from a footpath. From here the line is

arrive was the East Norfolk, in 1877, with a station to the southeast of the town. Next came the Eastern & Midlands, in 1887, with a new station called Cromer Beach, a style of naming that seems to have appealed to the E&M for they used it also for their Yarmouth terminus. Cromer's beach is in fact quite a long walk away, but the visitors probably did not mind. The station, a fine timber-framed building in the Arts & Crafts style with a *porte cochère* supported by cast-iron M&GN

brackets, is still there but no longer in use, the British Rail trains stopping at a new brick structure round the back. The final arrival was the Norfolk & Suffolk Joint Railway, whose trains began to use Cromer Beach station from 1906. This was a joint venture between the M&GN and the GER, set up in 1898, that operated the coastal services between Cromer and North Walsham via Overstrand and Mundersley, and between Yarmouth and Lowestoft via Gorleston.

Above *The North Norfolk Railway has brought a section of the old M&GN back to life. Harlaxton, a tank locomotive painted in M&GN colours, hauls its train towards Weybourne in the autumn of 1994*

Left *Quite near the road between Corpusty and Oulton, and half hidden by trees, is an old stone platelayers' hut*

MELTON CONSTABLE TO YARMOUTH

The line eastwards from Melton Constable to Yarmouth had a convoluted history typical of railways in East Anglia. Work was started in 1876 by a company called the Great Yarmouth & Stalham Light Railway which built a short stretch and then turned itself into the Yarmouth & North Norfolk Light Railway. After another change or two this was absorbed in 1883 into the Eastern & Midlands Railway, and it was they who actually completed the line. Building railways to Yarmouth seems to have been a popular Victorian activity. The first, the Yarmouth & Norwich Railway, opened in 1844. One of its backers was a brewer who stipulated that every station should have a public house, including Berney Arms – then, as now, one of Britain's most inaccessible stations, with no road anywhere near it. As very few trains stopped there, the publican had a rather quiet life. In the end he took the railway to court and, after years of wrangling, he won the case and the trains were then compelled to stop there. Other railways then followed, and by the end of the century there were five lines making their way into Yarmouth.

Today, there is not much to be seen of the line as it leaves Melton Constable. Large sections have been ploughed back into the fields and elsewhere it has been absorbed into back gardens, or taken over by farm tracks. South of Briston a bridge still stands, with bits of its embankment, but in the village the level crossing has largely vanished, along with its keeper's cottage. One new house has in its garden a very decorative old cast-iron lamp, which might well have come from a station. A short stretch between Rookery Farm and Blackwater Bridge is now a incorporated into a local footpath circuit, with new access steps beside the bridge, but this does not include the isolated and attractive wooded section west of Corpusty. The trackbed comes back into view as it enters the village beside the road. Corpusty & Saxthorpe station is now the changing room for the local sports ground, and a football pitch has taken over the trackbed. Presumably the platform makes a rather good grandstand. Across the road the trackbed has been taken over by gardens and ducks.

After Corpusty the line vanishes back into the fields and then reappears to run beside the B1149 for a while. Here, visible from the road but half hidden by trees, is a real treasure, an old platelayers' hut, finely made from carefully cut stone and an unexpected survivor. A bit further on a track leads to Oulton station, now a private house hidden in woods, but instantly recognisable from its style. The trackbed then curves round and, according to the map, skirts the runways of a Second World War satellite airfield. On the ground the picture is very different, both railway and runways having largely disappeared under the plough, recent history obliterated with great efficiency. Soon the trackbed reappears as a local footpath and then cuttings take it south of Blickling, to the bridge that carried the B1354 over it. The road has been re-aligned, leaving the bridge, a fine skewed one in red and black brick, isolated in the bushes. Across

the road the Weavers' Way joins the line, and follows the trackbed for some miles from here. This is a 56-mile bridleway and cycle path that links Cromer and Yarmouth, with much of its route along former railways, well made for easy going, and well signposted.

From here the track skirts to the north of Aylsham, crossing over the River Bure. Like so many other small towns in Britain, Aylsham ended up with two stations on separate lines, operated by competing railway companies. Neither was particularly well placed for the town centre and, with no physical link between them, passengers changing from one to the other had to make their own way across the town. Aylsham South survives in good

Below *In the bare fields of early spring the line of the old embankment near Corpusty is clearly visible*

Above *On a late June afternoon in 1957, Ivatt class 4 No. 43160 draws out of North Walsham station with a Fakenham to Yarmouth local. North Walsham still has a station, on the Norwich to Sheringham line, but the leisurely route taken by this train has long disappeared*

order as the headquarters of the Bure Valley Railway, described earlier, but the M&GN's Aylsham North has disappeared, its site taken over by an industrial estate. There is a car park for walkers and cyclists just off the B1145, near the station site.

After Aylsham the trackbed, in its new guise as the Weavers' Way, crosses the undulating landscape in a series of cuttings and embankments. One such cutting leads to Felmingham station, boarded up but complete, its building and yard now used as a footpath maintenance depot by the local council. A set of wooden steps leads up to the platform, where there are a couple of picnic tables. It is a quiet and peaceful spot, with a good view along the track towards North Walsham Wood, and must have been a delightful place to sit and wait for a train on a summer's evening. Felmingham is a very small village, just a cluster of houses around the church and at the best of times the station cannot have seen much traffic. Besides, it is only a couple of miles from here to North Walsham.

Until the 1950s, North Walsham was the meeting point of no less than five lines. First to arrive was the East Norfolk Railway's line from Whitlingham Junction,

to the east of Norwich, which reached North Walsham in 1874 and was then extended to Cromer five years later. Next came the Eastern & Midlands, and later the M&GN, Yarmouth line and finally, in 1906 the Norfolk & Suffolk Joint Railway's coastal route to Cromer. This last arrival was the first to close, followed by the M&GN but, miraculously, the old East Norfolk line is still open, clinging to life somewhat precariously. North Walsham still has, as a result, a living station, a pretty building somewhat the worse for wear, standing on an embankment to the south of the town, with plenty of local railway atmosphere. There is a signal box, proudly painted in green and cream and decorated with plant pots and bird feeders. More surprising still, there is an active freight depot with a network of sidings handling oil tank traffic. Old goods sheds stand around, mostly given over to various non railway activities. One houses the Norfolk Motor Cycle Museum.

Not so easy to find are traces of the other lines that met at North Walsham. The Weavers' Way leaves the M&GN just to the west of the former junction with the East Norfolk Railway, after the site of a level crossing, and the trackbed then degenerates into a local footpath before coming to a dead end. Originally this, and the Norfolk & Suffolk Joint line, looped round to the east but little of that route survives. South of the station the M&GN ran parallel to the East Norfolk line for about a while before turning away to the east, but all of this seems to have vanished beneath the new A149. There is nothing to be seen until the end of this new road at Bengate, and then the trackbed appears again as a battered and overgrown embankment to the east of the road. At the next crossing, on a minor road, the Weavers' Way takes over again.

This is the start of a particularly attractive stretch, with the scene set almost at once by the bridge that carries the line over the old North Walsham and Dilham Canal. Opened in 1826 to connect North Walsham with the River Ant, and thus with the waterways of the Broads, this canal enjoyed a leisurely life throughout the nineteenth century with occasional visits from both commercial and pleasure craft. There has been little traffic since the 1930s and the section north of Honing has been derelict for years. A feature of the canal was the series of large mills that were built beside the locks, to make the most of the water supply, and the remains of one of these can be seen at Briggate, just to the south of the railway bridge, and adjacent to the lock whose broken gates still hang open at the end of the chamber.

Canal and railway then run across the fields to Honing, and there the trackbed plunges into woods and passes beneath a decorative old iron bridge. There is no sign of Honing station but the trackbed continues across the low-lying marshlands, broadly following the canal to East Ruston. Here, it all comes to an end, and from now on the line becomes increasingly elusive, thanks to the combined efforts of road-makers and farmers.

For several miles the A149, sweeping southwards through Stalham, Catfield and Potter Heigham, lies on top of the trackbed and has effectively obliterated it. It is very difficult to make sense of the scant remains that survive. All three stations have gone without a trace, although in Potter Heigham a Station Road gives a clue to where it used to be. There are occasional glimpses from the car of concrete railway fencing posts and railway gates, now serving no real function, and two former crossing cottages can be spotted beside the road. The road has also taken over the former railway bridge across the River Thurne just south of

Right *A footpath runs under an overbridge near Honing. Its decorative cast-iron supports were once blackened by smoke*

(18)—V 20—11-06.

[W. & S. Ltd.]

MIDLAND & GREAT NORTHERN RAILWAYS JOINT COMMITTEE.

TO

STALHAM

Above *Near Hemsby a grand bridge lifts the road over empty fields, leaving everything to memory and the imagination*

buried in the hedge. The last few miles into Yarmouth must have been spectacular, with the line running along the dunes, right beside the beach. The trackbed survives, erratically and generally unrecognisable, as a rough path across the dunes, passing through Caister-on-Sea, disappearing into a massive caravan park and then swinging inland to enter Yarmouth via the race course.

The Norfolk coastline north and south of Yarmouth was largely undeveloped when the railway arrived, and the interminable miles of bungalows and caravans that characterise the region today can be blamed on the railway, fair and square. Holiday traffic was vital to the Great Eastern, and its smaller rival, the M&GN, and it was the latter that was responsible for the opening up of the Yarmouth coast. This traffic flourished before World War I, but its heyday was between the wars, when holiday camps and caravan parks became a part of the British way of life. So rapid and dense was the development that the M&GN had to open special halts to serve the camps, notably California and Caister. The equally rapid decline in this traffic from the 1950s was a major nail in the railway's coffin.

The line used to sweep into Yarmouth as a broad swathe through the northern suburbs, spanned by generous bridges standing proud above the terraces and seaside hotels. Looking down from these bridges today, it is possible, just, to imagine the M&GN locomotives pounding by below, at the head of important-looking trains setting off across rural Norfolk to distant destinations, to King's Lynn perhaps, or Peterborough. New estates have taken over some parts, along with their approach roads, Great Northern Close and Midland Close.

Potter Heigham, and there is nothing to tell passing boaters that a railway once ran here. The old road bridge, famous for its narrowness and bearing, as a result, the scars of many boating mishaps, can be seen to the west.

South of the river, the line has gone. Only an unusual weatherboarded crossing-keeper's cottage remains, with a tiny section of trackbed still visible in the garden. All around are huge fields, running uninterrupted to the horizon. There is nothing to be seen in Martham, although a pretty wooden building in a private garden just by the site of a level crossing looks as though it may be part of the station. Between Martham and Hemsby it is the same story, with the trackbed simply ploughed away to nothing. It is extraordinary that a line still in use thirty years ago can have been obliterated so totally by farmers who cannot have been short of land in this vast and empty landscape. Just outside Hemsby the road rises steeply to cross a high and imposing bridge, but it is now a bridge over nothing, just a convenient link between fields that roll away to the horizon. Surprisingly, and for no good reason, this still carries its bridge plate, numbered 158.

New estates have been built over Hemsby's station but the line can at least be placed by a sign saying 'Old Station House, B&B'. South of Hemsby the trackbed reappears, briefly, and is visible either side of the former level crossing on the B1159. On the southern side it is an unofficial footpath, leading down towards Ormesby and to another Station Road with no station. It was in Ormesby that the line turned sharply towards the coast, and there are a few traces to be seen between here and California, notably some old gates and a short line of fence posts

PRACTICAL INFORMATION

OS Landrangers
133, 134

Information points
Cromer Tourist Information Centre: Bus Station, Prince of Wales Road, Cromer, Norfolk NR27 9HS. Tel 01263 512497.
Norwich Tourist Information Centre: The Guildhall, Gaol Hill, Norfolk, NR2 1NF. Tel 01603 666071, fax 01603 765389.
Sheringham Tourist Information Centre: Station Approach, Sheringham, Norfolk NR26 8RA. Tel 01263 824329.
Great Yarmouth Tourist Information Centre: Marine Parade, Great Yarmouth, Norfolk NR30 2EJ. Tel 01493 842195 or 846345, fax 01493 846332.

Official cycle/walkways
Marriott's Way: from Drayton to Aylsham (21 miles). Follows the trackbed of the M&GN as far as Themelthorpe (11 miles) with access points at Freeland Corner, near Taverham, Whitwell and Reepham station (near Themelthorpe).
Weavers' Way: a long distance footpath between Cromer and Yarmouth (56 miles); follows the M&GN trackbed from south of Blickling to North Walsham (7 miles).

Nearby attractions
Bure Valley Railway: Norwich Road, Aylsham, Norfolk Tel 01263 733858. A 15-inch gauge railway with steam and diesel locomotives between Aylsham South station and Wroxham, stopping at Brampton, Buxton and Coltishall by request (9 miles). Open Apr–Sep daily in summer; phone for other times.
North Norfolk Railway: The Station, Sheringham, Norfolk. Tel 01263 822045. A 10½ mile round trip by steam and vintage diesel trains, from Sheringham to Holt, via Weybourne and Kelling Heath Park. Narrow gauge line, museum signal box. Open Mar–Oct daily in summer; phone for other times.
Norfolk Motor Cycle Museum: Norwich Road, North Walsham Station Yard. Tel 01692 406266. A collection of about seventy bikes dating from 1922 onwards. Open all year daily, 10–4.30.

The end of the line was Yarmouth Beach station, with the sea breaking on to the sand a couple of streets away. This was a grand terminus, worthy of its name and its setting, and far more central than Yarmouth's other main station, Vauxhall, the terminus of the Yarmouth & Norwich Railway. A late addition was a link line, branching away to the west just outside Beach station, crossing Breydon Water on a large steel viaduct and curving round the town to join the lines south from Yarmouth to Lowestoft and to Beccles. This closed in the 1950s, but the viaduct remains, surrounded by scrap yards and industrial buildings. Vauxhall is Yarmouth's only station today, and the grand Beach terminus is but a memory, an empty space now used as a car and coach park. Flanking the road that runs beside it is a series of small rectangular spaces defined by low brick walls. Each contains a short section of railway track, complete with wooden sleepers set into ballast. Towering above them are four cast-iron canopy pillars, holding out decorative brackets bearing the initials E&M and M&GN. This bizarre structure is the memorial to Norfolk's most idiosyncratic, and much lamented, rural railway network.

Above *During the autumn of 1958 the 11.11am Peterborough to Yarmouth train nears the end of its journey as the Ivatt class 4 No. 43158 drifts its train past the caravan parks and the racecourse. Today, the trackbed survives, along with some of the overbridges, but the site of the line's grand terminus, Yarmouth Beach, is now just a car and coach park*

Left *No. 1, the first of the M&GN class C locomotives leaves Yarmouth in June 1937 at the head of a long fish train, one of the mainstays of the railways of East Anglia*

THE ATLANTIC COAST

◆

Okehampton to Bude via Halwill Junction
Halwill Junction to Wadebridge via Launceston
Padstow to Wadebridge and Bodmin (the Camel Trail)
Bodmin to Wenford Bridge (the Camel Trail)

The highpoint of a cycle ride along the Camel Trail today is Petherick Bridge, seen here from Tregonce, near Padstow

HISTORY

The railway history of northwest Devon and north Cornwall is curiously uneven. The lines that were built spanned a great period of time and represented the ambitions of many companies, both great and small. First on the scene, and indeed one of the first locomotive-hauled railways in Britain, was the Bodmin & Wadebridge, opened in 1834. It was an intensely local affair, built primarily to serve the needs of quarries and clay pits around the River Camel but also carrying passengers from its early days. Two of its early passenger carriages, direct descendants of horse-drawn coaches, are preserved in the National Railway Museum in York. Until the 1880s the Bodmin & Wadebridge existed in isolation, with no direct access to the national railway network, and all its freight movements were tied to ships sailing to and from Wadebridge.

All this came to an end after 1888, first with the opening of a line linking the Bodmin & Wadebridge with the Great Western Railway's main Plymouth to Penzance route, via Bodmin Road station, and then, seven years later, with the arrival in Wadebridge of the London & South Western Railway's North Cornwall line via Launceston, later extended to Padstow. This, a latecomer in railway terms, had grown out of a scheme first authorised in the early 1860s, but never proceeded with, and its laborious construction through the 1880s and the 1890s represented almost the last shot in the long battle for West Country traffic fought between the GWR and the L&SWR. Its route from Halwill Junction was the last phase of the L&SWR's four-pronged assault on the West Country from Exeter, the earlier phases being the route southwards to Plymouth via Tavistock, the line northwards to Barnstaple, Bideford and, ultimately, Ilfracombe, and the line to Holsworthy and Bude from Halwill Junction. With holiday traffic always important, these routes were the domain of the famous Atlantic Coast Express, Waterloo's answer to Paddington's Cornish Riviera Express and a train necessarily of great complexity to serve the needs of all the north Devon and north Cornwall resorts. Its great days were during the interwar Southern Railway years but it ran on into the era of British Railways, through the 1950s and into the early 1960s before being brought to the end of the line by changing patterns of holiday traffic. With the holiday and freight traffic steadily reducing, the lines were seen as no longer viable and most were closed in 1966, including those to Bude and to Wadebridge and Padstow.

Ironically, it was the oldest line, the Bodmin & Wadebridge, that lasted the longest. Freight services to

Left *Clipping the points near Boscarne Junction in July 1960 while the locomotive waits*

Wadebridge lingered on into the 1970s but the Wenford Bridge clay line, part of the original route of the Bodmin & Wadebridge, did not finally close until 1983, along with the route linking it to Bodmin Road, or Parkway as it was by then called. Today, this link line is open again, thanks to the Bodmin & Wenford Railway, and other parts of the old Bodmin & Wadebridge network may follow. Lost irretrievably are the lines to Bude and Padstow, and with them the ambitions of the old London & South Western Railway.

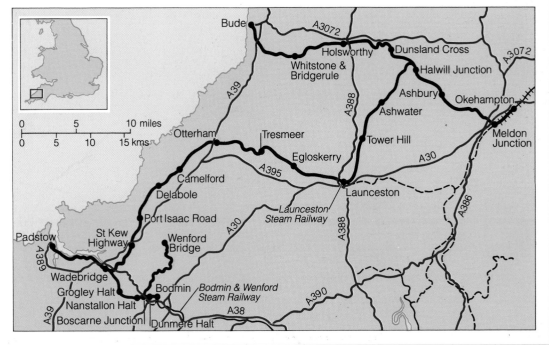

Far Right *Nearly seventy years later, Okehampton station still looks much the same, despite having been closed to passengers for thirty years. The buildings remain, faded ghosts from another era watching the stone trains rumble through*

IN THE STILL, early morning air the hoarse shriek of a diesel locomotive's horn came clearly across the valley, an unmistakable sound quickly repeated. Taken by surprise as I was filling the car on the forecourt of a rather rundown garage on the old A30 (now the B3260), I stopped and looked around. It was a grey morning, with the colours all merged together into indistinct shapes on the steep hillside to the south of the West Okement River, on the outskirts of Okehampton. I knew the line was up there somewhere but I had not yet bothered to seek it out and was, in any case, thinking about lost rather than active railways. Looking properly now, I saw the line of mineral wagons half-hidden by the bushes and as I watched they began to move, at first almost imperceptibly and then slowly up the steep gradient towards the quarry, whose buildings towered on the skyline. Soon the locomotives, a pair working hard together, came from from behind the trees and I watched until the whole train had disappeared from view. Beyond the quarry the line turns west to cross the valley, carried high on the six wrought-iron spans of Meldon viaduct. With its towering trestles and delicate lattice-work of wrought iron, the viaduct looks as though it belongs in America. I half expected to see Buster Keaton come steaming across at the controls of *The General*. Built in the 1870s, and by far the better of the only two such structures surviving in Britain, Meldon is one of the essential sights of this part of England. The minor roads that lead to

Meldon village offer plenty of good views and on very rare and lucky days trains do cross on to the viaduct. Today was not one of them, so I finished filling the car and drove on into Okehampton.

OKEHAMPTON TO BUDE VIA HALWILL JUNCTION

Okehampton station is to the south of the town, at the end of a steep climb between suburban villas up a long street named, conveniently for railway hunters, Station Road. High above the town, I parked in the forecourt of what appeared to be ghost station. Rather the worse for wear, but still in the fading cream and green paint of British Railways' old Southern Region, it survives intact from a distant and vaguely remembered past. Handsome brick buildings with glassless canopies stand on the platforms, linked by a fine footbridge. Across the rusty tracks, a network of sidings leads to old goods sheds, and in the distance a signal box keeps watch. Concrete name boards are still in place and all that is missing are the green and white enamel signs that identified the ticket and parcels offices, the waiting rooms, and the lavatories. I could almost hear the platform number signs creaking in the wind, and the distant whistle of the West Country class locomotive pounding westwards with the Atlantic Coast Express. Trains do still pass through, heavily laden with stone ballast from Meldon quarry, but it is many years since any passengers have disturbed Okehampton station's quiet decay.

The mineral line that is still in use, from Coleford Junction on the Exeter and Barnstaple route to west of Meldon quarry, is all that survives of a once-extensive network, laboriously constructed in bits and pieces during the latter part of the Victorian era to fulfill the ambitions of the London & South Western Railway. It represented the climax of the battle between the two giants of western Britain, the L&SWR and the GWR, for the freight and, above all, the burgeoning holiday traffic west of Exeter.

The story starts in 1862 when the Okehampton Railway was authorised to build a line from Coleford Junction to Okehampton and then on to Lydford, where it would meet another local undertaking, the Launceston & South Devon. A long branch, from Meldon to Bude, was also authorised. In the event, not much happened and by 1865 the line had only reached North Tawton, not even half way to Okehampton. In 1870 the company renamed itself the Devon & Cornwall Railway and then sold out, two years later, to the L&SWR. Things then happened quite quickly. The line to Lydford was completed in 1874 and this, by a series of connections with other local railways, became in due course the L&SWR's main line to Plymouth from Waterloo, a route striking deep into the

Below *In the summer of 1928 this London & South Western locomotive was working hard for its new master, the Southern Railway. Here, it rests briefly at Okehampton with the 9.27am Tavistock to Exeter train*

traditional territory of the GWR. The L&SWR also completed the line from Meldon to Bude as part of its attempt to gain control of the developing holiday traffic to the Altantic coast resorts. The same ambition inspired the building of the branch from Barnstaple to Ilfracombe in north Devon. Later came the third prong of this attack on the Atlantic coast, the line running south from Halwill Junction to Padstow.

In the years before World War I, in the 1920s and 1930s, and in the 1950s these routes all enjoyed considerable success and until the early 1960s the departure of the daily expresses for Plymouth and the Atlantic coast resorts represented the glamorous highlight of British Railway's busy Waterloo timetable. However, changing patterns of holiday traffic and increasing competition from roads brought a rapid decline and in the mid-1960s much of the old L&SWR network west of Exeter was closed, including the main line to Plymouth and the Atlantic coast routes.

On departure from Okehampton, trains bound for the Atlantic coast crossed the Meldon viaduct and then swung north at the junction on to the tightly curving embankment that marked the start of the climb across the hills towards Halwill. Today, although the route can be traced on the ground, there is not much at all to be seen. The first couple of miles are fairly inaccessible and the best place to pick up the traces is Thorndon Cross, where the B3218 crossed the line on a big stone bridge. The bridge is still there, over a trackbed now converted to farm paths and a garden, but there is no sign of the small halt that was here until the 1930s. From this point road and railway run side by side and the overgrown trackbed is often in view. Tangible relics, in the form of the crossing-keeper's cottage, concrete gate posts and a decaying kissing gate, can be seen at the site of a level crossing just south of Venn Down, but much more exciting is Ashbury station. Two or three miles south-west of its village, the station survives as a private house, now painted white and with platforms incorporated into a decorative gardening scheme which features conifers and a trackbed lawn. It is all easily admired from the parapet of the adjacent road bridge. From here the trackbed curves onwards to Halwill Junction through cuttings and along embankments, generally visible but inaccessible, and occasionally filled in. The approach to Halwill is beside the road and then the line vanishes beneath the new housing development described on page 28.

North of Halwill the line to Padstow branches away westwards and then the lines to Bude and Barnstaple separate deep in the woods. Woods and Forestry Commission plantations surround the line for the first couple of miles and these limit access. The only practical place to find the track is at the end of a minor road off the AA3079 that runs into the woods north of Cookworthy Moor Plantation. Here, at the start of a series of forest paths, there is a picnic site and small car park beside the trackbed, which lies deep in an overgrown cutting and was flooded to the point of looking like a river when I saw it. Now the road bridge has gone, the whole site has virtually lost the links it once had with the railway.

The clue to the site of Dunsland Cross station is a row of railway cottages alongside the main road as it runs due north to the junction with the A3072. A turning at the end of this row leads to the station site, much changed by the arrival of new houses. Bits and pieces survive – a goods shed half hidden in the bushes and various smaller relics – but much is now private and detailed exploration is therefore impossible. Beyond the station the line crossed the road, but the bridge was removed years ago and broken embankments stand back in the fields. In this remote and hilly region the track is quite easy to follow, there being little incentive for anyone to do other than let it slowly revert to nature. The big cuttings generally survive, densely filled with brambles and young trees flourishing in the boggy earth. The grey brick bridge at Hollacombe, just by the church, offers a fine view into just such a wilderness, but by comparison

Above and Right *Another former London & South Western locomotive at work in 1926, hauls its train over the high trestles of Meldon viaduct. This remarkable structure, shown well here in its landscape setting, is the only surviving bridge of its kind on this scale*

the next cutting, by West Coombe, is being used as a landfill site and is vanishing. At Holsworthy, however, the old railway really comes to life. The town is set on top of a hill, with the big church tower its focal point. The railway ran to the south of the town, maintaining its level by two massive viaducts that carried it across the valley. The approach to Holsworthy along the A3072 brings the first of these dramatically into view as a series of tall and surprisingly delicate arches. The second, equally delicate and sitting beautifully in the rural landscape, can be seen from the minor road leading westwards towards Derriton. In between the two viaducts is the station, abandoned and crumbling away in a scene of dereliction. The buildings are still fairly complete, despite the attentions of the local vandals, and there are bits and pieces of all sorts of relics, to be enjoyed by those who want to root around and can interpret what they represent. The platforms are an unofficial car park and the huge former goods yard sprawls into the distance, a sad sight as it all awaits its fate.

West of Holsworthy the line is largely inaccessible in its private landscape, with only occasional glimpses of overgrown embankments and cuttings from bridges on minor roads. The

SOUTHERN RAILWAY.
Stock 787
(2/40) 48M
TO
BUDE

Above *Holsworthy stands above the grand east viaduct, a towering but now inaccessible structure*

next site of interest is Bridgerule, where the station survives as a private house. As so often, it is well over a mile from its village, hidden at the end of a very minor road that branches eastwards to Merrifield, off the B3254. The tall grey brick bridge gives an excellent view of the station with its canopy, still in faded Southern Region cream, and its grassed-over platforms. The trackbed can be seen curving away in the distance towards its former crossing of the Tamar. For most of its course, the river marks the border between Devon and Cornwall, but for some strange boundary reason, just at this spot Devon bulges into Cornwall for a couple of miles.

The line next appears east of Titson, the clue to its presence being a long section of 1930s Southern Railway concrete fencing, pleasantly overgrown and lichen-covered, right beside the road. Then it disappears completely, obliterated by farmers. It reappears again shortly, east of Trelay, as a curving embankment against the green hills, well defined as it makes its way to another fine viaduct across a broad valley and easily enjoyed from a road west of Trelay. To the north is Marhamchurch and the route of the old Bude Canal network, famous for its inclined planes and wheeled tub boats, all built for the transport of sea sand to inland farms – an inconceivable enterprise in the context of modern economics. South of Bude the canal survives, and its towpath forms a pleasant walk into the town from Helebridge. This makes a welcome escape from the new road which has, in any case, wiped out any remaining vestiges of the old railway for a while. Beyond Helebridge the line appears again, and it follows the canal along the valley, visible from the A39/3073 as a low and largely inaccessible embankment until it vanishes into a mess of new estates, old factories and car graveyards that have taken over the station site. It is hard to make sense of anything, and little, if anything, survives of a major terminus of the Atlantic Coast Express. The only clue to this glorious past was a road in the middle of a new estate, named Bulleid Way, a pathetic reminder of the Southern Railway's great locomotive designer.

Below *Trelay viaduct carried the line on its approach to Bude*

HALWILL JUNCTION TO WADEBRIDGE

The third of the Atlantic Coast Expresses' three routes from Halwill Junction was the least successful. It was a remote and little-used railway, dependent for much of its life on the seasonal holiday traffic for Padstow and on the carriage of slate from Delabole. Its inland route was not particularly convenient for Atlantic coast towns such as Boscastle and Tintagel, and resorts west of Padstow were well looked after by the Great Western Railway's extensive network. It has long been known by railway enthusiasts as 'the withered arm', a rather unappealing title that at least expresses the unfulfilled ambitions of the London & South Western Railway in their long-running territorial battle with the GWR. Cornwall had always been close to the Great Western's heart, and the L&SWR's long branch snaking westwards from Launceston must have been seen as a serious invasion. In fact, by the time it opened, the war was largely over, and it came too late to affect traffic patterns in the region. It probably even benefited from its junction with the GWR at Launceston. However, the line had originally been authorised over thirty year earlier, in July 1864, as the Launceston, Bodmin & Wadebridge Junction Railway. A year later an extension was proposed and the line was renamed the Central Cornwall Railway, but nothing happened and not a sod was turned until 1882 when the whole scheme was relaunched as the North Cornwall Railway. With the backing of the L&SWR, construction started at the Halwill end but progress was always painfully slow and it took four years to complete the section to Launceston. Over the next nine years the line crept slowly westwards, finally reaching Wadebridge in June 1895. It then took another four years to build the final few miles from Wadebridge to Padstow, far too late to have any serious impact upon the region. Despite this uncertain start and its inadequate traffic, the line lingered on and it was not until October 1966 that it was finally closed, along with much of the former L&SWR's network west of Exeter.

Since then, not much has happened. The trackbed largely survives, sometimes in a wild and overgrown state and sometimes given new life as a farm track. It is generally private, but there are plenty of minor roads that cross it between Halwill Junction and Launceston. This is a particularly attractive stretch, with the line following closely the broadening River Carey whose wooded banks place it firmly in north Devon. It would make a wonderful footpath or cycle trail, but any such development does not seem likely. Minor roads initially stay close to the trackbed south from Halwill, and there are glimpses of it in the valley below. More rewarding is Ashwater, where the station survives as a smart house. It is a distinctive building, well constructed in stone and looking like a large family house, its

round arched windows being one of a number of attractive features. As I progressed along this line, it became apparent that all the stations had been built to the same architectural plan with the same decorative features, the only variant being the material used, sometimes stone, sometimes brick. Remarkably, nearly all of them survive, and their generous proportions indicate a sense of style surprising in a railway of so late a date. The goods yard at Ashwater now houses a coal merchant, perhaps a link with the railway's past.

West of Ashwater the line follows a private route through the woods, and the next place I saw it was from a minor road near Virginstow. The view from the bridge was delightful, the trackbed well defined and grass-covered beside the river, and all around were woods and plenty of early spring flowers. Of the next station, Tower Hill, a remote one serving a few houses and

a scattering of farms, not a trace remains. Old photographs show it looking much the same as the others, but it has been completely obliterated, along with its associated works.

From here the line continues southwards beside the Carey, leaving the hills and the woods as it approaches Launceston, to become a low green embankment across the fields, scattered with sheep. It swings west to cross the Tamar and enter Cornwall, and then becomes rather hard to find in Launceston's suburbs and industrial estates. At some point here it met the Great Western's line from Plymouth via Tavistock and Lydford, and then the two came together for the last mile or so into Launceston. The town once boasted quite a substantial station, with a generous canopy over the platform and extensive sidings. Today the site is still there, with parts in use as a car park or taken over by industry, but there is no sense of the railway's past in the fragmented trackbed.

Above *In the summer of 1960 an ancient class T9 locomotive, No. 30719, then over fifty years old, waits at Tower Hill, near the Devon–Cornwall border, with the 9.56 Okehampton to Padstow local. Today, not a stone of this scene remains, and the view from the bridge is over farmland and fields*

London and South Western Ry. 787

FROM WATERLOO TO

EGLOSKERRY

However, all is not lost. Signs on the A388 and directional notices on the old trackbed, now a footpath from the car park, led me step by step towards the Launceston Steam Railway. This starts with a will just beyond the old bridge carrying the A388, in a flurry of old signals, sidings filled with wagons and open-sided carriages, engine sheds, nostalgic notices and a little station rather dwarfed by a large canopy of standard North Cornwall style. From here trains run westwards for a couple of miles, along the steep-sided valley of the River Kensey. It is a narrow gauge line, and so journeys are a slow meander behind elderly locomotives that once earned their living in mineral and slate quarries, far removed from the great days of the Atlantic Coast Express. When I was there everything was quiet, and the trains were still deep in their winter hibernation. However, the sight of rails, albeit small ones, glistening in the damp and grey light, and sleepers bedded in fresh ballast, was sufficient to bring it all to life.

When the rails stop, nature takes over again. The trackbed continues alongside the river and in and out of the woods, easily seen from the minor road that runs parallel to it on the south side of the valley. This road leads straight to the next station, Egloskerry, built in the same style but this time in brick. Now a private house, it has a fine garden and a greenhouse set between the platforms, one of which still boasts its concrete Southern Railway name board. Also on show was the familiar cast-iron 'Beware of the Trains' notice, an essential accessory for former railway buildings enjoying a reincarnation. There used to be a level crossing here but by some reversal of the usual order of things the trackbed beyond the crossing has become a car graveyard.

Leaving the river, the line winds its way through the hills, a natural component of the landscape whose softly rounded shapes and secret green valleys have all the quality of Devonshire. Only the place names are firmly Cornish. Driving the route involved, as usual, stopping at every bridge and looking over the parapet. The view was generally one composed of tangled undergrowth and mud or a grassy trackbed flanked by gorse but there was the occasional surprise. From the stone parapet of an ordinary bridge east of Tresmeer there was the unexpected sight of a cutting turned into a small reservoir, and completely filled with water. Not far from here another curving cutting leads to the next station. This is actually sited right in the middle of a village called Splatt, but the railway company presumably found the idea of selling tickets to a station called Splatt hard to stomach and called it Tresmeer instead, after another village over a mile to the south. The building, again in brick, is as

usual a private house now, with a grassy platform garden that includes a trackbed pond supervised by a plastic heron. Station name boards and gradient posts complete the picture, and in the distance is the old goods shed, now in some ill-defined industrial or agricultural use.

Beyond Splatt the hills become steeper and the trackbed more remote in its winding route across the landscape. A good place to enjoy it is from the bridge on a minor road between Trewonnard and Treneglos. This is really the end of the hills for, after a few more curves, the landscape opens out towards the bleak, windswept plains of the north Cornish coast. Otterham Station is, surprisingly, still the name of a small settlement on the A39, indicating that it must have been the station that created the settlement. Otterham village is away to the north. The station is still there, now in charge of a caravan park that spreads out along the trackbed. Across the road there is nothing, the railway having been removed by farmers, but soon it reapppears as a low embankment crossing the fields. Farmers seem to have been the winners when the railways were closed. In some places, fields and estates that were inconveniently divided a century or more ago have been easily reunited by bulldozer, while in others the well-built and firmly surfaced trackbed has become a useful access road. It was near here that the value of the latter was perfectly demonstrated. I had stopped the car near the site of a demolished bridge to look at the surviving embankments, which stretch away in opposite directions towards the horizon. Both carried well-made tracks, uncluttered by bushes, and both had sloped approaches, with gates on to the road. As I looked, a tractor appeared in the distance, coming along the top of one of the embankments. It approached quickly, dropped down to cross the road – the driver stopping to open and close the gates – and then climbed the slope on the other side and drove off along the other embankment. Some of these reclaimed tracks have become sufficiently established to be marked on the map as white roads.

The next station, Camelford, now houses the Museum of Historic Cycling, with over 200 elderly and classic machines sharing the building with various railway relics and ephemera. Although called Camelford, the station is in the middle of nowhere, inconveniently placed over a mile north of the town and several miles south of Boscastle and Tintagel, a compromise that cannot have pleased anyone. No wonder the line was never a great success.

From here the line crosses increasingly inhospitable terrain as it nears Delabole, the quarrying town that was one of the main justifications for the railway's existence. The legacies of the slate industry today are a rather rundown town adrift in north Cornwall and struggling to survive without its *raison d'être*, and one of the largest holes in the world. The line skirted the

London and South Western Ry.
—
FROM WATERLOO TO
DELABOLE
787

Left *On that July day in 1960, the photographer, R C Riley, followed the train westwards. Here, No. 30719 rests at Delabole. The station buildings still survive, now an island from the past isolated in a surrounding sea of new houses*

Below *The trackbed curves round the hills near Treskellow, between Tresmeer and Otterham*

northern rim of this vast hole, and passengers enjoying their tea on the Atlantic Coast Express must have had a wonderful view down into it. Safety barriers and piles of rubbish make this rather harder to do today but the view is still spectacular, and it is not hard to imagine it as a hive of activity. There were extensive sidings here for the slate traffic but they have disappeared beneath a new housing estate called, inevitably, The Sidings. Isolated in the centre, decoratively built from local stone but rather decayed and fenced in like some dangerous creature from the past, is the old station.

Fine stone bridges south of Delabole offer an interesting variety of views on to the remote and generally overgrown trackbed. From one, near Pendoggett, there was the unexpected sight of a cutting filled to the brim with yellow gorse, a broad, bright band of colour curving away towards the next station, Port Isaac Road. This large complex of buildings – including the station, which is now a private house – is quite disproportionate to the relative emptiness of the landscape. Port Isaac is a small place several miles away, and its harbour had probably passed its peak by the time the railway arrived. Traffic can never have been heavy at the best of times at these remote but generously built stations.

Leaving behind the bleak countryside of north Cornwall, the line crosses an increasingly domestic landscape to St Kew Highway. Here road widening has significantly altered the

Right *Old Town Cove on the Camel Trail*

Far Right *With Battle of Britain class 66 Squadron, No. 34110, in charge, the Atlantic Coast Express trundles along beside the estuary near Old Town Cove soon after leaving Wadebidge in May 1962, on the last lap of the long journey from Waterloo to Padstow*

Below *In September 1964 the line was nearing the end of its life but still the Atlantic Coast Express ran on. West Country class Pacific* Exmouth, *No. 34015, has reached the buffers at Padstow*

setting, but the station is still there, sheltered by trees and, now separated from any railway context, having the appearance of another large family house. The next few miles are marked by deep cuttings, the line carved through the hills to drop down to the Camel Valley. Some of these cuttings are still quite dramatic when seen from the bridges high above, but others have been completely filled in and levelled with the surrounding fields, a process involving an amazing amount of work considering the small amount of usable land regained. The last of these cuttings, all overgrown, is at Pendavey, where there is a bridge at the end of a steep and muddy track just south of the A389. From here the railway swept out of the cutting, crossed the Camel on an iron bridge and curved across the field to its junction with the Bodmin and Wadebridge railway, a flowery place beside the Camel, now marked by a farmer's gate and ambling cows. It is a lovely little piece of secret and peaceful railway landscape, where a sense of the past lingers quietly in the air. It can all be seen from the Camel Trail (see below). From the junction the trains swept on into Wadebridge, and then alongside the sandy estuary of the Camel to Padstow, the end of the line and the end of the London & South Western's West Country ambitions. This section has now become part of the Camel trail, and is best treated as such, on the following pages.

THE CAMEL TRAIL – PADSTOW TO BODMIN AND WENFORD BRIDGE

The first locomotive-hauled railway in Cornwall, and one of the earliest in Britain, was the Bodmin & Wadebridge, whose 22-mile route was opened in September 1834. It was an

essentially local undertaking, simply constructed with iron rails laid on granite sleeper blocks and its route, from Wadebridge to Wenford Bridge with branches to Ruthern Bridge and Bodmin, was for mineral traffic. For the next forty-four years it carried on in its own private world, isolated from the rest of Britain's railway network, and then, in 1888 and 1895, it was linked via Bodmin to the GWR and via Wadebridge to the L&SWR. Much of the network closed in the 1960s and the 1970s, but the Wenford Bridge line survived until 1983, carrying clay right up to the end. Today, much of the Bodmin & Wadebridge's network has been successfully brought back to life as the Camel Trail, a 17-mile route for walkers, riders and cyclists that also includes the former L&SWR line from Wadebridge to Padstow.

On a wet and cold day, I was not in a cycling or walking mood and chose to follow the route of the trail as closely as I could by car. I started at Padstow and quickly found the former station, a building in the familiar North Cornwall line style now housing the Customs & Excise. It stands on its platform, isolated in the middle of a car park and overlooking the old goods sheds and fish market which now houses the Padstow Shipwreck Museum and other centres of maritime activity. The trail starts here and sets off along the southern shore of the Camel estuary, which it follows all the way to Wadebridge. This is a spectacular journey, through rock cuttings and along embankments with a series of wonderful views across the estuary, and plenty of flowers and birds. A highlight is the crossing of Little Petherick Creek on the high girders of the big iron bridge, the sight of which can be enjoyed from afar, against a distant view of Padstow, from the minor road leading to

BODMIN AND WADEBRIDGE RAILWAY.

RETURN TICKET. 4. K.

SECOND CLASS.

NOT TRANSFERABLE.

Above *Part of Wadebridge station survives as the John Betjeman Centre, but there is no sense today of the scale and complexity of what used to be there. In 1960 it was still thriving, its extensive display of buildings and lineside equipment a suitable setting for the ancient London & South Western class T9, No. 30313*

Right *The distinctive quality of the Wenford Bridge clay line is captured in this July 1960 photograph, as Beattie well tank No. 30585 pauses for water in Pencarrow Woods. This venerable class of locomotive, unusual in having its water tank beneath the boiler, survived on the Wenford Bridge line until the early 1960s*

Tregonce. Another good spot is Oldtown Cove, where there is a small car park and access steps beside the creek. At Tregunna a substantial bridge carries a minor road that stops abruptly at the water's edge.

From here the trail turns south and then meets a minor road built on the trackbed. This leads into Wadebridge via an industrial estate and ends by a cycle hire depot. Walkers and cyclists have to make their own way through Wadebridge's busy traffic, passing the restored station, now an over-60s day centre, and then following the appropriately named Southern Way, which leads to the trackbed, and the beginning of the next part of the Camel Trail. After the junction with the North Cornwall line, described earlier, the Trail enters a delightfully private and wooded section close by the river, whose winding course often contrasts with the straighter, economical route taken by the railway's early nineteenth-century builders. Sturdy stone bridges in vernacular styles also indicate the line's early date.

A platform survives at Grogley Halt but the next halt, Nanstallon, has much more and is now a tea garden. Away from the woods, the track is framed by the curving sweep of Penaligon Down, and then it comes to Boscarne Junction, the site of once-busy sidings for the clay trains from Wenford Bridge. Here, the Bodmin & Wadebridge's original route turns to the northeast, up the Camel Valley, while the loop line built in 1888 to connect Wadebridge to the GWR's Bodmin General station swings away to the south. A little further on, just after

the bridge over the Camel, is the site of another junction, Dunmere. Here, the original line to Bodmin branched away, passing through Dunmere Halt, whose platform still survives, to climb up a steep gradient to the terminus at a station that became known as Bodmin North, in the shadows of the old gaol. Nothings remains of this station, long buried beneath a supermarket and industrial complex, but Bodmin still has two other stations.

For much of the nineteenth century, Bodmin's only railway link with the outside world was via Bodmin Road, or Parkway as it is now known, an inconveniently placed station remote from the town on the Great Western's main Plymouth to Penzance line. In 1887 this came to end when the GWR opened Bodmin General station, just to the south of the town centre, a small terminus at the end of a short branch from Bodmin Road. Following a period of closure, Bodmin General is flourishing again, as the headquarters of the Bodmin & Wenford Railway, a preserved line that operates steam trains on the branch to Bodmin Parkway. It is an enjoyable journey, climbing through woods, with the advantage of a direct connection wth BR at Parkway that means the line also has a social value. An ambitious company worthy of its Victorian ancestors, the Bodmin & Wenford is also restoring the loop line to Boscarne Junction, partly for passenger use but also to revive the china clay traffic from Wenford Bridge. This scheme has neatly divided the environmental lobby for, on the one hand, the revival of the rail traffic would mean the loss of six miles of the Camel Trail and on the other it would remove 3,000 lorry journeys a year from unsuitable narrow roads. A public enquiry found for the maintenance of the Trail, but this decision was

PRACTICAL INFORMATION

OS Landrangers,
190, 191, 200, 201

Information points
Bodmin Tourist Information Centre:
Shire House, Mount Folly Square,
Bodmin, Cornwall PL31 2DQ.
Tel/fax 01208 76616.
Bude Tourist Information Centre:
The Crescent Car Park, Bude,
Cornwall EX23 8EL.
Tel 01288 354240.
Launceston Tourist Information
Centre: Market House Arcade,
Market Street, Launceston,
Cornwall PL15 8EP.
Tel 01566 772321.
Padstow Tourist Information
Centre: The Red Brick Building,
North Quay, Padstow, Cornwall
PL28 8AF. Tel 01841 533449,
fax 01841 532356.
Wadebridge Tourist Information
Centre: Town Hall, Wadebridge,
Cornwall PL27 7AQ.
Tel 01208 813725.
Camel Trail: Camel Valley
Countryside Service, 3–5 Barn
Lane, Bodmin, Cornwall
PL31 1LZ. Tel 01208 78087.

Official cycle/walkways
The Camel Trail: 17 miles, open
all year round. The trail is in three
sections: Wadebridge to Padstow
(4½ miles); Wadebridge to
Boscarne, Bodmin (5 miles);
Boscarne, Bodmin to Poley's
Bridge (7½ miles).

Cycle hire
It is advisable to book cycles at
any time of the year, and essential
in summer months.
Cycle Revolution, Church Square,
Bodmin. Tel 01208 72557. All

year, Mon–Sat 9–5.30.
Glyn Davis Bike Hire, Unit 5–6,
South Quay, Padstow. Tel 01841
532594. All year, daily 9–5.
Bridge Bike Hire, The Camel Trail,
Wadebridge. Tel 01208 813050.
All year daily (9–5 in summer;
phone for winter hours)
Cycle Revolution, Eddystone
Road, Wadebridge. Tel 01208
812021. All year, daily 9–5.30.

Nearby attractions
Museum of Historic Cycling: The
Old Station, Camelford. Tel 01840
212811. Collection of 200 cycles
plus cycling memorabilia, library
of books. Open all year, Sun–Thu
10–5.
Padstow Shipwreck Museum:
South Quay, Padstow station. Tel
01841 532663. Open Apr to Oct,
daily 10–5. The story of local
shipwrecks and a collection of
salvaged items.
Camel Trail Tea Gardens,
Nanstallon: Tel 01208 74291.
Open Mar–Oct (weather
permitting).
The Bodmin & Wenford Railway,
General Station, Bodmin. Tel
01208 73666. Steam-hauled trains
run between Bodmin General and
Bodmin Parkway (connection with
BR main line) via Coleslogett
Halt. Jun–Sep, daily; Easter, Apr,
May, Oct; specials (phone for
further details).
Launceston Steam Railway: St
Thomas Road, Launceston. Tel
01566 775665. 4-mile steam-
hauled round trip; locos, model
railway, motor and motorcycle
museum. Jun–Sep, Sun–Fri
10.30–4.30; Easter, Oct, Tue,
Sun 10.30–4.30.

overturned in November 1994 by the Transport Secretary and the way is now clear for the line to be re-instated. Having had, in the course of my travels for this and other books, a number of close encounters of the unpleasant kind with thundering clay lorries, I am wholly on the side of the railway. Railways are the natural carriers for minerals in bulk and it was an act of madness to close the line in 1983. For walkers there are alternative footpaths on the western bank of the Camel that follow much of the railway's route and offer very similar pleasures. The reopening cannot come too soon.

The Wenford Bridge line is remarkable in a number of ways. Its active life of nearly 150 years was quite an achievement but what is more extraordinary is that throughout that time it never saw any regular passenger traffic. Its entire working life was spent in the mineral trade. The route is a delight, a gentle meander up the wooded eastern bank of the Camel, isolated for much of the way from roads or houses. Until the demise of steam the line was the last recorded habitat of a distinctive and rare type of locomotive, the Beattie Well Tank. There were a few level crossings and curiously these still have their warning signs and their rails in place even though the rest of the track

Above *At Helland Bridge the track is still in place on the level crossing, waiting for the Wenford Bridge reopening*

is long gone. This should certainly simplify the reinstatement of the railway. One of the best of these crossings is at Hellandbridge, where the line seems to burst through a row of cottages before going over the minor road. The end of the line is now at Poley's Bridge, in the shadow of the extensive buildings of the clay works. There is a car park, and information about the Camel Trail. It is a beautiful walk or ride, particularly in spring, but it would be even more heartening to see the china clay wagons rolling again, and to hear the diesel locomotive muttering through the trees and hooting shrilly as it crawls over the level crossings.

THE WILDS OF WALES

The Great Western Railway and its predecessors
Ruabon to Barmouth Junction
Blaenau Ffestiniog to Bala Junction

Towards Trawsfynydd the trackbed clings to the hillside, high above the Prysor Valley

HISTORY

The Great Western Railway, ambitious to add central Wales to its growing empire, was the inspiration and the driving force that brought into being the lines from Ruabon to Barmouth and from Bala to Blaenau Ffestiniog. From the 1840s there were various proposals to drive lines westwards into Wales from Chester, Ruabon and Shrewsbury. Some were supported by the Great Western's major rival, the London & North Western, but it was a Great Western scheme for a line along the Vale of Llangollen from Ruabon, on the Shrewsbury & Chester Railway, that won the day. Thomas Brassey was the engineer and work started in 1859. The railway was opened throughout in 1862 and from the outset was worked by the Great Western, a pattern to be maintained as the route expanded westwards. Next came the Llangollen & Corwen Railway, completed two years later despite difficult and expensive engineering along the Dee Valley. There were a number of proposals for lines from Corwen to the west coast but again it was the GWR-backed Corwen & Bala Railway that carried the line westwards. This opened in 1868, along with the Bala & Dolgelly Railway, the next link in the chain. The last stage was more complicated for the previous year has seen the opening of a branch from Barmouth to Dolgellau by the Aberythwith & Welsh Coast Railway. Shortly before the line's completion, this company was absorbed by the Great Western's rival, the Cambrian Railways, and so the Great Western lost control of the final stage of the route. The result was a stand-off in Dolgellau, with separate stations facing each other across the tracks, and no possibility of trains running over the whole route. For years passengers and freight had to change trains to complete the journey, a situation not resolved until 1922, when the Great Western finally gained control of the Cambrian network. From then on through running became possible.

Through the 1920s and 1930s the Great Western operated the Ruabon to Barmouth line as a typical country railway. Passenger receipts were never dramatic despite the expansion of tourism in the 1930s but there was enough freight to keep the route in profit. This pattern was maintained into the era of British Railways but by then the writing was on the wall. The line simply could not compete with road traffic, and it never realised its full tourist potential. Closure of the section from Barmouth Junction to Llangollen came in 1965, the excuse being flood damage to the track near Llandderfel. The remaining section, from Llangollen to Ruabon,

Right *A 1920s postcard view of Llangollen shows how little the scene has changed, particularly as the Llangollen Railway has brought the station back to life*

lingered on for another three years. Today, sections of the route have been brought back to life as preserved railways. The Llangollen Railway, a reincarnation of the rural Great Western, operates between Llangollen and Glyndyfrdwy and will soon be running trains to Corwen, while the narrow gauge Bala Lake Railway operates from Llanuwchllyn over a four-mile stretch beside the lake.

There were connections with two other railways along the route. The Denbigh, Ruthin & Corwen Railway, sponsored by the London & North Western, opened in 1865 and offered through routes to the north coast and Chester. After a somewhat chequered career this closed to passengers in 1953 but continued as a freight line for another nine years. More significant was the Bala & Festiniog Railway. Incorporated in 1873, this reflected the Great Western's desire to win a share of the north Wales slate traffic. Heavily engineered, this line took ten years to complete its 22-mile route to Llan Ffestiniog, where it met the short Festiniog & Blaenau

Railway. It took over this narrow gauge mineral line, rebuilt it, and finally reached its target, the slate quarries around Blaenau Ffestiniog. However, the London & North Western had got there first, via its Conwy Valley route, and the Great Western never really recovered its investment. It was a spectacular journey through a dramatic landscape but, as a long branch line it never attracted enough traffic. The route survived until 1961, when the building of a reservoir above Bala cut the line and gave British Railways the excuse to close it. The upper section, from Blaenau Ffestiniog to Trawsfynedd, was retained to serve the nuclear power station, and a connection was finally made with the former London & North Western line so that trains could be routed via the Conwy Valley. With the power station at the end of its life, the line now faces a precarious future.

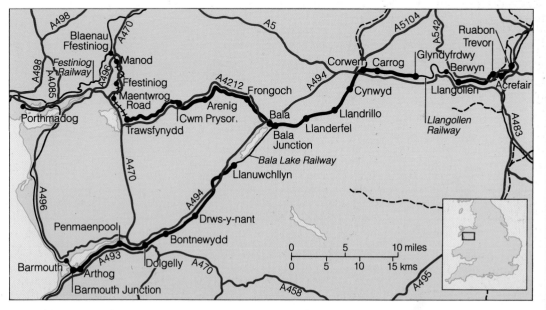

As a very small boy in the late 1940s, I stayed in Aberdovey for a couple of weeks. It was my first visit to Wales, and I have strong memories of the house and its views out across the sand dunes to the sea. There was another boy in the house, rather older than me and fanatical about birds, which he drew with great skill. Stuck with me for most of the time, he tried to share his enthusiasm and to teach me to draw, without much success in either direction. All I wanted to do was watch the trains. Living in Kent at the end of a local branch line, I had never really seen proper trains. In those days the Cambrian coast line was still very busy, and so I spent my two weeks completely enthralled by its continuous traffic. There were big expresses and pottering locals, but best of all were the goods trains, often double-headed, that pounded along the railway, just across the road from the house. The seagulls simply had no chance in this very unequal contest.

Railways continued to play their part in my subsequent visits to Wales, but the emphasis switched to the narrow gauge lines. I remember a journey on the Snowdon Mountain Railway a few years later, and other outings of the kind that are now so vital a part of the Wales experience. Marketing people have spent years promoting Wales as the land of the Great Little Trains, to the extent that the principality's few remaining real railways are over-shadowed and under-used. Diesel Sprinters scuttle to and fro on the lines that are still open, offering the best service that hard-pressed managers can afford but arousing neither interest nor enthusiasm. Most of Wales's huge railway network was destroyed during the Beeching era, and the lines that survived that holocaust,

usually for political rather than social reasons, face a very uncertain future. It is quite possible that in a few years' time the only trains left running in Wales, apart from those serving Holyhead and Swansea, will be on the narrow gauge lines or the preserved railways.

Some of the trains I watched as a child at Aberdovey may have travelled along the former Great Western line that linked Ruabon, Llangollen, Corwen, Bala and Barmouth, then one of the three routes across Wales open to traffic at that time. Remarkably, two of these, from Shrewsbury to Dovey Junction and from Shrewsbury to Swansea, are still in use, but the third, the Llangollen line, was a Beeching victim.

Childhood holidays introduced me to the Cambrian coast and to Snowdonia but it was another twenty years before I visited the Vale of Llangollen and the heart of Wales. I was drawn there then by canals and over a couple of years explored thoroughly the whole route of the Llangollen Canal and its associated waterways, past and present. By this time most of the railways of that region had gone, leaving just the line southwards from Wrexham via Ruabon and Oswestry. This had particular canal appeal, for trains on the route offered their passengers a grandstand view of the famous Chirk aqueduct. At this point, at the end of the 1960s, Llangollen station was largely derelict and the trackbed westwards towards Corwen and Bala, then as now easily explored by car, was already reverting to nature. An abandoned railway is often an adjunct to a canal, and the gentle speed of the boat allows ample time for indulgent and romantic consideration of what used to be. My first experience of the Llangollen line was exactly that, idle speculation about an imagined railway past as my boat ambled westwards along the canal from Pontcysyllte, with the trackbed generally in view.

Over subsequent visits to this part of Wales, undertaken for a variety of reasons, I watched the gradual rehabilitation and resurrection, first of Llangollen station and then of the line westwards to Berwyn and beyond, as the new Llangollen Railway got into its stride. Visitors now can enjoy the sight, and sounds, of a Great Western country railway as it used to be, with familiar chocolate and cream carriages slowly hauled by dark green locomotives along the valley of the Dee to Carrog, the present terminus. In the end, the line will be reopened as far as Corwen.

The restored section is, of course, only a part of a much longer route and its revival has to be seen against the background of the complex pattern of Victorian ambition that brought it into being. It all started in the late 1840s, with proposals for lines to Llangollen from Birkenhead and from the Shrewsbury & Chester Railway, whose route had been completed in 1848. However, nothing happened until about 1854 when this latter scheme was revived with the support of

Below British Railways' winter timetable for 1958/9, with the journey from Paddington to Barmouth taking up to ten hours

Table 187

RUABON, CORWEN, BALA, DOLGELLEY and BARMOUTH
WEEK DAYS ONLY

Stations (from Ruabon): 152London (Paddington), 152Birmingham (Snow Hill), 152Wolverhampton (L.L.), 152Shrewsbury, 152Birkenhead (Woodside), 152Chester (General), Ruabon, Acrefair, Trevor, Llangollen, Berwyn Halt, Glyndyfrdwy, Carrog, Bonwm Halt, Corwen, Cynwyd, Llandrillo, Llanderfel, Bala D, Llangower Halt, Glan Llyn Halt, Llanuwchllyn, Llys Halt, Garneddwen Halt, Drws-y-Nant, Wnion Halt, Bonnewydd, Dolgelley, Penmaenpool, Arthog, Barmouth Junction, Barmouth, Pwllheli

Notes:
- **A** On Saturdays dep Birmingham (Snow Hill) 9 50 am and Wolverhampton (L.L.) 10 15 am
- **B** Buffet Car for a portion of the journey only
- **C** ½ mile to Blaenau Ffestiniog
- **D** Passengers to and from Bala change at Bala Junc. by most of the Trains
- **dd** Calls to set down from beyond Ruabon on notice being given to the Guard at Ruabon
- **E** Except Saturdays
- **aa** Calls to take up or set down passengers during hours of daylight only. Passengers wishing to alight must give notice to the Guard at previous stopping station and those desiring to join should give the necessary hand signal to the Driver
- **R** Restaurant Car for a portion of the journey only
- **S** Saturdays only
- **t** Arr 12 20 pm
- ***** Arr 7 42 am
- **‡** Arr 4 minutes earlier
- **§** Arr 3 minutes earlier
- **②** Second class only

Table 188

BALA and BLAENAU FFESTINIOG
WEEK DAYS ONLY

Stations (from Bala): Bala, Frongoch, Tyddyn Bridge Halt, Capel Celyn Halt, Arenig, Cwm Prysor Halt, Llafar Halt, Trawsfynydd, Trawsfynydd Lake Halt, Maentwrog Road, Festiniog, Teigl Halt, Manod Halt, Blaenau Ffestiniog Cen. C.

Stations (from Blaenau Ffestiniog Central): Blaenau Ffestiniog Central, Manod Halt, Teigl Halt, Festiniog, Maentwrog Road, Trawsfynydd, Trawsfynydd Lake Halt, Llafar Halt, Bryncelynog Halt, Arenig, Capel Celyn Halt, Cwm Prysor Halt, Tyddyn Bridge Halt, Frongoch, Bala

OTHER TRAINS between Barmouth Junction and Barmouth see Table 189

the London & North Western Railway. There followed a typical territorial battle, with the Great Western backing the rival Vale of Llangollen scheme, and it was this that finally triumphed, receiving the Royal assent in August 1859. By the summer of 1862 passengers could travel between Ruabon and Llangollen. With its ambitions firmly on a route across Wales to the west coast, the Great Western operated this line, and its various westerly extensions, from the start.

The first of these was another Great Western puppet, the nominally independent Llangollen & Corwen Railway, whose route was completed in 1865. Three years later, the next section, from Corwen to Bala, was brought into use, along with the final stretch, built by the so-called Bala & Dolgelly Railway. By this time the Aberystwith & Welch Coast Railway, as it was named, had built its branch line from Barmouth to Dolgellau, and there the two lines met. The Great Western extended its sphere of influence by taking over all these companies between 1877 and 1896, but it was not able to acquire the vital final link, the Aberystwith & Welch Coast's Dolgellau branch, as that company had been absorbed in 1866 by the GWR's great rival, the Cambrian Railways. As a result, Dolgellau for many years had two stations, facing each other across the track, both fully manned but with no communication between them, and passengers were compelled to change trains. This anomaly survived until 1922, when the Great Western took over most of the railways of central and south Wales, including the Cambrian.

Apart from its junction with the coastal route via Barmouth, the line had two other major connections. The first was at Corwen, with the Denbigh, Ruthin & Corwen Railway, whose line northwards was opened in 1865, and later absorbed by the London & North Western Company, and the second was the Bala & Festiniog. This railway, despite massive backing from the Great Western who wanted a share of the north Wales slate traffic, took ten years to complete its heavily engineered and very expensive twenty-two mile line. By that time the slate industry was in terminal decline, and so the Great Western, in control from the early 1920s, accepted its lot and operated the lines as part of its huge network of Welsh country railways. Never particularly busy, the lines were closed progressively between 1960 and 1968.

RUABON TO BARMOUTH JUNCTION

On a warm spring day I drove along the familiar, but now much improved route towards Llangollen, pausing on the way to enjoy favourite landmarks, the Chirk and Pontcysyllte aqueducts, and the Eric Gill war memorial in the centre of Chirk. Then I turned north, towards Ruabon and alongside the

still active Wrexham line, to Ruabon to start looking for the Llangollen railway. From an overbridge on a minor road off the A483 there is a clear view of the site of Llangollen Line Junction, a grassy and overgrown cutting climbing away to the west being all that now remains. From here the line climbed sharply, and then began the alternating pattern of embankment and cutting that reflected the railway's route across the difficult landscape. A tight curve and a short tunnel led to Acrefair station, but it is hard to make much sense of what can be seen today. The trackbed is not always apparent or accessible, and the picture is confused by the embankment on the other side of the road that carried the Pontcysyllte mineral line. This, nearly four miles long and serving collieries, brick and tile companies as well as other local industries, was in its day extremely busy. From here, the hard red brick and terracotta that is characteristic of the Ruabon region was taken by train all over Britain. Today, all these local industries and much of the railway that served them have vanished beneath the enormous modern chemical complex. This wandering and steeply graded mineral network joined the main line at Trevor. Here there is a Station Road, but it only goes to a new estate. However, a glance over the parapet of the adjacent A359 bridge revealed an overgrown wasteland with the two

Above *A Great Western tank locomotive, No. 1628, pauses at Trevor with a mixed freight from Llangollen*

Above *The 4.30pm Chester to Llangollen train reaches its destination on a May evening in 1932, in the care of GWR's No. 7308*

Far Right *The evocative quality of the Great Western's rural railways is shown in this 1958 view of the 2.35pm Barmouth to Chester train approaching Berwyn tunnel, hauled by the first of its class, No. 7800 Torquay Manor*

Inset Far Right *One of the unchanging views of the Vale of Llangollen is shown in this 1905 postcard of Berwyn*

roadside trees until they are buried under a housing development shortly before Llangollen. Trains used to enter the town right beside the river, wheels screaming as they negotiated the sweeping curves that preceded Bishop Trevor's bridge and the station. Today this area has been changed beyond recognition by landscaping and the building of a public park and riverside walkway, and it is hard to believe that trains were still running here in 1968. With its splendid riverside setting, hard by the bridge and looking out across the Dee to the town centre, Llangollen was always an important station, with plenty of tourist and freight traffic. It was probably at its peak during the decade before World War I, when it had twenty staff and, in its extensive network of sidings, handled nearly 20,000 tons of freight per year. At one time there was a branch west of the station leading to a canal wharf that was used primarily for slate traffic, but in the 1920s this was converted into carriage sidings, necessitated by the town's increasing importance as a tourist centre.

Today, the view of the station from the bridge, familiar from so many old postcards, is apparently unchanged. The handsome buildings with their tall chimneys, the broad platform canopy, the signal box, the old lamps, benches and enamel signs and floral displays, are all still there. There may even be a train in the platform, a few Great Western carriages waiting behind a quietly steaming dark green locomotive with gleaming brasswork. The sense of time warp, so carefully developed by the Llangollen Railway, is very effective and must be quite startling for anyone who comes across the sight unprepared. The reopening of the line is one of the triumphs of the preservation movement, for the railway, like the canal, seems such an integral and essential part of the Dee Valley landscape that it is hard now to remember it not being there.

From here the line, single-tracked from Llangollen, sweeps along beside the river and through the trees, visible in tantalising glimpses from the adjacent A5. There is a clear view of the iron viaduct that carries it across the Dee, but train spotting is a hazardous activity on this busy road. The first station after Llangollen, Berwyn, is also largely unchanged, and its tall timber-framed building towers over the road and the sharply curving platform. This was always primarily a tourist station, serving visitors to the famous Horseshoe Falls built by Telford to feed water from the Dee into the Llangollen Canal, and today the tradition is maintained by the many walkers that crowd the platform in summer.

From Berwyn the line enters the line's major tunnel, 689 yards long and cut on a curve through thick rock with very limited headroom. This guarantees that modern travellers on the Llangollen Railway can experience to the full the smoke and smell of steam haulage.

platforms still well defined. Gone for ever are the station buildings, the signal box, the circular water tower with its conical top, and the meandering sidings that led to the start of the mineral line.

From Trevor, the road and the trackbed run side by side, with the latter generally visible but at a lower level. After about a mile the Llangollen Canal swings in along its contour line to pass under the railway. Just beyond here is the site of Sun Bank Halt, a little-used and unstaffed wooden station that was opened in 1905. At this point, where railway, canal and road ran close together, there was a serious accident in the early hours of 7 September 1945. During the night the canal burst its banks and the water pouring through the breach swept away a stretch of the railway embankment, but left the rails and sleepers suspended in mid-air, along with the signal cables. The first train of the day, its driver and crew completely unaware of what had happened, steamed straight on and plunged into the gap in the embankment. The driver was killed and the goods wagons caught fire and burned out. The wreckage, including the locomotive was cut up on the spot, the embankment was rebuilt and two weeks later the line was back in use.

From here the line ran steadily down into the Vale of Llangollen and its remains are generally visible among the

Berwyn, Llangollen

Climbing steadily, the reopened railway continues beside the river to Glyndyfrdwy and then on to Carrog, currently the end of the line. Both stations survive, surprisingly substantial structures considering the size of the villages they served, and both are characterised by the tall chimneys and decorative polychrome brickwork that reflect the desire of the line's original builders to make their mark on the unchanging rural architecture of the Dee Valley. During the restoration process other buildings have been added, to bring back the true Great Western flavour. At Glyndyfrdwy these include a signal box and a wooden station building rescued, respectively, from Leaton, near Shrewsbury, and Northwich. There were considerable sidings, underlining the importance of goods traffic for the railway. Much of this was agricultural, with the line being the prime mover of livestock to market, but there were other regular cargoes, such as slate from the Moelferna quarry near Glyndyfrdwy. Beyond Carrog the track, always in view from the nearby A5, is currently being relaid in preparation for the line's reopening to Corwen, its chosen terminus. In the 1920s a small halt was opened at Bonwm, midway between Carrog and Corwen, but there is little to be seen of this wooden structure whose platform was only one carriage long.

Corwen was a substantial station, stone-built and with decorative platform canopies, serving both the Llangollen line and the London & North Western's route northwards to Rhyl and Chester via Denbigh and Mold. The junction was just to the east. Traffic was at its peak before and after World War I, and in 1923 the station had twenty-eight staff. The Denbigh line was to be an early casualty, closing to passengers in 1953. There were extensive sidings, goods warehouses and cattle pens, two signal boxes, a large engine shed and turntable and a clutter of other buildings and structures. Today, some of these buildings survive beside the A5, but there is no sense of their ever having been part of a major station complex. The line has been swept away, along with the bridge that carried it over a minor road by the war memorial park, just to the east of the town centre. Time will tell whether the Llangollen Railway can breathe some kind of new life into these shattered fragments.

After Corwen the railway followed the River Dee to the southwest, leaving the A5 for a landscape of quieter country roads and fields full of sheep and sheepdogs. Much of the railway's route was on a low embankment, raised above the river's floodplain, and this is generally clearly visible, though often overgrown or broken by farmers. The next station was Cynwyd, a small single-storey structure with one platform and a few sidings, sometimes used by trains loading timber from the local forests, a regular traffic in this region. The buildings have mostly gone but the yard remains, now the province of Ifor Williams, the well-known maker of horse and livestock trailers.

Llandrillo was a more substantial station with two platforms, a signal box, a large goods shed and a station master's house, yet it served a small village well away to the south. Today the site and the surviving buildings are occupied by a sawmill, reflecting the continuing importance of a local traffic that the railway was already losing to the roads in the years immediately preceeding the final closure in 1964.

Following a rather remote route along by the river, which it crossed twice, at Cilan and Dolgadfa, the line made its way to Llandderfel. Queen Victoria came here in August 1889 in the royal train, to stay at nearby Pale Hall, but she would not recognise it today. The station site, then comparatively open and with fine views of the distant hills that flank the valley, is now overgrown and decrepit. The station buildings and the signal box have gone, along with the platforms, but a curious and unexpected survivor is the wooden staircase that linked the platform with the road bridge above.

Leaving Llandderfel, the line curved away sharply, hard by the river, passed through a short tunnel and then ran along an embankment that carried it into the broadening valley towards Bala. It was track damage by the flooding River Dee near Llandderfel in December 1964 that brought about the premature closure of the line. With

Above *In the summer of 1963 Ivatt class 2MT No. 46509 draws into Bala Junction with the single-coach shuttle service from Bala. The diverging line to Barmouth is clearly seen on the left*

Far Left *A timeless Vale of Llangollen scene as Standard class 4 No. 76079, a visitor from the East Lancashire Railway, sets off for Llangollen from Glyndyfrdwy in the summer of 1992*

Above *Today Llanuwchllyn station has a new life as the headquarters of the Bala Lake Railway. In the early morning a diesel shunter prepares the first train of the day*

the huge expanse of Lake Bala glittering in the distance, the single line track opened out into four as it approached Bala Junction. This large station with its three platforms, particularly decorative canopies and elegant footbridge, water tower, large signal box and grand array of signals was built to serve the meeting point between the Llangollen and the Bala to Ffestiniog lines. Curiously, for so impressive a structure, it was set in open fields beside the river, had no road access and could be reached only via a long footpath from the road (B4391) to the south. This did make sense, however, because the bulk of its traffic came from the interchange between the two lines. Bala itself was served by another station a few hundred yards up the Festiniog line, and there was a shuttle to link the two stations. This remained in use after the closure of the Ffestiniog line, and so the Junction station never lost its character and sense of isolation. Today, the site of Bala Junction station is equally inaccessible and much of it, along with the line towards Bala, has disappeared beneath an industrial estate.

From the junction, the line followed the river to the eastern end of Lake Bala, passing under the B4391. It was in this area that the Corwen & Bala Railway had its original 1868 terminus, but this was swept away long ago. In 1934 a new station appeared here, Bala Lake Halt, inspired by the needs of tourist traffic, and this is now the eastern end of the narrow gauge Bala

Lake Railway, laid along the trackbed between here and Llanuwchllyn. This, maintaining the popular image of Wales as the home of Little Trains, offers a leisurely journey along the lakeside, making use of the halts built by the Great Western at Llangower and Glan Lynn to encourage tourism. Llangower stands by the lake, decorated with a surprising profusion of signals for so small a railway, and early on a spring morning the only signs of life I saw were a sheep and its lamb nibbling the lineside grass. The other halt was originally private, built for Sir Watkin Williams-Wynn, one of the railway's original directors, who retained the power to stop trains whenever necessary. Beyond the simple platform with its rusticated timber shelter was a landing stage, with a flag to summon a boat from Glan Lynn, the Williams-Wynn house on the lake's western shore. This gave the station its original name, Flag Halt, changed to Glan Lynn in 1950. The Bala Lake Railway had added an additional halt, at Pentre Piod where there is a camp site.

West of Bala the landscape changes, becoming much more rugged as it nears the coast. The gentle slopes of the meandering river valley give way to dramatic and bare hills, rising to over 2,000 feet, and the railway's builders in the 1860s had little choice but to force a route along existing river valleys, first the Dyfrdwy and then the Wnion, all the way to Dolgellau. The result was some steep gradients, compelling the locomotives and their crews to work hard. They used to hit the first of these, a straight climb of 1 in 70, near the western end of Lake Bala, and this certainly makes demands on the little narrow gauge locomotives of the Bala Lake Railway before they can slow down for the more gentle approach to Llanuwchllyn, the line's headquarters. Seen from the road that runs across the hills to the south, it looks an impressive station with a big signal box, a variety of surrounding structures and some sidings filled with a scattering of rolling stock. A former industrial diesel locomotive was sorting out some carriages and by the shed a little steam engine was slowly coming to life. If anything, the station looks better today than during its GWR past. It now boasts a large platform canopy, built for Pwllheli and then subsequently put to work at Aberdovey in 1909 before coming to rest here in the early 1970s. Llanuwchllyn, originally called Pandy, is very much the end of the line for, just beyond the station, a new house straddles the trackbed and the bridge over the B4403 has gone.

From here, the A494 is never far from the track and there are good views as it climbs steeply towards the summit at Garneddwen. On the way it passes the site of Llys Halt, a little single platform beside a level crossing on a very minor road, now marked by the former crossing-keeper's house. In winter, trains sometimes required the help of a pilot engine to bank them up to the summit, and these were kept ready at Bala and Penmaenpool. At the Garneddwen summit there was a passing

With the widening river ever present and increasingly a major feature in the landscape, the line ran on to Bontnewydd, another remote but surprisingly well equipped station. Today the site survives, but everything to do with the railway has disappeared without trace. Even the trackbed is hard to determine here for the road seems to have encroached on to it by the river bridge and the former level crossing. The down platform was exciting, a timber structure built mostly from old sleepers, with supports made from redundant rails, and with its corrugated-iron shelter hanging out over the river. West of here is a wonderful stretch of trackbed, a secret route through woods that in spring are filled with bluebells, wild garlic and the sounds of the river and the lambs, the lost railway at its best. Also lost today is the final station before Dolgellau, Dolserau Halt, added in the 1930s for the tourist traffic. It was built to serve the Torrent Walk, a popular path southwards up the rocky valley of the River Clywedog, and its name board said as much.

Approaching Dolgellau, this delightful idyll is rudely shattered by the familiar outburst of new roads, surpermarkets and trading estates that have taken over completely the station site. This was where the Great Western met the Cambrian Railways' branch from Barmouth head on but, until 1922, they were rarely on speaking terms. Dolgellau (Dolgelly until about 1896, Dolgelley until 1960) was, therefore, two stations in one,

loop controlled by a very isolated signal box, and a couple of small platforms which cannot ever have seen many passengers. Trains stopped only on request in any case. It must have been a bleak spot for the signalman on duty.

The line now drops steeply, and continues to descend all the way to Dolgellau, with gradients up to 1 in 53. Today, the trackbed is often overgrown and lined on both sides by thick woods which limit visibility from the road. The next station was at Drws-y-Nant, just by the stream that will soon become the River Wnion. It is hard today to visualise this station in its railway days, with two platforms, a range of buildings, some sidings, a signal box and, in winter, a roaring fire in the waiting room. It is also difficult to imagine that many passengers ever needed all these facilities. In fact, the revenue for all these remote stations came largely from freight, and in particular the timber traffic.

The steep descent continued through the woods to Wnion Halt, a little single platform station opened in 1933 and graced with just a name board and rudimentary corrugated iron shelter. Over the last thirty years the trackbed has reverted to nature, and it is hard today to find many tangible remains of active life. Typical railway concrete fencing is often still in place, striding through the encroaching woods, but in general it is a private world, despite the constant proximity of the main road.

Above *A fine stone bridge carries the trackbed over the River Wnion at Pont Rhyd-ddwl, one of the few surviving structures on this part of the line*

Right *In the early 1960s, No. 7822* Foxcote Manor *draws a Barmouth to Ruabon train into Dolgellau. Everything is now beneath the road or under the industrial estate*

west to cross the tidal mudflats on a low embankment. Penmaenpool was the first station on this stretch and, remarkably, much of it survives today, including the brick-built station buildings and house on the south side, the signal box, now used as a bird observatory, an old signal and, by the hotel, the station name board, a postwar example in brown and cream enamel. Gone are the platforms, the goods shed and a charming little wooden engine shed which was just big enough for a couple of locomotives. In the eighteenth and early nineteenth centuries Penmaenpool was a busy port and shipbuilding centre, but the coming of the railway in 1865 killed off this already dying trade.

West of Penmaenpool the line cut across to the estuary and then ran for several miles virtually on the shore. Erosion by tides and storms meant that the railway engineers had to battle constantly to maintain the embankment that carried the track along this stretch. At Arthog, the point where the line left the estuary for its final approach to Barmouth, there was a little station, a pretty timber structure with decorative barge boarding set beside the single wooden platform. There was also a surprisingly long siding. Today there is just the grassy trackbed, an old bridge and lovely views out across the estuary. However, the GWR station name board survives, attached to a private shed near Morfa Mawddach.

A sharp curve took the railway northwards to its junction with the Cambrian coast line and a remote station was built here, mainly for passengers changing trains. Originally it had no road access and was known, until 1871, as Barmouth Ferry. It then became Barmouth Junction, which in turn became Morfa Mawddach in 1960. An important interchange station for both passengers and freight, it boasted a number of quite substantial buildings. The track at the junction formed a triangle, to allow for the turning of locomotives, and as a result the platforms were Y-shaped. Today these platforms survive, along with buffers and other hints of former railway life, one still in use and the other an overgrown and forgotten adjunct to the car park used both by train travellers and walkers. The footpath ends just before the station, but it is possible to walk on through the car park and on to the splendid 113-span wooden viaduct that strides across the bay to Barmouth. This is a magnificent but rather windswept walk of about a mile, with the practical and, for this book unusual, alternative of catching a train.

Above *Plenty survives on the Morfa Mawddach Trail at Penmaenpool, including this GWR lower quadrant signal. The toll bridge is in the background*

with the Great Western occupying the buildings on the up side and the Cambrian the down side. There were two station masters with their staffs and, until 1925 when a footbridge was added, passengers crossed from one platform to the other via the road bridge, The stations were distinct in style, and very different in their use of architectural detail. It is very sad that all this has been lost.

From Dolgellau to Barmouth Junction the trackbed is now an official walkway, the Morfa Mawddach Trail, with a well-graded and level surface. Part of the Snowdonia National Park, it follows the southern shore of the Mawddach estuary, a wide expanse of tidal water noted for its bird life. There are wonderful views, across to the hills on the north side of the esturay and westwards towards Barmouth. There are signs to the walkway from the tourist information centre in Dolgellau, on a public footpath that joins the trackbed west of the town. It crosses the Wnion on the old railway bridge and then swings

BLAENAU FFESTINIOG TO BALA JUNCTION

In the 1870s both the London & North Western and the Great Western companies had their eye firmly on the north Wales slate trade. At that time the only access to the huge quarries around Blaenau Ffestiniog was via the narrow gauge Festiniog Railway and its line to the coast at Porthmadog, a situation that both companies found highly unsatisfactory. The L&NWR mounted its attack from the north and backed an extension to the existing Conwy Valley line to Betws-y-Coed, while the GWR put its weight behind the Bala & Festiniog Railway, whose proposed route up from Bala in the south had received parliamentary approval in July 1873. Both lines proved to be very expensive and laborious to construct, and both companies must often have wished they had never started. In the event, the L&NWR won the race, its trains reaching Blaenau in 1881. A year later the Bala & Festiniog reached Llan Ffestiniog, where it met the short Festiniog & Blaenau Railway. This little three-mile narrow gauge line had opened in 1868, initially as an adjunct to the Festiniog Railway. Bought by the Bala & Festiniog and converted to standard gauge, it finally enabled the GWR to reach Blaenau Ffestiniog in 1883. From that date on until 1960 Blaenau was able to boast two large standard gauge

Above *A busy scene at Blaenau Ffestiniog Central in 1958, with the train for Bala waiting to leave. Today this station is used as a joint terminus by British Rail's Conwy Valley line and the Ffestiniog Railway*

Left *From Blaenau Ffestiniog the freight line to Trawsfynydd curves away, on a long viaduct, from the town and its backdrop of slate-covered hills*

BALA

PISTYLL CAIN, DOLGELLEY

ARTHOG

11

BERWYN

Above *Contrasting views of Wales reflected by a page from a GWR holiday brochure of the 1920s and a postcard of about 1905, showing Ffestiniog with mixed freight on the Great Western's line*

Far Right *High on the hills near Cwm Prysor, bridges and viaducts survive in splendid isolation, memorials to the line's rugged quality*

southwards towards the village of Ffestiniog. This was where the little Festiniog & Blaenau Railway met the Bala & Festiniog's new line, and was absorbed by it.

At Maentwrog Road the station survives, its platform and buildings looking good from the parapet of the bridge carrying the A470, and it is all given an unexpected reality by the existence of the track. This station has found a new life as a garden centre, a domestic interlude in a landscape notable for its wildness. From here the line runs close to the road, its route partly hidden by woods and then, as it reaches the northern edge of Trawsfynedd Lake, it comes to an abrupt halt, beneath a large gantry used for loading the nuclear flasks on to the speical transporter wagons. With Trawsfynedd power station at the end of its active life, the railway now faces a very uncertain future. The section south from Blaenau Ffestiniog seems likely to disappear sooner or later, and it is quite possible that, deprived of its nuclear lifeline and exposed to the harsh realities of privatisation, the whole route up the Conwy Valley from Llandudno Junction to Blaenau may go as well.

The transition from active to lost railway is immediate, and just past the buffers the former trackbed is little more than a path through the trees. When it emerges from the woods to make its way southwards round the lake, it is just the familiar overgrown embankment, richly coloured in greens and browns, with the occasional bridge still in place. At Trawsfynedd the former station, well away from its village, is now a house, with a fine lawn well established between the platforms, and the canopy glazed in to form a conservatory. Here the trackbed swings to the east, to follow the course of the River Prysor up into the hills. In the increasingly wild landscape the trackbed can sometimes be followed as a grassy path through old rock-strewn cuttings, and at other times disappears completely.

Seen from the B4212 down in the valley, the next section is spectacular as the line climbs steadily high on to the hillside, sweeping round generous curves as it sticks to the contours. At times it is little more than a shelf cut into the rocks, above precipitous walls of scree and in the shadow of a series of rounded peaks that rise up to 2,000 feet. On one of the curving sweeps into the hills, it crosses over the plunging course of the Prysor on a viaduct worthy of the Alps or the Andes. The road then climbs to meet the line, and where they come together is the site of Cwm Prysor station. Nothing remains of what must have been one of the most remote and little-used stations in Wales. Briefly, the road has taken over the trackbed, and then they separate again with the line now to the south, running across the barren landscape towards the softer green of the valley of the River Tryweryn. A minor road branches down into the valley to accompany it, passing a huge old quarry where the trackbed broadens into an expanse of flattened stone,

stations a couple of hundred yards apart but with no rail link between them. The link was finally made in 1961, when the old GWR route south to Bala was closed due to the building of a reservoir and the decision was made to service the nuclear power station at Trawsfynydd via the Conwy Valley line.

Blaenau Ffestiniog now has one station, recently rebuilt on the site of the old GWR one, and shared by both British Rail's Conwy Valley trains and the Ffestiniog Railway. Blaenau Ffestiniog is the end of the line for passenger services, but the track continues southwards for some miles to Trawsfynedd Lake. It is almost a ghost railway, fully equipped but rarely used, its only traffic being either maintenance trains or those carrying nuclear flasks. The route through Blaenau Ffestiniog is dramatic, with the line winding its way through the town high on a hillside, and this sets a pattern for the whole journey. The first station was at Manod but new bungalows have taken over the site, leaving the line curiously isolated. Here the railway leaves the town behind, carving its way in sweeping curves through a landscape of hills and farms. There are good views of the route from a minor road south of Teiliau, sweeping

presumably the site of the quarry sidings, and the station house at Arenig, another one that seems to have served nothing at all.

From here the line alternates between cuttings and embankments and then, as it curves away from the road, it simply disappears into the waters of Lake Celyn. It was the building of this reservoir that brought about the line's closure, for British Railways were understandably reluctant to go to the expense of building a deviationary route for a railway that can never have repaid its huge construction costs. When it reappears at the lake's eastern edge, it is in the more gentle setting of the woods of the Tryweryn Valley, as an embankment path overlooking a canoeing centre.

The line descends through the woods into a greener landscape of lush riverside fields. Frongoch station, the last before Bala, survives as a house, complete with old signal box and a platform decorated with rusty milk churns and a porter's trolley. Here, a section of trackbed has become a drive leading to a number of houses. It follows the B4212 down into Bala, occasionally visible but generally inaccessible, crossing the road near Rhiwlas, and then entering the town on a low green embankment, an unofficial tree-lined path much enjoyed by local children. This is really the end of the line, for the railway's route through Bala and on down to the junction has been changed beyond recognition. Bala Town station is just a memory, even though it outlived the rest of the line by a few years. Its site is a flattened area of grass just to the south of the A494, and there is nothing to indicate that this was the starting point of one of the most dramatic railway journeys in Wales.

Right *In May 1958 the 9.15am Blaenau Ffestiniog to Bala train, a single carriage hauled by GWR tank locomotive No. 5810, scuttles along the single track near Cwm Prysor*

Far Right *West of Cwm Prysor a grand brick viaduct still stands in wild country, high above the River Prysor*

THE NORTH YORKSHIRE COAST

Saltburn-by-the-Sea to Whitby
Whitby to Scarborough

Approaching Ravenscar, the trackbed, now a footpath, climbs round the hillside towards the old tunnel and passes under a bridge half hidden in the gorse

HISTORY

The development of the railways of North Yorkshire and its coastline spanned almost the entire Victorian railway age. First to be opened, in 1836, was the horse-drawn Whitby & Pickering Railway, an entirely local and isolated operation built to encourage the use of Whitby's growing harbour. More significant in terms of later developments were, firstly, the eastwards expansion between 1830 and 1861 of the Stockton & Darlington Railway, initially to Middlesbrough and then along Teesside to Saltburn, and, secondly, the opening up in the 1840s of Scarborough and the coast by George Hudson's York & North Midland Railway. This line from York had a branch to Pickering, bringing to an end the individuality and independence of the Whitby & Pickering Railway, which was rebuilt for steam operation by 1847. During the 1850s there was further expansion of inland routes, notably by the Middlesbrough & Guisborough and the Cleveland Railways, with many lines being opened to serve the mines and industries of the region. In 1861 the Cleveland Railway received authorisation for a line along the coast to Loftus. Built in stages, this reached Skinningrove in 1866 and Loftus a year later. Connecting lines also linked this to Guisborough and to Saltburn. The next phase, the continuation of the line southwards along the coast to Whitby, was undertaken by the Whitby, Redcar & Middlesbrough Union Railway. Always short of money, this company could not begin work until 1871 and had to stop in 1874 when the contractor went bankrupt. By now the major player in the region was the large North Eastern Railway, formed in 1854 by the amalgamation of a series of small, local companies, and this stepped in to acquire the Whitby, Redcar & Middlesbrough Union and completed the line to Whitby. This took a long time, owing to the complex and expensive engineering involved, and the line did not open fully until 1883. In a route of a little over sixteen miles there were three tunnels and a series of American-style steel viaducts.

The first, unsuccessful, scheme for a line linking Whitby and Scarborough appeared in 1865. The Scarborough & Whitby Railway started on a more modest scheme in 1871 but made slow progress. Work stopped, then started again in 1880 but it was not until 1885 that it was finally completed, with long delays caused by the expensive and difficult engineering involved. From the start, the line was operated by the North Eastern Railway, and in 1898 it acquired the Scarborough & Whitby and took full control, paying less than half the line's construction costs.

Industry and tourism combined to keep the railways in business throughout the early years of this century. In the amalgamations of 1923 the whole network came under the control of the London & North Eastern Railway and services were considerably expanded during the 1920s and 1930s. The coastal route lived on into the era of British Railways but as traffic fell so its future looked less secure. The first closure, of the line northwards from Whitby to Loftus, came in 1958, followed two years later by the withdrawal of passenger services over the remainder of the route to Saltburn. The southern section, from Whitby to Scarborough, fared better but it too was finally axed in 1965. After a long campaign the Middlesbrough to Whitby line along the Esk Valley, originally scheduled for closure, was reprieved, and so Whitby was able to retain one of its three railway routes.

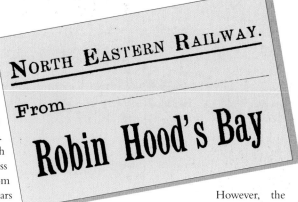

However, the line south from Grosmont to Pickering, the original 1836 route of the Whitby & Pickering Railway, was also closed, only to be reopened some years later as the North Yorkshire Moors preserved railway. Also still alive is the freight line from Saltburn to Skinningrove, which was extended in 1974 to serve the potash mine at Boulby.

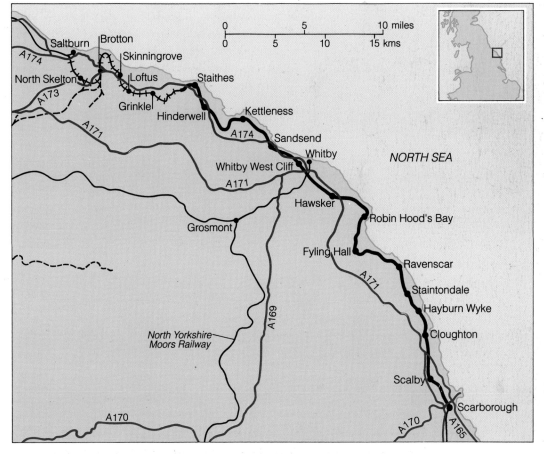

NORTH EASTERN RAILWAY

From Saltburn

I HAVE always liked Whitby, ever since my first visit thirty years ago. In evening light through the windscreen of an old Bedford van, my first view of the town – the houses tight round the harbour, the cluster of fishing boats, the gaunt silhouette of the abbey ruins up on the clifftop – was unforgettable, love at first sight. A friend and I were travelling around Yorkshire and the Northeast, nominally hunting for antiques but really just making the most of a chance to visit a region hitherto unknown. We drove up from the South and Whitby, tacked on to the itinerary because of a vague interest in Victorian jet, was the climax of a day of rich diversity. Our approach along minor roads gave tantalising glimpses of a large railway viaduct spanning the steep Esk Valley, but this was soon forgotten as the town came into view.

Over the following years there were subsequent visits, and I always came to Whitby with the same sense of anticipation, and was never disappointed. There were changes, inevitably, as the town became more tourist-conscious and acquired supermarkets and a brazen new road bridge high over the river, but in essence it was always the same place. It was many years later that I first came to Whitby by train, a low level approach along the Esk Valley that really showed the town at its best as a theatrical sequence of splendid

vistas. It was then that I appreciated for the first time the magnificence of the great Larpool viaduct, whose curving brick arches play as vital a role in the town's visual excitement as the abbey itself. Immediately I wanted to know more about it, and to take a train over it. But I was too late. The last train had gone years before, and all that remained of a once-thriving network was the Esk Valley service from Whitby to Middlesbrough, railcars slipping in and out of the town's grand classical station a few times each day. I did not know at that time of the other station, Whitby West Cliff, set high above the town to the north, or that this had been the place to take a train that crossed the Larpool viaduct.

Some reading and a bit of work with a map soon made sense of it all, and I vowed then to walk one day the old coastal line all the way from Saltburn south to Scarborough. I have not done it yet, but exploring the route for this book has been the next best thing.

The history of the railways around Whitby is, as ever, rather complicated. It all started on 26 May 1836 with the opening of the horse-drawn Whitby & Pickering Railway, whose route, engineered by George Stephenson, included nine bridges over the River Esk and a rope-worked incline at Goathland. Until 1845 this existed in peaceful isolation but that year the York & North Midland Railway, owned by the entrepreneur, George Hudson, completed its York to Scarborough line, with a branch to Pickering. During the same year the York & North Midland acquired the sleepy Whity & Pickering Railway, and rebuilt it entirely for double-tracked steam operation. Twenty years later a new route to Goathland replaced the incline, which had been for far too long an archaic impediment to modern travel.

The next stage was the building of a line towards Whitby from Middlesbrough. From the 1840s there were various schemes promoted by various companies, including the Stockton & Darlington, but the one that got off the ground, albeit in a rather devious manner, was the Cleveland Railway, whose route via Guisborough to Skinningrove and Loftus was sanctioned in 1858. This was completed throughout nine years later, by which time the Cleveland had been absorbed by the rapidly expanding North Eastern Railway. In the early 1870s this route was extended northwards to Saltburn, whose station, the terminus of a Stockton & Darlington Teesside line from Middlesbrough, had opened in 1861.

Another company, the grandly named Whitby, Redcar & Middlesbrough Union Railway, was authorised to extend the line southwards from Loftus in 1866. Always short of money, this company did nothing for a while and, when work did start, it was plagued by problems. Part of the line was built along the cliff-edge past Kettleness and Sandsend, but this fell into the sea

Below Timetable from the 1922 Bradshaw

before it was even completed. In the mid-1870s the North Eastern Railway took control and the heavily engineeered line, which included three tunnels and five steel viaducts, was finally opened in 1883. Yet another company, the Scarborough & Whitby Railway, began to build the line southwards from Whitby along the coast but this too faced all sorts of difficulties and it was twenty years before the dramatic route, which included the Larpool viaduct, steep gradients of up to 1 in 41 and a tunnel under Scarborough, was completed in 1885. The North Eastern was again involved, initially as the operator of the line, and took it over completely in 1898.

SALTBURN-BY-THE-SEA TO WHITBY

It was unseasonably cold and raining intermittently when I drove into Saltburn to start my exploration of the line to Whitby. Much of the town was developed by Alfred Pease, the Quaker industrialist and entrepreneur, and the railway was at the heart of his plans to create a great seaside resort, and a rival to Scarborough. As a result, the station, perhaps designed by Thomas Prosser, was a grand Italianate structure in stone-dressed buff brick with a three-arched *porte cochère*. This was not hard to find and it still carried a large enamel sign in the orange and white of the former British Railways' northeastern region saying 'Railway Station'. This turned out to be a lie, for the active station is a new and unremarkable little building to the west, while Prosser's ambitious façade leads only to a shopping centre and supermarket. However, still present, if paved over, was the long platform extension that enabled carriages to be shunted right up to the back door of the Zetland Hotel, another grandiose Pease speculation in typical high Victorian style. It is no longer a hotel, but still attached to the back of the building is the pretty little glass-roofed train shed.

Saltburn had always been at the end of a short branch and so, when the closures started in the late 1950s, it made sense to make it the end of the line for the Teesside route from Middlesbrough. All the lines southwards to Whitby, Guisborough and Scarborough, built with great difficulties and at enormous expense, were swept away bit by bit and now the only trains that visit Saltburn are the railcars that shuttle to and fro, barely keeping alive the town's tradition as a railway resort.

Just west of the station there is a junction. Here the Middlesbrough trains go straight on along the coast, while a mineral line, formerly the route to Whitby, branches away to the south. When this line was closed to passengers in 1960, the track was retained to serve various mines and industrial complexes in the Skinningrove area, ironically the main reason for the building of the railway in the first place. Remarkably, this freight line is still in business and, even more remarkably, it

has even been extended south from Skinningrove to Boulby, where there is a major potash mine. This extension involved the reinstatement of four miles of track and the rebuilding of a number of bridges, work that was completed in 1974. Since then the line has been used by several bulk hopper trains a day, carrying potash to the Teesside docks for export. It is refreshing that here the railway, the natural carrier for this kind of cargo, has been able to keep at bay the predatory lorries.

The line is, as a result, easy to follow as it makes its way southwards out of Saltburn. The first major feature is the big Upleatham viaduct, which carries it high above Skelton Beck. As I stood looking at the viaduct's graceful and remarkably slender brick arches rising high above the wooded valley, I heard the rumble of an approaching train. Very slowly a big class 47 diesel, painted in one of those strange liveries currently favoured by British Rail in its fragmented form, hauled its line of potash hopper wagons across the viaduct and away round the curve leading to the junction – a satisfying confirmation of railway reality.

The first station was North Skelton, a relatively late arrival, opened only in 1902. Just beyond it is the site of a former junction that used to give access to some connecting and bypass lines, built in the 1870s to simplify journeys between Guisborough, Saltburn and Middlesbrough, and to mineral lines to various mines around Kilton and Lingdale. All these

Above *The day before the line closed in 1958 the Reverend Rokeby, a Norfolk clergyman who was an enthusiastic rail traveller and amateur photographer, visited Kettleness. Here, a train from Whitby, hauled by LNER class L1 No. 67766, pauses while he takes his photograph. A friend looks on*

closed years ago, but sections of the surviving trackbed can be explored via local footpaths.

The railway now embarked on a series of great meandering curves that took the route high above Brotton and round Warsett Hill on a dramatic clifftop loop. Brotton station survives, with some recognisable buildings and a couple of platforms. From the cliffs there are wonderful views over the roofs of Brotton and back to Saltburn, framed by the distant horizon of industrial Teesside. The line then sweeps back inland and runs beside the A174 to Skinningrove, at one time called Carlin How. There is plenty of railway life here in the form of signal box, signals, sidings and related structures maintaining the spirit of the past, thanks in part to the local steel works. There were always mines and related industrial activities around here, some on the upper level and some down in the valley. When the railway arrived it had to serve all these, and so the company built a complicated and steeply graded South American-style zig-zig system down into the valley. It must have been exciting to watch two or even three locomotives working hard together to get the loaded wagons up the 1 in 28 gradient.

The reopening of the main line in 1974 involved the building of an unusual curving, concrete bridge to carry it over the A174 south of Skinningrove, but far more impressive must have been the original viaduct across Kilton Beck. Twelve stone piers carried the line on iron girders 150 feet above the river. However, by 1911 subsidence caused by local ironstone mining had made the structure unsafe and so the whole thing was buried in a huge new embankment. This takes the line across the valley and then it swings eastward through the woods below Loftus. The station, for some time the line's southern terminus, is now a house, but there is not much to see. There is even less at the delightfully named Grinkle, the first station to have been built by the Whitby, Redcar & Middlesbrough Union Railway. Next comes Grinkle tunnel, 993 yards long, and then the line turns north again, to run beside the woods above Easington Beck. It all comes to an end in a mass of sidings at Cleveland Potash's huge Boulby mine complex, whose tall chimneys have been visible for miles. There is a good view from the A174 of the the diesel shunter sorting out the hopper wagons.

Much harder to see is what happened next, for the old trackbed has completely disappeared. There is no sign where it crossed the road, and a length of about a mile seems to have been ploughed or landscaped out of existence. When it does reappear at Cowbar, west of Staithes, it is as an isolated section

Below *Just before closure, in March 1958, another L1 tank, No. 67754, leaves Staithes viaduct to enter the station with the 12.27 Middlesbrough to Scarborough train*

of embankment, set in the open fields like some prehistoric earthwork. This was actually the approach to the great Staithes viaduct that strode across the valley on seventeen tubular steel piers, 790 feet long and, at its highest, 152 feet in the air. Impressive though this structure was, it must have completely dominated Staithes and rather spoiled the secret charm of this traditional, and then rather inaccessible, fishing village. High and exposed, the viaduct suffered from severe cross-winds and trains were not allowed over it when the wind pressure reached 28lbs per square foot. A wind gauge on the viaduct rang a bell in Staithes signal box when the danger level was reached and the signalman stopped all traffic. All that remains today is the western abutment, forming a precipitous end to the grassy embankment. Housing developments have buried the eastern end, along with some of the trackbed above the village.

From here the line swung back inland, but little can be seen until the site of its crossing of the A174 just north of Hinderwell. A well-defined trackbed runs beside the road into the village, where some elements of the station can still be seen at the end of country lanes. It then diasappears again for a while, to reappear near Runswick Bay and run parallel to the curving coastline as a series of wooded cuttings on the hillside.

Above *Across the valley, the western abutment is all that remains of Staithes viaduct*

Left *From a distance, the formal symmetry of Kettleness's old station gives it the appearance of a country house beside the sea*

The trackbed comes to life as a farm path to the west of Kettleness, but the best approach to this clifftop settlement is down the minor road from Goldsborough, passing the site of the Roman signal station. The view across the steeply sloping fields to the empty cliffs and on to the wide expanse of sea is wonderful, and at its heart there is what appears to be a small but elegant country house, quietly classical in the symmetry of its central block and matching wings. This is Kettleness station, all dark red brick with purple detailing, still looking out over its platforms, outbuildings and overgrown yards. Close to, there is more to see and to discover, including the curving line of the trackbed disappearing to the west, and the site of the old level crossing, now guarded by a pretty little weather-boarded cottage, probably nothing to do with the railway. As I watched, the sound of shots drew my eyes to a farmer in the distance, shooting rabbits from the trackbed. Presently he climbed back into a Landrover and drove into the village, passing along between the platforms.

East of Kettleness there is, by comparison, little to see. After the collapse of the early, clifftop route, the railway's builders moved back inland and pushed the line across the headland in two tunnels, the first quite short, but the second, Sandsend, a major undertaking 1652 yards long. The only way to visit the sites of these tunnels today is by foot along the clifftop route of the Cleveland Way.

Approaching Sandsend, the trackbed appears from the woods as a broad path cut into the cliff side, leading directly to the station, in matching style to Kettleness. Now a house, this is set high to the west of the village. On a clear day, there is a good view of this, and the line of the trackbed, from the cliff path west of Whitby. From the station, another tubular steel viaduct carried the line across the river valley and Sandsend village, the first of four viaducts in little over a mile between here and Whitby. Sandsend, the shortest, was followed by East Row, which at 528 feet was the longest. Next came Newholm Bank and finally Upgang, just outside Whitby by the golf links. Some traces remain to identify the sites of the viaducts, occasionally an abutment or a section of embankment, but only old photographs can recapture the extraordinary nature of this stretch of coastal railway. It was the cost of maintaining these viaducts in the hostile seaside atmosphere that gave British Railways the excuse for closing the line between Whitby and Loftus in 1958. From Sandsend, the track disappears briefly beneath the road, and then swings away along the cliffs, to approach Whitby at a high level. Its route can be seen through the golf links, where an overbridge remains to carry golfers and their impedimenta between the greens. Surprisingly, it can also be traced through Whitby's smart West Cliff suburbs practically all the way to the station, a handsome structure in polychrome

brick and stone at the end of Station Avenue, now in use as a depot for Yorkshire Water.

As it was now lunch time and the sun had come out, I allowed myself some time in Whitby. The town was as welcoming and endearing as ever, and pleasantly full of people making the most of the spring weather. I drove around for a while then parked on the south side, across the old harbour bridge. A large coaster was moored at the quay while a single crane unloaded its cargo, and yachts and fishing boats came and went. I went to a café that offered 'the best fish and chips in Whitby' and found this to be a reasonable claim. There was also another reason for spending some time in Whitby. Not far from the bridge is a junk shop, old-fashioned and rather dishevelled but therefore very tempting. This shop includes in its stock old railway signs and other relics, and on several previous visits I have peered at them through the rather grubby windows. So far, on five or six visits, I had never found the shop open. Every time there was a different scrawled notice on the door, listing opening times that had never included the day I was there. This time I was quite hopeful. It was a Wednesday, and I remembered

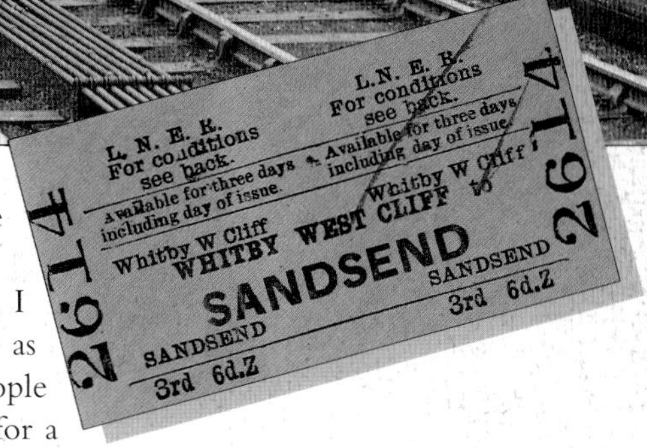

Above *High above the town, Whitby's West Cliff station, seen here shortly before closure, was the meeting point for trains from north and south. Some of the buildings survive today*

Far Left *Class B1 No. 61115 propels an inspection saloon backwards out of Kettleness station in 1958, with a misty Runswick Bay in the background*

that had been one of the open days listed on my previous attempt, a Tuesday in January. I approached the shop, my heart sinking as I saw its gloomy interior. Sure enough, there was a new notice on the door, and Wednesday was now the only day in the week the shop did not open. To make it worse, there was a big handwritten notice inside saying '30% reduction on all railway items.'

Trains leaving West Cliff in a southerly direction had a choice. They could continue straight on, pass to the west of the town at a high level and then cross the valley on the Larpool viaduct, or they could swing to the west at Prospect Hill Junction, pass actually beneath the signal box and drop steeply down into the valley along the sharply curved single-track link that ran under the viaduct and then joined the Esk Valley line at Bog Hall Junction for the final approach to Whitby Town station. Some through trains between Scarborough and the Teesside towns called at Whitby Town and so had to carry out this manoeuvre, which often involved complicated reversing operations. At other times a shuttle service linked the two Whitby stations.

WHITBY TO SCARBOROUGH

The approach to Larpool is marked by sections of embankment and cuttings, often glimpsed over garden walls. Like most viaducts, it looks best from below, but there are good views, particularly in winter, from the minor road that runs parallel to the river's southern shore, but at a high level. This road then drops down to pass beneath the trackbed. The bridge here is a starting point for the Scarborough and Whitby Trailway, which follows the track all the way to Scarborough. At this point you can turn the other way and walk back towards the viaduct. As is normally the case with viaducts, Larpool is for safety reasons sealed off by metal fences at both ends, but it is nevertheless possible to enjoy the magnificent views along the Esk Valley. The descending curve of the old link line can be traced through the trees on the opposite hillside, along with the site of the former junction. Something that looked like the base of an old turntable, but much too large, was, I realised later, the base of one of the gasometers of the former gas works. The sight of Whitby and the abbey in the distance is particularly enticing, marred only by the inelegant lines of the new road bridge over the river.

Running first past woods and then alongside the road, the now well-surfaced trackbed leads to Hawsker station, actually nearer Stainsacre and now a private house near the main road. Beyond the station the line crossed the A171, but the bridge has gone and so walkers now have to cross on the level. From here the trackbed swings away from the road towards Hawsker

Bottoms and the sea, passing by the Seaview Caravan Park, the first of a number along the route. The approach to Robin Hood's Bay is, characteristically for this line, at a high level, the trackbed running along beside the sea and then sweeping in across the top of the village. The bridge has gone and its site is the temporary end of the trail, which now joins the streets for a while and makes its way past the former station. This survives as a house, along with some of its associated structures. The waiting room had been in use as a gallery but was looking empty and woebegone when I was there. Particularly appealing was an old turn-of-the-century timber shop building tacked on to the side, and presumably at one time the station newsagent. Sadly, this was also out of use, but still active was the coalyard, a traditionally essential part of station life. Signs from here direct walkers to the place where they can rejoin the trackbed path, up the hill beyond the station.

A feature of Robin Hood's Bay station in its railway days had been its camping coaches. For those who experienced the delights of spending a week in a converted railway carriage on a siding at some remote and generally scenic station the memories will live on for ever. Luckily my grandmother was a long-established camping coach enthusiast. She had stayed at several with her own children during the 1930s and when my generation had reached the right age in the late 1950s, she started the whole process again. For several years we had a

Above and Right *Whitby's greatest railway feature is the Larpool viaduct. In this 1931 view an LNER tank hauls its train up the steeply curving link line from Town station to West Cliff. Today, Larpool's slender piers are still a masterpiece of Victorian brickwork*

Est., 4772 5M. 8/37

B 877

L.N E.R.

LUGGAGE

From YORK

To WHITBY

were exploited by the railway marketing people in both pre- and post-nationalisation eras. It was often included on special tours and excursions, and these continued to operate right up to the final closure in the spring of 1965.

At its peak in the late 1930s and early 1950s the line was kept very busy during the holiday season. The summer timetable for 1950 shows up to fourteen trains a day between Middlesbrough, Whitby and Scarborough, with the fastest journey time for the 58 miles being 2 hours 27 minutes. In the winter, this was cut back to three trains each way on weekdays only, an imbalance that made it hard for the line ever to be financially viable.

There follows the most spectacular part of the journey, with the line twisting through the woods to Fyling Hall station, and then climbing up to the moors and tackling the steep gradients on both sides of Ravenscar. Walking up and down the steeply sloping trackbed today can give some idea of the hard work faced by locomotives and their crews, particularly when the lines were made slippery by the fogs and sea mists of autumn and winter. The approach to Ravenscar is dramatic, the trackbed carved into the hillside and curving round to enter the short tunnel that preceded the station. Now busy with caravans, this was quite a remote and bleak spot before the war, the station, which at one time was called Peak, serving only isolated farms and the Raven Hall Hotel.

In a windswept landscape bare of trees, the colours of sea and moorland are in spring heightened by the bright yellow of the gorse that flourishes in the relative shelter of every cutting. With nothing but sheep between it and the cliff edge, the line makes the most of the view out across the wide expanse of sea, dotted with fishing boats and tankers bound for Teesside. It then drops down in to the softer greens of Staintondale, where the station survives as a house, half hidden by woods. From the road on the hillside above there is a fine view of the trackbed's route through the trees and of the station dwarfed by the sea beyond.

By comparison, Hayburn Wyke station is, and must always have been, practically invisible. The approach is down a narrow lane that plunges into dense woodland through a series of hairpin bends, and then levels out as it reaches the trackbed. Enough of the station survives to identify the scene, and beyond is the rather grand Hayburn Wyke

Above *On the line's last day, 6 March 1965, the 12.50 Middlesbrough to Scarborough (via Battersby) diesel railcar pauses at Robin Hood's Bay, for once filled to the brim*

wonderful week in the quiet, and sometimes not so quiet, sidings of Hampshire and Dorset.

The LNER were the camping coach pioneers, putting their first ten vehicles to work in 1933. Included in the programme for that first year were coaches on the Whitby to Loftus section, based at Sandsend, Kettleness or Staithes, and on the Scarborough to Whitby section, based at Cloughton, Stainton Dale or Robin Hood's Bay. In those days camping coaches could be moved around, spending days at different locations along the line, but the complications this entailed soon encouraged the railway company to place them on fixed sites. Robin Hood's Bay was always a favourite. It had three coaches in 1938 and by 1963, the year before the whole camping coach operation was abandoned, it had five. Towards the end there was a concentration of coaches on this line, with other sites at Ravenscar, Stainton Dale, Cloughton and Scalby. Today, the tradition has been maintained by the North Yorkshire Moors Railway's single camping coach at Goathland. Indeed, tourism was such a growing force during the 1960s that it is surprising the Whitby to Scarborough line did not survive longer. Its scenic qualities had always been enjoyed, and

NORTH EASTERN RAILWAY.

Hayburn Wyke

From YORK.

PRACTICAL INFORMATION

OS Landrangers
91, 104

Information points
Scarborugh Tourist Information Centre: St Nicholas Cliff, Scarborough North Yorkshire YO11 2EP. Tel 01723 373333, fax 01723 376941.
Whitby Tourist Information Centre: Langborne Road, Whitby, North Yorkshire YO21 1YN. Tel 01947 602674, fax 01947 606137.
Saltburn by the Sea Tourist Information Centre: 3 Station Buildings, Station Square, Saltburn, Cleveland TS12 1AQ. Tel 01287 622422, fax 01287 622422.

Official cycle/walkways
The Scarborough and Whitby Trailway: approximately 20 miles along the old railway line, with several access points. A leaflet, giving details, along with a history of the line and its surviving features, is available from the information points listed above. The Cleveland Way: part of this national trail is a coastal path between Saltburn and Scarborough. It follows the railway's route closely between Kettleness and Sandsend.

Cycle hire
Pedal Power: The Everly Hotel Workshop, Hackness, Scarborough. Tel 01723 36929. Jul–Aug, daily 10–4; Sep–Jun, Sat–Sun 10–4.
The Purple Mountain: Applegarth, Castleton, Whitby. Tel 01287 660539. All year, daily 9–9.

Nearby attraction
North Yorkshire Moors Railway: Pickering Station. Tel 01751 472508. Steam trains operate on 18 miles between Pickering and Grosmont. Access to moorland and forest walks from Newtondale Halt. Loco sheds at Grosmont. Apr–Oct, daily; specials.

Hotel, presumably the reason why a station was put in this utterly remote spot in the first place. There was only ever one platform, with some wooden station buildings. When the station was opened in 1885 this was on the eastern, or sea side of the track. For some reason, about ten years later, the whole station was moved across to the other side of the track, but rebuilt exactly as it had been before. There are no other buildings around, and the woods continue right down to the inaccessible cliff edge.

The next station, Cloughton, makes much more sense. A big village has spread itself along the main road, considerably enlarged since the railway's demise, but always substantial enough to warrant a station. This is down a lane to the east of the village and it turned out to be quite a treat. The station buildings are now an immaculate house with a fine trackbed garden decorated with cast-iron notices and other ephemera. The former goods shed, quite a grand building, survives as well, presumably now in horticultural or garage use. The footpath goes round the house, and then rejoins the trackbed at the end of the garden. Seen from across the fields to the east, the buildings almost have a semblance of reality.

When it was built, Scalby was another station serving a remote and self-contained village, but over the last few years Scarborough has expanded northwards and has absorbed much of the hithero undeveloped land by the river. The station and the viaduct that carried the line across the valley have gone, and part of the trackbed has vanished beneath a new housing estate. As a result the footpath has to follow a diversion through the village, but this is adequately signposted. From here the trackbed follows a private route through suburban Scarborough

and towards the town centre, much of which is in a cutting hidden from houses and back gardens. It passes under a series of increasingly busy roads and then finally comes to an end after a particularly substantial bridge. Beyond it is a childrens' playground, a car park and the inevitable supermarket. In railway days the line continued on through the town and then plunged into the short Falsgrave tunnel, to emerge again at Falsgrave Junction, just to the south of Scarborough's massive Central station. Just beyond the junction was Scarborough's other station, Londesborough Road.

The Central station, which dates back to 1845, was originally an elegant classical structure with the fine detailing typical of its architect, G T Andrews, whose friend and patron was the entrepreneur, George Hudson. The success and growth of Scarborough as a resort caused the station to be steadily altered and expanded, with most of the adaptations being made within the boundaries of the original site. The result was a complex and irregular structure, with platforms in apparently unrelated groups, behind the calm of Andrews's symmetrical façade. When the Whitby line was opened, its trains tended to use platform one, the most northerly and the most convenient for Falsgrave Junction. Even so, some complicated reversing procedures were a normal part of journeys in and out of Scarborough on the Whitby line. Today the station, along with its services, is much reduced, but it is still marked by its most familiar feature, the rather vulgar baroque-style clock tower added in 1884. Still one of Scarborough's most visible landmarks, it is a lasting reminder of the role played by the train in making the town famous.

Top Left *Set in woods above the sea, Stainton Dale station is now a private house*

LMS

E R O. 21556/130
O.P. 3

SCARBORO'

THE IRISH MAIL

◆

Castle Douglas to Stranraer and Portpatrick
The Newton Stewart to Whithorn Branch

The Big Water of Fleet viaduct, the line's most remarkable feature, is one of Britain's best railway views

HISTORY

The inspiration for the railways across Galloway came from the Irish trade, with Scottish and English railway companies ambitious to develop rail-connected harbours to exploit the short sea route to northern Ireland. A main line linking Carlisle, Dumfries and Glasgow had been opened in 1850 by the Glasgow & South Western Railway and in 1856 this company had received parliamentary approval for an extension westwards from Dumfries to Castle Douglas. The same year saw the authorisation of a line from Castle Douglas on to Stranraer and Portpatrick, and this was finally completed in 1862 by the Portpatrick Railway, with the support of the Glasgow & South Western company, who were also the line's operators. There were in addition branches to Kirkcudbright and to Whithorn, the latter built by the Wigtownshire Railway and completed in 1877.

From 1864 the Portpatrick Railway was operated by the Caledonian Railway, Glasgow & South Western's great rival. Delays in the development of Portpatrick harbour by the government and the admiralty, and the resultant lack of facilities for the handling of mail, brought financial problems. This was resolved, however, by switching the emphasis to Stranraer and establishing a regular steamer service from there to Larne. In 1875 the railway began to carry mails to Ulster. Further problems were caused by the opening of the Girvan & Portpatrick Junction Railway, a more direct route to Stranraer from Glasgow, and in 1885 the Portpatrick and Wigtownshire Railways merged to form a new company operated by a committee made up of the Caledonian, Glasgow & South Western, London & North Western and Midland Railways. With the introduction of through sleeper services from London to Stranraer and the expansion of the ferry service to Ireland, with connecting trains, the line finally prospered. The growth of tourism brought additional benefits, and from 1907 the ferry service could also handle motor vehicles. Heavily used by the government during both World Wars for the transport of troops and military equipment, the line seemed to have a secure future. However, with the coming of British Railways the decline set in and the first closures came in 1950. The Portpatrick branch closed west of Colfin, and passenger services were withdrawn on the Whithorn branch. Freight services remained on those lines until 1959 and 1964 respectively, but by that time the end was in sight. Once the decision had been made to retain only the northern access route to Stranraer via Glasgow and Ayr, the southern route had no future. It was closed throughout from Dumfries westwards in July 1965.

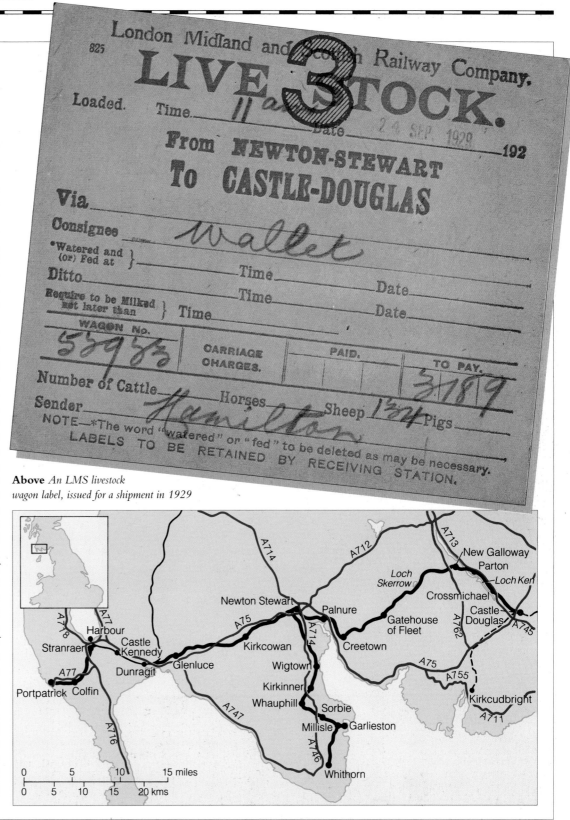

Above *An LMS livestock wagon label, issued for a shipment in 1929*

P. P. & W. Joint Rys.
This ticket is issued subject to the regulations
& conditions stated in the Co's Time Tables & Bills
NEW GALLOWAY TO
CASTLE DOUGLAS
Third] 4(S) FARE -/8½ [Class
CASTLE DOUGLAS

IN THE summer of 1964 a friend and I decided, at rather short notice, to have a week's holiday in Ireland. I had recently acquired a Honda motorcycle, all smart red paint and sporting looks, and it seemed a good way to try it out. There was some discussion as to whether the trip should be to the south or the north, where my friend had some relatives. In the event we decided, on the toss of a coin, to go to Eire and so a few days later we drove to Euston and put ourselves and the motorcycle on to the evening train to Holyhead, prior to taking the night ferry. Had the fall of the coin favoured the north we would instead have taken the alternative Euston departure for Ireland, via Stranraer and Larne. The result of this was that I missed my only chance to experience this southern route, via Castle Douglas, for less than a year later it was closed, leaving the great loop via Glasgow and Ayr as the only way to Stranraer.

A few years later I did finally get to Galloway, during the early stages of a long exploration of all of Scotland's western coast. Travelling in an old van with, as it happened, the same friend, and sticking mainly to minor roads, we visited Kirkcudbright, the Whithorn peninsula, Gatehouse of Fleet, Portpatrick and Stranraer without fully appreciating their former railway associations. Throughout that trip railways were, in any case, way down my list of priorities, the most pressing of which were to get to Cape Wrath in one piece and within the tight deadline imposed by the guidebook we were researching.

Later, as more and more of the Scottish railway network disappeared, along with its tangible remains, I came to regret both those missed opportunities. I like to think that I did take the time to look at surviving railway structures in Whithorn and Portpatrick for there were, then, still things to see. If I did, I cannot remember much about it. I did, however, see the route of the old line to Ballaculish, and I treasure the memory of Oban's original great timber summer-house of a station, with its soaring clock tower. The trip also introduced me to the special qualities of the lines to Mallaig and Kyle of Lochalsh, both of which I came to know well in later years.

The closures of the Beeching era were severe in Scotland, leaving large parts of the country with no rail service at all. Particularly hard hit were the regions north of Aberdeen, southeast of Edinburgh and west of Dumfries. Of these, the biggest surprise at the time was probably the the virtual removal of Galloway from the national railway map. The line to Stranraer via Dumfries, Castle Douglas and Newton Stewart was both quicker and shorter than the northern alternative and, as one of the primary routes to Ireland, it must have seemed secure. With its branches and connections, this line was also the backbone of the region's transport infrastructure. Roads were inadequate and journey times for the increasing freight traffic struggling to Stranraer were notoriously slow. After a rather shaky start, the railway had become well established, thanks to the Irish mail and the sleeper services from London, its mainstay and consistent revenue earners, and it was widely felt that the line had a future as long as Stranraer remained in business as a port. This it showed every intention of doing, and so the announcement of the line's closure was a shock that provoked a strong rearguard action, with questions asked in parliament – all, of course, to no avail.

Ferry services to northern Ireland had been the main inspiration for the building of the line in the first place. It had all started in 1850, with the opening of the Glasgow, Dumfries & Carlisle Railway. The same year this company merged with the already established Glasgow, Paisley, Kilmarnock & Ayr Railway, whose line south from Glasgow had been completed some years earlier. Together, as the Glasgow & South Western Railway, they offered the public a new main line route betweeen Glasgow and Carlisle. This company, always the main rival in commercial terms of the better-known Caledonian Railway, grew to become the major railway in southwest Scotland with, at its peak, routes covering over 1,100 miles and supported by a network of steamer services. From an early date the Glasgow & South Western had its eye on Galloway and its various ports and harbours, and a number of schemes were considered during the 1850s. However, the move westwards actually began in 1856, with the authorisation of the Castle

Below *On the line's last day, the crew of the 3.35pm Stranraer to Dumfries train collect the single line token at Creetown, while Standard class 4MT No. 76074 waits quietly*

Douglas & Dumfries Railway. Nominally independent, this line was completed three years later, with the full backing of the G&SWR, who also operated it and were to take complete control if it in 1865. Meanwhile, another important milestone had been reached the year before with the opening of the branch south from Castle Douglas to Kirkcudbright, always an important goal for the railway's promoters and backers.

The next stage was the extension of the line westwards from Castle Douglas, the ultimate target being the harbours at Portpatrick and Stranraer. A number of large and well-established companies had expressed an interest in this route, lured by the possibilities it offered for the development of trade with Ireland via the short sea crossing. Those prepared to back it included the Glasgow & South Western, along with two important English railways, the Lancaster & Carlisle and the Great Northern. All this, along with plenty of local support, carried the plan quickly through Parliament, and so the Portpatrick Railway received its authorisation in August 1857. Construction work began the following spring, with teams of navvies working at various places along the route. Particularly demanding was the long stretch across wild and uninhabited countryside north of Gatehouse of Fleet, and the whole undertaking proved to be very expensive, with much money being swallowed by the various bridges and viaducts. However, the backers' fears were mollified by Government promises to improve and greatly enlarge Portpatrick's limited harbour facilities. At that time, and for a few years to come, Portpatrick was seen as the principal port for the Irish trade, and the railway's ambitions were tied up with its redevelopment. However, when the line was completed throughout in 1862, including a short branch leading down to Portpatrick's quayside, the Government and the Admiralty had still done nothing and their promises remained unfulfilled. Portpatrick's little harbour was quite unsuitable for the anticipated traffic, and so the railway was compelled to live for a while from revenues far below expectations.

By this time the Post Office had begun to use the Holyhead to Kingsdown route for the Irish mails, and had little interest in an alternative that included no means of crossing the sea. In any case, with the local needs of Scotland, as always, a low priority in Westminster, the Government was content to make promises, but do little. With Portpatrick unable to be used, interest began to switch to Stranraer, whose sheltered location on Loch Ryan seemed to be more suitable for the long-term development of the Irish trade. Local support for Portpatrick also gradually evaporated with the increasing awareness that the Irish traffic would never support two harbours so close together. In the end, the Government was persuaded to put up some money, and some limited improvement works were started.

However, these were never really enough to make the port viable and the Government soon lost interest again, preferring instead to pay a lump sum directly to the Portpatrick Railway as compensation for broken promises. This left the company in an unenviable position as the owner of a long line, built at great cost in order to connect two ports to the railway network, neither of which could actually be used. With no boat services available, there was no point in the railway even bidding for the Irish mail traffic.

Below *British Railways' summer 1964 timetable for the line*

Table 8 — DUMFRIES, CASTLE DOUGLAS, KIRKCUDBRIGHT, NEWTON-STEWART and STRANRAER — British Railways summer 1964 timetable

In 1862 the railway company had bought an old iron steamer, the *Briton*, and had tried to set up a service to Ireland off its own bat, but after a few months of losses this venture was abandoned. Faced by this potentially disastrous series of circumstances, and seeing its resources draining away, the directors of the Portpatrick Railway sought help. This came from two unexpected quarters, first from the Glasgow & South Western's great rival, the Caledonian Railway, who in October 1864 took over the task of operating the line, and secondly, and less directly, from the London & North Western Railway, keen to expand its hold over the Irish traffic. In the late 1860s two further attempts were made to establish a regular steamer service from Portpatrick, but both ended in failure. It was not until July 1872 that this service finally got under way, with the introduction of the first ship custom-built for the route, the *Princess Louise*. This ship sailed from Stranraer, setting a pattern that was to be followed by all subsequent ferry services to Larne, and so Portpatrick, the railway's original inspiration, remained a little fishing port and a very pleasant backwater largely unaffected by the trains that continued to serve a station that had been laboriously carved out of the cliffs high above the town. The short harbour branch line soon fell into disuse, and was eventually removed.

In 1875 the Post Office finally agreed to send mails to northern Ireland via the Stranraer route and this, combined with the steadily improving ferry traffic, finally brought the railway into profit. The same year saw the opening of the Wigtownshire Railway's line south from Newton Stewart to Wigtown and along the Wigtownshire peninsula, a useful source of extra revenue and, via the connection to the harbour at Garlieston, a further expansion of maritime traffic. Four years later this line was completed to its Whithorn terminus.

However, the always uneasy relationship between the Caledonian and the Glasgow & South Western was considerably worsened by the construction of the Girvan and Portpatrick Junction Railway. Authorised in 1865 and opened twelve years later with the backing of the G&SWR, this offered a far more direct route to Stranraer from Glasgow, cutting over fifty miles from the journey. This new line met the Portpatrick Railway at Challoch Junction, six miles east of Stranraer. Long disputes about the use of this joint section were finally settled in court in 1880.

As a result of disputes and other problems, both the Portpatrick and the Wigtownshire Railways experienced financial difficulties during the 1880s, compounded by the forthcoming expiry of the operating agreement with the Caledonian Railway. After long and frequently acrimonious discussions a formula was reached that would secure the future of both companies. In August 1885 the two amalgamated as the

Portpatrick & Wigtownshire Joint Railway, to be operated by a committee formed by all the interested parties, namely the Caledonian, the Glasgow & South Western, the London & North Western and the Midland Railways. Under the committee's careful control, the line began at last to enjoy the fruits of prosperity. Traffic increased steadily, thanks to the new growth in tourism, and this was matched by constant improvements in the ferry service to Larne. From 1907 the ships began to carry cars and by 1914 there were three daily crossings each way during the summer season.

During World War I the emphasis switched to troop carrying, and the line, serving the safest crossing to Ireland, became busier than ever, despite shortages of locomotives and rolling stock and the requisitioning by the Government of some of the ferries. When peace returned, the railway struggled with its maintenance backlog and had just about sorted itself out when the amalgamations occurred and it was absorbed into the newly formed giant, the London, Midland & Scottish Railway. During the 1930s tourism further expanded, and the end of the decade saw the introduction of the first ferry able to load motor vehicles through stern doors. World War II brought all this to a close, and the line became a major troop carrier, serving army, navy and airforce bases in the region. A wartime development was the building of a secondary harbour at Cairnryan, on the eastern side of Loch Ryan, planned initially as a replacement facility for Glasgow or Liverpool, should either have been closed by bombing. A rail link was opened to it, which was then closed again soon after the war. Little used as a harbour after the war, Cairnryan became a shipbreaking base and then started a new life as a ferry port for the burgeoning car and lorry traffic on the Larne route.

With the return of peace, traffic on the railway returned to normal. New ferries were introduced, the most important of which was the new large Glasgow-built stern-loading vehicle carrier, the *Princess Victoria*. This entered service in 1947 but was destined for a short life. On 31 January 1953 the ship was lost, with all hands and many of the passengers, in a violent storm off the mouth of Loch Ryan, the worst British ferry disaster until the capsizing of the *Herald of Free Enterprise* off Zeebrugge in 1988. The subsequent enquiry found that the force of the sea had broken open the stern doors, flooding the vehicle deck and making the vessel unstable – a sequence of events to be repeated in subsequent ferry disasters all around the world.

In 1948 the Stranraer line became part of British Railways, and the next two decades witnessed a steady decline to eventual

Right *The trackbed of the Whithorn branch climbs away from Kirkinner against the backdrop of the estuary and the peaks of Knockeans and Cairnholy*

Above *On a spring morning in 1959 the 8.15 for Kirkcudbright takes the junction line away from Castle Douglas station. Nothing remains of this scene and its rich array of period detail*

Far Right *Still standing near Parton are the three arches of Loch Ken viaduct*
Inset Far Right *Approaching Parton from the Loch Ken viaduct in 1961 is the 2.20 Stranraer to Newcastle train, headed by Jubilee No. 45718,* Dreadnought

CASTLE DOUGLAS TO PORTPATRICK

I started my exploration of the line's remains in Castle Douglas, and it was not a promising beginning. There was nothing to see in the town, with only the Station Yard industrial estate hinting at what had been there before, but a bridge survived to the north, carrying the A75 over the trackbed. Also completely obliterated is the former junction with the Kirkcudbright branch. However, the trackbed appears not far from the town, as a low embankment running parallel to the A713, which it then follows closely to the eastern shores of Loch Ken. At one point it crosses the road, but little remains to establish the precise site, the road having absorbed sections of the line. The first station was at Crossmichael, and this survives as a house, at the end of a small private track ambitiously called Station Yard. The track then ran along beside the Loch, sometimes right on the shore line, with another small station at Parton. The best way to enjoy this stretch is from the minor road that runs all the way along the loch's western shore from Glenlochar. This offers fine views out over the loch and to the backdrop of wooded hills, and it is possible to make out the surviving sections of trackbed. It must have been a beautiful part of the journey. At the narrowest part of the loch the line crossed it on a big viaduct, three iron bowstring arches supported on chunky rusticated stone piers that cost over £12,000 when it was built in 1860. Rather surprisingly this still stands, adding an element of excitement into the landscape, and it can be seen either from the adjacent A713, or as a distant and rather picturesque view from fields on the western side of the loch. From here the line plunges into woods and is largely invisible, although from the private grounds of Hensol House there must be a good view of the track as it runs alongside the river, the Black Water of Dee.

The trackbed reappears as it curves round to Mossdale, the site of New Galloway station. From the road bridge there is a good view over the former yard and the surviving platform, now part of the garden of the old station house. The single-storey station building has gone. The remoteness of this station is typical of this section of the route and it marks the beginning of a wild and often inaccessible stretch, with the line running through great tracts of isolated forest and across bleak and inhospitable moorland. The view westwards from the bridge gives a good sense of this, with the trackbed, now used as a long farm access path, climbing away towards the distant hills. This path runs for several miles, finally ending at Loch Skerrow, where the railway had an isolated passing loop, signal box and a water tower, a vital necessity for the locomotives that had struggled up the long climb from Loch Ken.

When the line was built, the landscape was one of bare hills. Since then massive afforestation has radically changed it, and

closure. First to go, in February 1950, was the Portpatrick branch, although freight traffic continued to serve the creamery at Colfin for another nine years. Next was the Whithorn branch, closed to passengers in September 1950 and to freight fourteen years later. By this time the future of the whole line was in doubt, despite the increasing use of Stranraer as a port. In June 1965 it closed completely, the decision having been made to route all rail traffic to Stranraer via Glasgow and then down the former Girvan & Portpatrick Junction line via Challoch. With hindsight it is possible to see that this decision, like so many made during the Beeching years, actually doomed the line to a lingering death. At Stranraer the emphasis switched increasingly from rail to road. With the end of through sleeper and express trains and with all freight coming to the port by road, the railway steadily degenerated into the little local service it has now become. It remains to be seen whether the line to Stranraer will survive the process of privatisation.

Left *An eastbound train heading for Dumfries approaches the Big Water of Fleet viaduct in May 1964. Clearly visible is the brick cladding, added to strengthen the piers*

Right *A typically remote station was New Galloway, seen here in the autumn of 1964. Today the view from the bridge shows the same landscape, but all the buildings have gone, except the station house, off the photograph to the right*

hidden the trackbed from view for miles. As a result, the only way to explore it is on foot, but it is not an official walkway, and access is often only via established footpaths, forest tracks and other rights of way.

Equally inaccessible are the series of famous viaducts, the construction of which made this section so expensive. The first, a mile west of New Galloway station, crossed the Black Water of Dee near Loch Sloan. More dramatic were the nine stone arches of the Little Water of Fleet viaduct, a mile or so west of Loch Skerrow, demolished some years ago. However, still standing is the line's most spectacular feature, the Big Water of Fleet viaduct, twenty great stone arches with later brick strengthening, striding across the bare hills. There is a famous view of this, indeed one of the most famous of all Britain's railway views, from the B796, the remote road across the hills that leads to Gatehouse of Fleet station. Seen in the distance, and contributing so much to the landscape, the viaduct fully expresses the full drama of Victorian railway engineering and its somewhat tentative survival is a fitting memorial to the hundreds who toiled to create the railway network through such inhospitable terrain.

The road virtually ends at Gatehouse of Fleet station, with only a narrow single track leading westwards from here over the hills towards Creetown. The road was built to serve the station for there is absolutely nothing else here at all. The town of Gatehouse of Fleet is over six miles away to the south, and so the station, along with the road leading to it, was really little more than a gesture by the railway company. Even they must

have been aware of the inadequacy of this gesture. Indeed, for the first few years of its life the station's name regularly alternated between Gatehouse and Dromore, a tiny settlement a mile to the east. Today, the station building survives as a house, and to the east is the visitor centre of the Cairnsmore of Fleet Nature Reserve, which probably attracts more people than the station ever did during its active life.

From Gatehouse of Fleet station the trackbed is never far from the road. It crosses it twice, but only one bridge survives, the other having been levelled. At Culcronchie, road and railway crossed the Culcronchie Burn side by side, but the railway bridge with its four brick arches has disappeared. The line then swings away to the west, to pass well to the north of Creetown. The route is almost perverse in its avoidance of centres of civilisation. A long lane leads to Creetown station, the main building just recognisable as a much-extended house, called, in case there was any doubt, Railway House. Anything else that survives is now in farm use, and there is no trace of the well-shaped hedges and elaborate flower beds that used to decorate the platforms.

The trackbed, generally in view from the A75, turns north to run along on the level beside the extensive floodplain of the River Cree. There were several bridges along this stretch, and the most bizarre today is just to the east of Muirfad, where the line crossed the Cairnsmore Burn. Originally this was called the Graddoch viaduct and it was a substantial structure of eight low sandstone arches. When it was demolished some time ago two arches were left, for no reason that is immediately apparent, and

these now stand in isolation on a perfectly manicured bit of grass, neatly severed at each end, and bearing a plaque calling it the Cairnsmore viaduct. There are houses near by that have nothing to do with it. The result of all this curious endeavour is that it looks like some carefully tended Roman relic, or a medieval ruin maintained in the rather excessive style sometimes associated with conservation bodies. The last thing that comes to mind is that it is in fact part of a Victorian railway bridge. The next bridge, over the Palnure Burn, is a more conventional iron structure that looks good against the backdrop of hills. Just beyond, where the line crossed the A75, is the site of Palnure station, never more than a small single-storey stone building and a couple of platforms. Two of the railway's few serious accidents happpened near Palnure. The first was the derailment of a goods train in 1866, with one fatality – the fireman was crushed by the tender as it rolled down the embankment with its train – and the second was the derailment of a passenger train as it crossed the Cree viaduct. This time there were no injuries but the engine, having broken away from the train, carried on along the line for some distance

Above *Miles from the town it was meant to serve, Gatehouse of Fleet station was notably isolated. Today the station building survives as a private house, but the signal box is long gone. A particular feature of the station was the adjacent chapel, seen here in 1963, formed from the body of an old clerestory coach*

Right *The two remaining arches of the Craddoch viaduct, carefully preserved and manicured, have the look of some Roman or medieval ruin*

without either driver or fireman being aware that they had left their train behind. After Palnure the line crossed the floodplain and then the tidal river itself on the three spans on the Cree bridge. This no longer exists, but those determined to see its site can do so by following a farm track. The line then swung north again for the approach to Newton Stewart, on an embankment beside the A714.

It is hard today to make any sense of Newton Stewart's railway past. Parts of the line have disappeared beneath new roads and Station Road leads, as so often, to an industrial estate. The abutments of a bridge survive, along with other buildings that may once have had railway connections, but the overall

picture is not exciting. There is no sign of the junction with the Wigtownshire Railway's line to the south, whose trains came and went from the bay platform at Newton Stewart station. However, the trackbeds of both lines become quickly apparent once the town is left behind. The Stranraer line ran along parallel to the A75 for some miles, and the track is often still visible. There are secret and appealing stretches through the woods, marking the noticeable change in the landscape away from the browns of the moorland hills to the softer greens of the river valleys. Gorse flourishes by the track and often fills the cuttings with a mass of dense yellow. Railway and road crossed the River Bladnoch together at Shennanton, but the line's

Above *A freight train from the Whithorn branch rumbles through Newton Stewart in May 1964, passing beneath the elegant iron footbridge. Nothing of this scene survives today*

girder bridge is no longer there. From here the track turns south across the open fields to Kirkcowan. Some of the station survives by an old stone bridge but the trackbed is inaccessible, and occasionally invisible. A minor road that wanders across the fields roughly following Tarf Water offers views of the bridge that carried the line over the river, surrounded by a landscape empty of habitation. After some woodland the line crossed the A75 and then accompanied it to Glenluce, but the trackbed keeps generally out of sight to the north before sweeping down on an embankment into the valley of the Water of Luce. Glenluce station is now just a flattened piece of waste ground, but it is worth taking the time to follow the trackbed westwards for it soon reaches the eight arches of the Glenluce viaduct, carried on elegant tapering piers of stone patched with brick. There are several ways of seeing this. There is a distant view of it up the river valley from the A75, exciting but made hazardous by the continuous lorries thundering to and from Stranraer. A

minor road actually winds in and out of the viaduct's piers and across the river, offering various angles from below. Best of all is the walk along the trackbed that leads directly on to it, with access, unusually, barred only by a gate. A proper footpath, complete with stile, leads directly up to the viaduct from the minor road below and so it is not difficult to approach it. When I was standing on the road below the viaduct, a group of boys ran across it, pausing now and then to look down and sending voices shrill with excitement echoing down the valley.

West of the viaduct there is a wooded embankment and then the line dropped down towards the sea and on to Challoch Junction. From a minor road near Whitecrook there is a wonderful view of the old embankment as it crosses the green fields against the distant expanse of sand and sea. Near by is the site of the junction, still just about visible as modern Sprinters rattle by, starting the long haul northwards to Ayr and Glasgow.

Far Left *The tall arches of Glenluce viaduct still stride across the river valley just west of the town*

Left *The view out across the sandy beach to the sea beyond from a point near Challoch Junction, where the still active Glasgow to Stranraer line meets the old trackbed*

The last few miles from Challoch to Stranraer represent the only active part of the old Portpatrick and Wigtownshire network. There were two intermediate stations, Dunragit and Castle Kennedy, both probably built to satisfy local landowners who were also supporters of the railway, Sir James Dalrymple Hay of Dunragit House and the Earl of Stair of Castle Kennedy. Both have been closed for years, but some buildings survive. The approach to Stranraer is via woodland and lochs and then the town's suburbs take over. Just discernible is the site of the former junction with the Government's wartime branch to Cairnryan, and then the train passes a sprawl of sidings and a huddle of old buildings. This, a Scotrail engineering depot now, was Stranraer Town station and the company's workshops and headquarters. All journeys ended or, to use modern railspeak, terminated here, with only boat trains or Portpatrick services continuing beyond the Town station. Planned as it originally was as a railway to Portpatrick, the main line went straight on through the station and then swung westwards. The line north to Stranraer harbour was initially only a secondary branch but, with the shift of emphasis towards Stranraer, this became the main line. Today, there is only Stranraer Harbour station, and a

Above *In June 1937, an LMS compound, No. 916, waits at Stranraer Harbour station, having just arrived from Dumfries*

Right *After the closure of the Portpatrick line, the Piltanton viaduct was partially blown up. Its shattered remains are now a picturesque folly*

pretty gloomy place it is too, stuck out at the end of the east pier and surrounded by the ghosts of its splendid past.

The line to Portpatrick, with its stiff gradients, was expensive to build and difficult to operate. From Stranraer the line climbed steeply to its summit at Colfin, and then it dropped even more steeply down its winding route to Portpatrick. Much of the route out of Stranraer has been lost, but it is possible to see the trackbed from the A77 as it climbs up through the hills, passing to the north of Lochans. From the road there is a good view of the shattered remains of the Piltanton Viaduct, the last one on the route. Partially demolished by explosives, the viaduct stands against the hillside, a picturesque and overgrown ruin. Not far on is Colfin station, named after a settlement well to the northeast. Here the single platform and some buildings survive, along with the site of the level crossing, but still dominant are the structures that housed the creamery, now a smokehouse. The creamery was set up on this site to make the most of the railway link, and it was this that kept the line from here to Stranraer open until 1959. From here the line descended through the hills, a continuous drop at up to 1 in 57. Today the trackbed crosses a golf course and then is carried straight towards the cliff-edge on a high embankment, surrounded by caravan parks. This is a pleasant walk that leads to the gaunt ruins of Dunskey Castle. From here the line curved round in a semi-circle to face back the way it had come, and to end at Portpatrick's station high above the town. With its single platform, its few buildings and its scattering of sidings carved out of the rocky cliffs, it was a terminus station far beneath the dreams of the railway's promoters. There was not even a turntable, so locomotives arriving from Stranraer had to return tender first. Originally there was a steep branch line down to the harbour, but this was closed and removed in about 1870 when it became clear that it was Stranraer and not Portpatrick that was destined to become the main port for the Irish trade. Traces of this can still be seen.

THE NEWTON STEWART TO WHITHORN BRANCH

The Wigtownshire Railway was the typical product of regional enthusiasm for railways in the mid-nineteenth century, with both support and money coming extensively from local sources. It was a feature of such railways that their promoters and backers

Below *Near Colfin the trackbed is a straight line of green across the rounded hills*

were always optimistic about both construction costs and traffic demand, and the Wigtownshire was no exception. Despite this, the line was built, with work starting in 1874. The same year the line was opened to Wigtown, but it took some time to raise the necessary finance to complete the southern extension and the nineteen-mile railway was not formally opened until July 1877. The route, although heavily graded, was quite straightforward, and the only major engineering feature was the two-arched bridge that had to be built across the River Bladnoch south of Wigtown. There was a short branch to Garlieston harbour. An extension of the line from Whithorn south to the Isle of Whithorn was considered, with an eye on the possibility of ferry services to the Isle of Man, but this was never built. Simple construction and economical management enabled to railway to keep its head above water during the late 1870s and early 1880s, but it was in trouble in the mid-1880s and it was only its merger with the Portpatrick Railway in 1885 that kept it alive. Passenger services to Garlieston were withdrawn in 1903 but the branch carried on as a freight line. All passenger services on the branch were withdrawn in September 1950, but freight kept the line open until the final closure in October 1964.

There is nothing much to see in Newton Stewart, but the trackbed appears by the former A75 crossing and its route southwards down across the low hills can be followed on farm tracks and footpaths to Barwhirran Croft. The approach to Wigtown was at sea level, along the estuary, but little remains to be seen today and some sections have disappeared completely. A good place to find the trackbed is on a minor road that follows its curving route round Wigtown. A short section here is a footpath, part of the West Galloway Wildlife Trail, and preserved primarily for those watching the birdlife on the estuary and mudflats. From Bladnoch there are good views down to the estuary, with the piers of the former bridge standing in the middle of the river. The next station was Kirkinner, but not much remains. Better are the views along the trackbed and out over the estuary from a bridge to the west, carrying a minor road. From here the line turned inland and climbed up to to Whauphill. Here, some battered old sheds indicate the site of the station, now overrun with derelict farm machinery. At one time there was a plan for a branch line from here westwards to Port William, but nothing came of it.

There is not much to see either at the next station, Sorbie, although creameries here, and at Whauphill, brought trade to the railway. It is difficult today to imagine that a railway could exist almost entirely on local agricultural traffic, but this line was a classic example. Every station, however small and insignificant, had a couple of sidings and a loading bay, and the local farmers made the most of these for the transport of livestock, dairy

PRACTICAL INFORMATION

OS Landrangers
82, 83, 84

Information points
Castle Douglas Tourist Information Centre: Markethilll, Castle Douglas, Dumfries and Galloway. Tel 01556 502611. Closed winter.
Gatehouse of Fleet Tourist Information Centre: Car Park, Gatehouse of Fleet, Dumfries and Galloway. Tel 01557 814212. Closed winter.
Kirkcudbright Tourist Information Centre: Harbour Square, Kirkcudbright, Dumfries and Galloway. Tel 01557 330494. Closed winter.
Newton Stewart Tourist Information Centre: Dashwod Square, Newton Stewart, Dumfries and Galloway. Tel 01671 402431. Closed winter.
Stranraer Tourist Information Centre: Bridge Street, Stranraer, Dumfries and Galloway. Tel 01776 702595. Closed winter.

Left *Standard class 2 No. 78026 waits to collect a freight from Whithorn in 1964. In the background the CWS creamery, one of the line's mainstays, is hard at work*

and other farm products, and agricultural equipment and machinery. Through this landscape of farmland the trackbed is often invisible, but glimpses from minor roads indicate its tortuous progress towards its terminus.

From Sorbie it cuts down towards the estuary again to Millisle, where there was the junction with the Garlieston branch. Millisle station, built really just for the junction, is now a substantial house with a rather formal garden. It is possible to see the trackbed as it follows the road into Garlieston, and just about possible to find the place where it crossed the road and curved round to the station, to the south. It is, however, hard to find much more of the original line to the quay, with its sidings and branches fed via a small wagon turntable. Although tidal, the quays could handle quite large ships and so there was

considerable traffic for the railway, especially before the outbreak of World War I.

The final approach to Whithorn is a steep climb, up to 1 in 58, to the line's summit, just north of the town. Parts of the trackbed are now in use for farm access, while other sections lie lost in the fields. Whithorn station used to stand in the fork formed by the junction of the A746 and the B7004. It had goods and engine sheds and plenty of sidings, along with a nearby creamery. Today, the site is occupied by fire and bus stations, and the only clue to the railway age is the grand old hotel. Whithorn is one of Scotland's smallest and oldest burghs, and it once had Scotland's southernmost railway station. That apart, little seems to have changed.

Far Left *The Whithorn branch was famous for its rural quality, gentle colours and fine views of distant hills*

ACKNOWLEDGEMENTS

Design Julian Holland
Editing Sue Gordon
Cartography Rodney Paull
Page make-up Avonset
Picture research Julian Holland

Author's acknowledgements

Several people have helped and encouraged me during the research and writing of this book. I am grateful to my daughter Zoë, who at Forcett Junction appreciated for the first time the lure of lost railways and then became an excellent embankment spotter, to my friend Caroline, a skilful navigator and ever tolerant of the need to explore muddy fields in unsuitable weather, to Sue Gordon, a far better editor than I deserve, to Barry McKay, for information about the railways of Cumbria, and, last but not least, to Julian Holland, whose idea it all was, and whose patience was sorely taxed by my erratic behaviour and poor sense of deadlines.

Julian Holland Publishing would like to thank these individuals for supplying the following material:
Paul Atterbury (luggage labels)
Basil Jeuda (railway tickets for pages 72–85)
Ian S Carr (railway tickets for pages 8–23 and 130–141)
David G Geldard/The Transport Ticket Society (railway tickets for pages 24–71, 86–129 and 142–159).

Photographic acknowledgements

(t = top, b = bottom, l = left, r = right)
Paul Atterbury: 13b, 15t, 17r, 20tl, 26, 27, 29t, 32, 34, 35t, 35b, 40, 46, 48, 74, 75t, 84b, 88, 90, 92t, 94t, 97, 98t, 115, 119t, 122, 126t, 130, 135t, 135b, 138/139, 141, 142, 143, 146/147, 149, 152b, 154, 155, 156b, 157, 158
Ian Burgum: 2/3, 5/6, 58, 60t, 65, 69, 73, 77, 79, 80, 84, 100, 103, 104/105b, 105, 106, 109b, 110/111, 113, 114, 123t, 124, 125b, 127, 128/129
Ian S Carr: 9, 10, 11, 14, 17t, 21, 22, 23, 134, 136, 137, 140
R M Casserley/H C Casserley: 36b, 54t, 87, 102, 104t, 118, 156t
Mike Esau: 60b, 61t, 125t
J S Gilks: 16, 89, 99t, 117, 119, 128, 148, 150/151, 153, 159
Julian Holland: 8, 12t, 12b, 13t, 18, 20tr, 36/37, 38, 42b, 43b, 44b, 50, 51b, 53t, 54/55, 71
Basil Jeuda: 72, 75b, 76, 78t, 78b, 82, 83t, 83b
S C Nash: 33t, 33b, 66, 110b, 111b
National Monuments Record Centre (The Rokeby Collection): 81, 133, 138b
Rail Archive Stephenson: 4/5 (Colling Turner), 15b (T G Hepburn), 18/19 (W J Verden Anderson), 56 (K L Cook), 59 (F R Hebron), 61b, 62/63 (E C Griffith), 64, 70 (K L Cook), 85 (Colling Turner), 86 (T G Hepburn), 91, 92b (John P Wilson), 96 (John Head), 98/99b (T G Hepburn), 121, 123b (W J Verden Anderson)
R C Riley Collection: 24, 25 (Dr I C Allen), 28, 29b, 30t, 30/31, 41, 42t, 43t, 44t, 45, 47, 48/49, 51t, 52, 53b, 57, 67, 69t, 101, 107, 109t, 112t, 112b
David C Rodgers: 120
W A C Smith: 144, 149b, 151t, 152t
N W Sprinks: 62b, 68
Sean Taylor: 93

SUSTRANS

All those involved in the creation of this book would like to acknowledge the work and aims of Sustrans, the railway path and cycle route construction charity devoted to the task of building traffic-free 'Greenways' for cyclists, walkers and people with disabilities, often on disused railway lines. Sustrans has built over 250 miles of paths and has researched thousands more miles of potential routes. For more information or to pledge your support contact Sustrans, 35 King Street, Bristol BS1 4DZ. Tel 0117 9 268893, fax 0117 9 294173.

NORTH EASTERN RAILWAY.

From

CLIBURN

PASSENGER FARES
FROM and TO
LONDON (Waterloo).
Children 3 and under 14 years; half-fare.

STATION	"MONTHLY RETURN"		ORDINARY SINGLE *	
	1st	3rd	1st	3rd
	s. d.	s. d.	s. d.	s. d.
Barnstaple Jct.	57/11	38/7	48/–	28/9
Barnstaple Tn.	60/8	40/5	50/4	30/3
Bideford	59/3	39/6	49/4	29/8
Braunton (for Saunton Sands)	52/9	35/2	43/11	26/4
Exeter (Cent.) (St. Davids)	62/–	41/4	51/6	30/11
Ilfracombe	61/2	40/9	50/10	30/6
Mortehoe (for Woolacombe)	62/5	41/7	51/10	31/1
Torrington				

*Ordinary Return Fares are double the above Single Fares. Ordinary Return Tickets are available on the outward or return journeys within three months from the date shown thereon.

"MONTHLY RETURN" TICKETS
between ANY TWO stations

Forward or return any day within one month (for one round trip) with break of journey at any intermediate station.

Tickets from London can be purchased in advance at any London or Suburban Station.

NOTICE.—These Tables are issued subject to the Conditions published in the Company's Notices.

No. 31A.
SOUTHERN RAILWAY

October 4th, 1943, to April 30th, 1944, both dates inclusive.

TRAIN SERVICE
AND FARES
BETWEEN
LONDON (Waterloo)
AND
EXETER
BARNSTAPLE JCT.
BIDEFORD (for Clovelly, Appledore and Westward Ho !)
TORRINGTON
BRAUNTON
(for Saunton Sands and Croyde Bay)
MORTEHOE
(for Woolacombe) and
ILFRACOMBE (for Combe Martin)

E. J. MISSENDEN,
General Manager.

7,000
9/9/43.

Waterlow & Sons Ltd.,
London & Dunstable.